Torah: A Way of Life
A Way to Life

Commentaries on the Sidroth

Torah: A Way of Life
A Way to Life

Commentaries on the Sidroth

by
Rabbi Shmuel Werzberger

KTAV PUBLISHING HOUSE, INC.
Hoboken, N.J.

Library of Congress Cataloging-in-Publication Data

Werzberger, Shmuel, 1917-
    Torah, a way of life: commentaries on the Sidroth / by
Shmuel Werzberger.

    p.   cm.
    ISBN 0-88125-347-2: $20.00
    1. Bible, O.T. Pentateuch—Commentaries. I. Title,
BS1225.3.W45   1989
222'-1107—dc20   89-24557
                                                      CIP

Manufactured in the United States of America

Dedication

I dedicate this book of Torah commentaries to my wife Manya Werzberger—may God grant her many years of good health—who during our almost fifty years together has been the solid foundation upon which I was able to build my life. It is only thanks to her complete and unselfish devotion, her unflinching loyalty and honesty—even during difficult years when economic necessities, leisure, and family life had to be sacrificed—that I was able to lead my life according to my desire.

Table of Contents

Foreword

In the days before the secularization of our society, it used to be a hallowed custom in most Jewish households to read *shneim mikrah achad targum*, meaning that the weekly portion was read twice, once in the original Hebrew, and a second time in the Targum, the authoritative Aramaic translation by Onkelos.

A second widespread source of biblical knowledge was *Ze'e-nah u-Re'enah* ("Come and See"), a late sixteenth-century work of enduring popularity, intended by its author, Jacob ben Isaac Ashkenazi, to "enable men and women... to understand the word of God in simple language." It contained discourses on selected passages from the weekly portions of the Torah, the *haftaroth* and other scriptural works, interspersed with midrashic stories and moralities.

Although originally intended for both sexes, *Ze'enah u-Re'enah*—which was written entirely in Yiddish—gradually came to be read mainly by women, which explains why many housewives were better versed in certain religious topics than the male members of their households, who were dependent upon a knowledge of Hebrew and Aramaic.

Apart from the linguistic and scholarly difficulties involved in gaining an understanding of our sacred writings, I have often noticed that mere reading, without a framework of examples from real life, easily causes one to miss the point of a Bible verse or commandment. Although the Tenach is not written in modern language, and despite the fact that many passages at first glance appear obscure, many people would be surprised to discover how remarkably simple and logical their meanings often are, and how relevant they are to many contemporary situa-

tions. For this reason alone I am saddened by the present aliena-
tion from our biblical heritage, because I know that all of us
would be enriched by a renewed confrontation with its lessons
and its profound topicality to our contemporary political, social,
and economic situation.

The decision to write this book was therefore a direct result
of my desire to help revive in every Jew a measure of interest in
the study of Tenach—in particular in the Five Books of Moses.
In the course of my studies over many years I collected many
volumes of handwritten outlines and notes on the various
weekly portions, which, added together, would have been sufficient to write four or five *divrei Torah* on each individual *parashah*.
However, being highly conscious of the pressures of modern
life, I restrained the urge to be too comprehensive, instead
selecting from the weekly portions those passages, and in some
cases even single expressions, that I considered to be the most
representative and topical as the basis of a commentary, while at
the same time attempting to provide as complete and clear a
reference as possible to halachic sources and midrashim, as well
as comments of sages and rabbis, wherever possible with refer-
ences to situations from everyday life.

It was this selection that, in fact, proved the principal challenge, for so fascinating, and so rich, and inexhaustible is the
material, that I could without any difficulty have covered ten
times as many subjects. However, as I already explained above,
this would have defeated my purpose.

I do not claim that all my commentaries are original; on the
contrary, in the course of my writing I was constantly reminded
that I might here and there be accused of having presented
certain ideas or conclusions as my own that in fact originated
with some of our sages and interpreters from earlier times. I
have been a student of Torah from the age of three, which
means that in the course of my life I have absorbed a variety of
ideas from sources too numerous to mention, to the point
where I almost cannot be blamed—although I do accept full

responsibility in cases where this has happened—for assuming certain thoughts as my own. Even so, I am sure that I may be forgiven if, in the process, I even partially achieve my purpose of kindling some renewed interest among my fellow-Jews in the study of their religious heritage.

My dream is that a new generation of Jewish families will once more know which *parashah* is read during a particular week, and take some time to read and discuss some of its lessons when seated around the Shabbath table. This is what my book intends to facilitate, not as a work of great literary pretense, but as an illustration in practical and down-to-earth language of some of the lessons the Torah contains for our contemporary existence. Even a few "converts" to this cause would mean a plentiful reward for my efforts, not for any greater glory, but because it would go some little way toward restoring the traditional Jewish "Torah way of life." Our sages long ago said, "A meal without a word of Torah is like idol worship." From this we can conclude that even "a word," in simple language, can help to turn the Shabbath meal once more into a holy meal, sanctifying God and the Jewish family.

It is a dismal thought, likely to cause despondency in the most optimistic person, to realize how many volumes of meritorious interpretations on spiritual subjects have been stacked away unused and forgotten in dark warehouses, in the face of a public that—insofar as it reads at all—seems to be drawn more and more to sensational bestsellers. Admittedly the Bible is still the biggest selling book of all time, but most of its understanding, and an insight in its lasting impact on the issues of our age—and all ages—must necessarily be lost without the accompanying commentaries and explanations, as seen through the eyes of those who have made the interpretation of our Scriptures their life's work. How sorry I feel for those who are thus deprived of the words of the Torah, the most vibrant and eternally relevant literary work ever written.

Having read the above, the reader will of course ask why I

have taken the trouble to prepare yet another volume on Torah commentary, and why—apart from the satisfaction of seeing my efforts in print—I should expect to find any readers willing to absorb its contents. Surely the reason cannot be the hope of large-scale public acceptance, or even praise for my effort—not to speak of the expectation of a financial return.

The answer is that, however conscious I am of a lack of popular acclaim and monetary reward, I do know that there continue to be countless people desirous of having the Bible explained in terms that they can understand and accept. I hope to attract them, in particular, while they browse in bookshops or search for some meaningful inspiration—in the expectation that, while leafing through these pages, they will be struck by these commentaries and the viability of some of their argumentation. I shall be fully recompensed if some of them will find their curiosity sufficiently aroused to follow up their interest by a closer study of the actual Torah portions that form the basis of the following discussions.

Tel Aviv, 1988

Acknowledgment

In writing this second book, I felt the need for a sounding board, to make certain that good intentions would not turn into mere preaching, and to avoid the risk that the idealism that invariably propels the author may overwhelm the everyday, moral lessons to be drawn from the Torah. For this reason I feel it my pleasant duty to record my indebtedness to Chanan Nijk, my editor and translator, who also assisted me with the preparation of my first book.

Ever since we started working together, now almost four years ago, our cooperation has deepened into friendship. Our often spirited discussions and his involvement and critical comments, based upon his own wide reading and varied life experiences, have helped to add yet another dimension to this work, enabling me to add focus and clarity to my arguments. I would like here to express my deep appreciation for his constructive contribution, and look forward—with God's help—to our further cooperation on my next project.

I want to record here with deep gratitude the practical and spiritual support of my dear friends Albert and Rivella Tavens during the preparation of this book. Knowing Albert Tavens' deep affection for his late parents, Ephraim and Anna Bracha Tavens ל"ז, I would like to commemorate and honor their memory on these pages.

A far more substantial memorial is that erected by the generosity and good works of their son, who proves himself unsparing in his readiness to help his needy fellowmen in the true spirit of *tzedakah*—Jewish charity.

Parashath Be-Reshith

בראשית ברא אלהים את השמים ואת הארץ: והארץ היתה תהו
ובהו וחשך על־פני תהום ורוח אלהים מרחפת על־פני המים:
ויאמר אלהים יהי־אור ויהי־אור: וירא אלהים את־האור כי־טוב
ויבדל אלהים בין האור ובין החשך.

"In the beginning God created the heavens and the earth.
Now the earth was formless and empty, darkness was over
the surface of the deep, and the Spirit of God was hovering
over the waters. And God said, 'Let there be light,' and
there was light. God saw that the light was good, and He
separated the light from the darkness."

One of our sages, Rabbi Eliezer, has said that the light that
God created on the first day of Creation would have enabled a
man to see from one end of the world to the other. However,
when God realized what would happen in the future, and how
He would have to destroy an entire generation in a great Flood,
because people were murderers and robbers, and "every inclination of the thoughts of their hearts was only evil all the time,"
He decided to hide this Great Light. He hid it for the future,
until there would be a time when man would recognize his
obligations to himself and his fellowman. Then He would again
open the Big Light that would enable man to see from one end of
the world to the other. Thus far the Midrash.

From this midrash we can learn that God has created man
with powerful eyes, which enable him to see what is near him
and what is far away. They enable him to see what is ahead of
him and use the knowledge that is thus gained for all his needs in

life. Through his eyes man can enjoy the beauties of nature as well as protect himself. How happy are people who have this gift of being able to use their eyes to observe all that is happening around them. How bitter, by contrast, must be the life of a blind man. Our sages expressed themselves in very extreme terms about this. According to them a blind man was like a dead person.

The main point, however, is not how much a man who is blind misses, but to what extent seeing people use their God-given eyes to see the right things in the right light. We know that one and the same person often does not observe the same thing in the same way from one day to the next. How much less do two different people see things the same way. I believe that there will hardly be two people in the world who look at their surroundings from the same perspective and react in the same way to what they think they observe. Objectively speaking, our world is not different, depending on who looks at it. We only think it is. If we are very honest with ourselves, we have to agree that our view is distorted, and that most of the time we behave as if we are blind.

There must be something wrong, not only with our eyes but with our psychology. The differences people observe are not in the object, but—as the saying goes—"in the eye of the beholder." What can we do, therefore, to get to know ourselves, to learn to see things as they really are; to learn to understand what we see and therefore also understand what we are doing. For we have to agree that what we see is often so superficial that we are also unable to control and guide our reactions.

Even less than our reactions are we able to control our thinking. Ever since he was created, man has been observing his physical surroundings. From the dawn of civilization, generation after human generation has tried to understand the world. Man has speculated, theorized, researched, and still he cannot say that he knows it. Every day somebody discovers or invents something new, but every new discovery strengthens our realization that our combined knowledge is still merely a drop in the ocean: total, ultimate knowledge of what God has created turns out to be a "moving target." In the course of the last few hundred years man has invented more things than during all the previous centuries together. Yet, everything we know today will prove to be negligible compared with what people will discover during the next few generations. Who knows what new inventions will be made—and what the world will look like—in the twenty-first century?

So it appears that we are still not really seeing; that we are not yet able to use our eyes. The treasures of nature that God created are still not properly exploited. The twentieth century is coming to an end, and we have not yet begun to exploit the ocean. The seas are not merely a means of transportation, or a source of fish; they are the world's largest reservoir of food-stuffs, energy and minerals! If we learned to use them, no people anywhere in the world would have to go hungry. Again, the big question is why God did not reveal immediately after the Creation everything that could have benefited man on this earth.

The Talmud makes a point of mentioning how much easier present-day life is compared with that in the Garden of Eden. Primitive man had to labor intensively to provide himself with even the most basic commodities—things like bread, which we can buy ready made, fresh, and cheap in unlimited quantities. How many generations had to pass before people invented elementary tools to ease their daily labor? In short, all our knowledge has come to us in bits and pieces, in the course of thousands of years of slow and painstaking evolution. In theory, how much happier would mankind be if it knew all the secrets of nature. We would be able to heal suffering from sickness or pain; we would not have to have unemployment; we would have the means—and the wisdom—for unrestricted communication, so that we could avoid wars; we would have the technical facilities for avoiding natural disasters. I am not even talking about another dream people have had ever since they began learning about the functions of the human body, namely the ability to prolong life.

So we come back to the question why God decided to hide the Big Light and "keep us in the dark." After all, the Torah teaches that God did not make the world for it to be a desolation to mankind. On the contrary, He created the world for us to live in it, and to enjoy his Creation. Complete knowledge of nature could also preempt people who claim that God did not create the world, but that the world was created by itself. Such a view of nature, and the full realization of its wonders, would cause humankind to recognize the existence of the Almighty. So again we must ask why He hid this knowledge from us.

There must have been a very good reason for God to prevent us from seeing everything from one end of the world to the other. The Torah says: ויאמר אלהים יהי־אור ויהי־אור (va-yomar ha-shem yehi or va-yehi or), "And God said, 'Let there be light,' and there was light." God did not place any limitations on His all-revealing light. His intention was to reveal the treasures of nature. Nature was created for one reason only: to serve man. But because God realized what people in their primitive state were capable of doing to each other, He hid the knowledge that could enlighten people and teach them the secrets of nature.

God hid the secrets of nature for the same reason that we cannot give a child a hand grenade. He would only hurt himself and others. Each and every one of us carries within himself the capacity to bring happiness to ourselves and our surroundings. If only we could learn that by harming a fellow creature or society at large we are also harming ourselves, the chances are that we would not do it. But until we have learned this lesson, and until we have learned to act accordingly, we shall have to grope our way—slowly and bit by bit.

Rashi says in connection with the verse וירא אלהים את־האור כי־טוב (va-yar' ha-shem eth ha-or ki-tov), "God saw that the light was good," that in order to understand these words we also need the interpretation of the Talmud, which says: God saw that it was not justified to use the Big Light for a generation of evil people. So He separated the Big Light from the regular light, in anticipation of a generation of *zadikkim*, sages, who would understand that using this Big Light improperly could endanger the existence and survival of the world. It is impossible to deliver the secrets of the universe to people who are capable of cruelty and committing sins out of sheer selfish interest.

Isn't it surprising how in our generation light and darkness are mixed together? For many centuries now, the vision of the civilized part of humanity has been that study and education would foster a more cultured world, with happiness and prosperity, a world in which there would be no more selfishness and exploitation. This was the vision of poets and romantic authors, who painted a rosy picture of the future world until the arrival of the גאולה הכללית (*ge'ulah ha-kelalit*), the Great Redemption for all humanity. Love and brotherhood would prevail, and man would be his brother's keeper. There would be no more hatred and jealousy, no ruthless competition, no killing, and no robbery. These poets and romantics promised us that there would be no more hunger or loneliness, and that people would live happily together, enjoying the benefits of their creativity and the inventions that made life easier.

It was a wonderful dream, but a dream nevertheless. How many people in their right minds today believe that this utopia will ever become reality? Surely nobody ever thought that civilization could bring so much destruction. Could anyone have believed that with our highly developed sciences and sophisticated inventions there would be so much evil and cruelty in the world? Did anybody imagine that the modern world could pass through so many crises, and that life would be so arduous for so many people? That there could still be so much enmity between nations, and that people would still give reign to their primitive instincts at the slightest provocation? Who could have imagined that civilization would not bring light, but darkness—not relief, but fear?

Now we can understand what Rabbi Eliezer said about the light that was created the first day: that one could look in this light from one end of the world to the other end, but that when God looked at the generation of the great Flood and their evil deeds, He decided to hide this Great Light, and the secrets of nature, until the time that man would recognize his obligations to himself and his fellowman.

Our prophets have assured us that a generation will come that will know how to handle this responsibility. Then the Big Light will be restored, and all the missing knowledge will be revealed, because God will no longer be afraid that mankind will abuse it to destroy the world. Our prophets have called this generation the דור דעה (*dor deah*), the "generation of knowledge," and this generation, through its combined responsibility and knowledge, will revolutionize our existence for the eternal well-being of all humankind.

Parashath Noah

אלה תולדות נח נח איש צדיק תמים היה בדרתיו את־האלהים
התהלך־נח: ותשחת הארץ לפני האלהים ותמלא הארץ חמס.

ויהי כל־הארץ שפה אחת ודברים אחדים: ויהי בנסעם מקדם
וימצאו בקעה בארץ שנער וישבו שם: ויאמרו איש אל־רעהו
הבה נלבנה לבנים ונשרפה לשרפה ותהי להם הלבנה לאבן
והחמר היה לחמר: ויאמרו הבה נבנה־לנו עיר ומגדל וראשו
בשמים ונעשו־לנו שם פן־נפוץ על־פני כל־הארץ: וירד יהוה
לראת את־העיר ואת־המגדל אשר בנו בני האדם: ויאמר יהוה
הן עם אחד ושפה אחת לכלם וזה החלם לעשות ועתה לא־יבצר
מהם כל אשר יזמו לעשות: הבה נרדה ונבלה שם שפתם אשר
לא ישמעו איש שפת רעהו: ויפץ יהוה אתם משם על־פני
כל־הארץ ויחדלו לבנת העיר.

"This is the account of Noah. Noah was a righteous man,
blameless among the people of his time, and he walked
with God.... Now the earth was corrupt in God's sight and
was full of violence."

At the beginning of *Parashath Noah* we are told why God
decided to destroy the earth and all its inhabitants in a big Flood.
After the floodwaters had subsided, and Noah and his family
had once again established themselves on dry land, the earth
soon became repopulated. As people moved eastward, they
found a plain in a region called Shinar and settled there. These

new inhabitants of the earth "had one language and a common speech."

At this point the Bible continues to tell how one day they said to each other:

"Come, let's make bricks and bake them thoroughly." They used brick instead of stone, and bitumen for mortar. Then they said: "Come, let us build ourselves a city, with a tower that reaches to the heavens, so that we may make a name for ourselves and not be scattered over the face of the whole earth." But God came down to see the city and the tower that the men were building. God said: "If as one people speaking one language they have begun to do this, then nothing they plan to do will be impossible for them. Come, let us go down and confuse their language so they will not understand each other." So God scattered them from there over all the earth, and they stopped building the city.

Surprisingly, in the same portion that deals with Noah, the Torah tells us about the building of the Tower of Babel, an event that took place only a short time after the Flood, with similar far-reaching consequences—not destruction, this time, but the dispersal of mankind all over the earth.

We have, therefore, two events dating from the very beginning of Jewish recorded history. The first is the story of Noah, about a time when, although both the world and mankind were young, people had already lost their innocence. Worse than that: they had made a travesty of the Creation, and murder and robbery were the order of the day.

The second narrative deals with the generation that repopulated the earth after the Flood and decided to build the Tower of Babel. Very little is known about this generation. However, the Torah tells us that God was displeased with them and decided to confuse their language, so that they could no longer understand each other. What was the sin of this דור הפלגה (*dor ha-falagah*), "the divided generation," as the generation of Babel is generally called? And why did God decide to scatter them all over the world? For even if their punishment was deserved, why did God choose to divide mankind, when His ultimate purpose has always been to unite it?

On the surface, the biblical narrative does not tell anything bad about the generation of Babel. On the contrary, our sages comment that—contrary to the דור המבול (*dor ha-mabul*), the generation of the Flood—"they conducted themselves in love and friendship, as it is said: 'they had one language and a common speech.'" Isn't this exactly what our present-day generation yearns for? Do we not say of people who live in harmony that they have "a common language"? The prophets foretold that a generation would come, the דור דעה (*dor deah*), when all people would understand each other. One of our biggest problems today is the lack of communication between people and their neighbors, and between nation and nation. Fear and suspicion are the hallmarks of the contemporary world society. Confusion reigns because of a "confounding of language."

In fact, we are suffering from a severe problem of semantics. The words that people use are the same—even in translation— but their meanings are not. The Western world speaks about peace, and so do the Communists. The Western world calls itself democratic, but so do the East Bloc countries. They even have adopted names such as "East German Democratic Republic." We speak of freedom, but so do some of the most repressive regimes in Europe or Africa, whose populations have been "liberated" from the imperialist yoke. So we see identical words, but opposite meanings.

According to the Midrash , Noah was still alive when the generation of the Tower of Babel revolted against God, and Noah asked God to destroy the entire generation. But God answered, "I do not have to destroy them, for they will destroy themselves through their deeds." How do we understand what the Torah and Midrash want to convey? What was the sin of the people? Where did they go wrong?

Some biblical scholars believe that God may have punished them for their presumptiousness in wanting to storm the heavens. Basically the people of the *dor ha-falagah* thought that they did not need God. Many people believe that they need God, to help unite and strengthen them, and to enable them to achieve their goals. Here was a generation that was united and even spoke the same language, and in short order it began to build itself a path to the heavens; the people of Babel felt like gods themselves, and they believed that they did not need the One God any more. They were going to rule the world according to their insights, without any need to subject themselves to divine supervision.

At this point God stepped in and said, "If as one people speaking one language they have begun to do this, then nothing they plan to do will be impossible for them." In other words, it would be impossible to prevent them from abusing their knowledge for base purposes. In fact, God had expressed a similar concern about man's misuse of knowledge on an earlier occasion, namely when He banished Adam and Eve from the Garden of Eden: "The man has now become like one of us, knowing good and evil. He must not be allowed to reach out his hand and take also from the Tree of Life and eat, and live forever." In other words, what God meant was that man should not regard knowledge as an end in itself, and use it the way he saw fit, for what he considered his benefit.

Our sages tell us that from the moment Adam had a taste of the Tree of Knowledge, and thus began to understand about good and bad, about beauty and ugliness, about what was permitted and what was forbidden, he began to be weighed down by life's problems. The first two portions of the Torah contain no fewer than three examples of fateful existential crises: the fratricidal struggle between Cain and Abel, the destruction of the דור המבול (*dor ha-mabul*), the generation of the Flood, and the dispersal of the דור הפלגה (*dor ha-falagah*).

Every one of these generations tried to solve its problems in its own way. Cain was the first to experience jealousy. He approached the problem in the most primitive and elementary way imaginable: he killed his brother. Ultimately he realized that this method of removing adversaries did not solve anything. His parents did not like him any better once Abel was no longer there to share their attention. More important is that Cain himself recognized that he had made a mistake, for he said גדול עוני מנשוא: . . . והיה כל־מצאי יהרגני (*gadol avoni me'neso . . . ve-hayah kol motz'e yahargene*), "My punishment is more than I can bear . . . and whoever finds me will kill me." What he meant was: I have committed a grave sin, and tomorrow someone stronger than me may come, and kill me in turn. He realized that he had chosen the wrong method of solving his problem. We simply cannot go through life removing everyone and everything that gets in our way. Unfortunately, though, Cain's system has not yet been abandoned. Even today we can witness how people everywhere take recourse to violent means in order to remove anything—or anybody—that disturbs them.

The generation of the Flood, by contrast, tried to solve its problems by utter licentiousness. They believed that it was possible to create a more convenient way of life by abrogating all moral categories. Why worry about problems such as what is allowed and what is forbidden; what is good and what is bad; what is beautiful and what is ugly; till where is mine, and where does somebody else's property begin? All those distinctions and restrictions were considered merely confusing. Anyway, who was to decide what was good or evil, right or wrong, beautiful or ugly, my property or the neighbor's? And if there was no one to give orders, concepts such as good and bad, or right and wrong, would not be needed anyway! There is only one word to describe such a situation: anarchy. ותשחת הארץ לפני האלהים ותמלא הארץ חמס (*ve-tishacheth ha-aretz lifnei ha-shem va-timale ha-aretz chamas*), "Now

the earth was corrupt in God's sight and was full of violence."
People said: Don't be afraid of God, just do what you want. Life
was cheap, and man reduced himself to the level of an animal.
God saw what was happening, and He sent the Flood to destroy
everything. Only Noah and his family survived.

Once the earth became repopulated, mankind once again ran
into problems, and again cast about for a solution. There was a
difference, however. The generation of Cain and Abel and the
generation of the Flood had done everything to degrade life and
create anarchy. The generation of the Tower of Babel at least
intended to respect human dignity, life, and property. ויהי
כל־הארץ שפה אחת ודברים אחדים (va-yehi kol ha-aretz safah echath u-devarim
achadim), "They had one language and a common speech." People
wanted to talk the same language, and have the same ideas, so
that there would be no differences of opinion, and therefore no
fighting. If there was one idea only, so they believed, there
automatically would be peace in the world and between
neighbors.

Human solidarity is a wonderful thing—provided that people do not rely exclusively on their own strength. What the
citizens of Babel had in mind, however, was a purely materialistic enterprise. God played no role in it whatsoever! "We will
build ourselves a city, with a tower that reaches to the heavens,
so that we may make a name for ourselves." Everything was to
be built on a materialistic—rather than on a spiritual—basis,
without any thought of God.

This was where they made their mistake. One language, in
the sense of *one single idea*, does not by itself yield a purpose in life,
or understanding among people. On the contrary, it produces
uneasiness, dissension, and hatred. In a world in which only one
idea is permitted to exist, there is nothing to talk about. Anyone
whose ideas or opinions differ from the rest will be very careful
to hide his feelings. Eventually a man will be afraid to talk to
strangers, and after that to friends, and in the end even to his
wife or children—as indeed was the case in Nazi Germany and in

China during the Cultural Revolution, and as it still happens in the Communist world.

Man is created as an individual, and if he is not allowed freedom to express himself, he will revolt. Therefore, one language is a good thing, given a prevailing belief that the world is ruled by God: a belief that man's own endeavors and those of his fellowman are guided by a proud and self-confident belief in self, carried by a firm faith in God. People who learn to live their lives in this manner will be more patient and more tolerant of others, and their own lives will be much more harmonious and resistant to all the problems with which life confronts each and every one of us every day.

Parashath Lech Lecha

ויאמר יהוה אל־אברם לך־לך מארצך וממולדתך ומבית אביך
אל־הארץ אשר אראך.

"God said to Abram, 'Leave your country, your people, and your father's household and go to the land I will show you.'"

Our sages comment that in fact God gave Abram the command to go twice: לך לך (*lech lecha*), "Go, Go." *Lech lecha* means "go for yourself," by which God wanted to indicate that Abram's departure from his home and homeland would be for his own benefit, for his own good.

It is interesting that even before Abram set out on his journey, God let it be known that the end result would be beneficial. We are reminded of another occasion when God sent Abraham (as he was later called) on a journey, namely when He told him to take his son Isaac to Mount Moriah. From the moment Abraham understood that he would have to sacrifice his son, his journey must have been an almost insurmountable burden. Yet the sages say that God did not tell Abraham that in the end He would not bring tragedy over his house, but—on the contrary—a blessing, as indeed He had promised him originally.

Why is it that לך לך (*lech lecha*) is interpreted the first time, when Abram left for Eretz Israel, as a good omen, and not when he set out on his equally unknown but far more difficult mission with Isaac?

We could argue that when God said to Abram, "Leave your home and your land," it was done with the purpose of testing

him, to see if Abram would listen and do what God told him—
but this only raises another question. For, if so, then why did
God reveal to Abram beforehand that his journey would have
such a good and beneficial ending? Once Abram was assured of
the outcome, it was no longer a test. Surprisingly, our sages say
that this test of leaving his country and his people was the
hardest of the ten trials with which Abraham was confronted in
the course of his life. How do we understand this, when according to the above interpretation of *lech lecha* it was not really a
test?

Rabbi Naphtali Zevi Berlin, the head of the great yeshivah of
Volozhin, whose acronym was 'הנצי"ב', the *"Neziv"* ("High Com-
missioner"), explains the circumstances surrounding Abraham's departure, and from them we learn the agonizing
hardships involved in this trial. The *Neziv* offers the following
interpretation of the words of the Torah: "God asked two things
from Abram—first, to leave the environment in which he was
born, his family and friends, and simply forget his entire past,
and second, to go and travel. Abram had to go and see for
himself how other people lived their daily lives, for the more he
looked and the more he saw, the better he would be able to
understand and help them.

As regards the first point: Why was it so difficult for Abram
to leave his familiar surroundings, in a time when people led
nomadic lives anyway?

To understand this we must first understand the relationship between Abram and his family, especially his connection
with his father Terach. Terach was not merely an idolator—an
idol worshiper—but an idol maker. Abram was the first man to
discover the One God and to recognize the existence of the
Almighty.

The Midrash gives numerous illustrations of the conflicts
between Abram and his father and family. The legend has it that
one night Abram went into his father's workshop where the
idols were made and smashed the images. When the following

day his father came and saw the destruction, he asked Abram who had broken his idols. Abram answered: It looks as if they quarreled among themselves, and one must have killed the other. His father became terribly angry and shouted at him: Why do you tell lies? I made them myself, and I know that there is not a breath of life in them. And now you want me to believe that they killed each other? Abram's reply was: If you know that much, then how can you believe that they are gods and can help you?

At this point our narratives state a very important thing, namely that from that day on his father Terach and his entire family never exchanged another word with him as long as he lived.

To understand the severity of this statement, we should remember the closely knit tribal society within which people spent their lives in ancient times. Tribes lived separately, and they were extremely jealous of their independence. The tribal society was governed by extremely strict and inflexible rules, and so if a tribe decided to excommunicate someone, he was totally on his own. There were no nearby settlements where he could go, and neighboring tribes refused to accept him. In other words, from the moment his family decided to ostracize him, Abram no longer had anyone to whom he could talk and relate. If something like this had happened to a weaker character than Abram who, as his later life shows, was quite resourceful and strong willed, he would have broken up completely, because a situation like this is worse than imprisonment for life. Society punishes criminals by putting them in prison and isolating them from society. But even a prisoner has fellow inmates; even in a prison there are some people one can talk to and befriend. In Abram's traditional tribal society nobody would have dared to talk to him. Such a *cherem*, a ban, or excommunication, meaning the total exclusion from all social and economic contact, was the worst punishment in the world, not only in antiquity, but until the nineteenth century.

However, Abram believed in the One God, and thus he was not scared of his isolation. His singular belief strengthened him and gave him a purpose in life. His God had told him, "Go from your land... to the land that I will show you." Start your life again as a new person, as if you were born today.

Now we understand the severity of Abram's test. Every refugee is distrusted and cold-shouldered by society. Except for his immediate family, Abram was truly on his own, without anybody to turn to or support him!

On the second point, the Talmud says that God wanted to teach Abram that man cannot live from bread alone. He had to travel, to get to know the world and his fellowmen to learn that it is not only the material existence that counts. Abram was not literally short of bread or the basic necessities of life, but he was missing something else.

One of our sages said, "Society can be divided any way one pleases, but I have found that the most useful distinction is between those who devote their lives to the verb 'to be!', and those who only think about the verb 'to have!'" Some people always seem to be thinking about "having," rather than about "being." Simply put, there are people who are continually preoccupied with having more and more. Their ultimate objective is to reach the top, socially and economically. By no means do I want to condemn material possessions, but the thinking of the people I am referring to seems to be that, since there is nothing wrong with being rich, nothing should stop them from trying to create more and more wealth and property. The point is, of course, that there is no yardstick for the meaning of "rich": one person's millionaire is the next one's pauper! Short of a definition of what is "rich," and what is "enough," nothing is to stop a person from taking everything—even at the expense of others, as well as of his own good name and morality.

On the other hand, those who devote their life to the word "to be!", show that they do have such a yardstick—that they care about others and want to be with other people for their mutual benefit. For them, it is not only a matter of individual existence, but of coexistence.

A great Jewish scholar once remarked, "Animals are merely concerned about their own needs. Man's concern is for the needs of humanity." Man is superior over animals depending on the degree to which he cares for others. "To be!", therefore, is to prefer people to things. Abraham and his wife Sarah introduced the recognition of the One God into the world. Even so, only a few of their contemporaries learned from them. They stayed with Abraham and Sarah, they ate with them, but they did not change their point of view as a result. They did not accept Abraham and Sarah's belief.

Because of this, and despite their advanced age, they asked for a child who would spread their message further across the world. God promised them a son, and Abraham and Sarah believed that they would get one. They never asked God to show them a sign, so that they could be sure.

When, however, God promised Abraham Eretz Israel for his children, Abraham asked God: How will I know that my children will inherit this land? We can be certain that Abraham did not doubt the word of God, so the question is why he asked. The reason is very simple. When God promised Abraham and Sarah that they would have a son, there was no reason to ask further, because children are a gift from God, and if God promises, it will be. A land, however, a country, is not just a gift. Land must be acquired; it must be occupied, populated, cultivated, guarded and protected by people. Abraham did not doubt that God would give him the land. He wanted to be certain that his children would do their share to *keep* the land. God's reply is most interesting. Instead of giving a direct answer, God said, ידע תדע כי־גר יהיה זרעך בארץ לא להם ועבדום וענו אתם ארבע מאות שנה (*yada teda ke-ger yihyeh zar'achah be-eretz lo lahem va-avadum ve-enu otam arba meoth shanah*), "Know for certain that your descendants will be strangers in a country not their own, and they will be enslaved and ill-treated four hundred years."

Why did God tell Abraham that his descendants would go to Egypt? The answer is that only through being oppressed and persecuted would the Jews know what it is to be free; only through living through an Exile lasting hundreds of years would they realize what it was to have their own country, and learn to cherish it and look after it.

I myself do not believe that the State of Israel was established because the nations, seeing how the Jews had suffered, decided to give them a country of their own. It is my belief that our people would not have been ready to sacrifice so much, had it not been for the Holocaust and the knowledge—and fear—that another Holocaust cannot be ruled out.

Abram learned two important lessons from his trial, which involved his forced departure from his homeland and his journey to an unknown destination where he started an entirely new life. Through it, God wants to teach people of all generations that if they want to live, they must be prepared to sacrifice—both for their own sake and for their fellowmen.

Parashat Va-Yera

וירא אליו יהוה באלני ממרא והוא ישב פתח־האהל כחם היום: וישא עיניו וירא והנה שלשה אנשים נצבים עליו וירא וירץ לקראתם מפתח האהל וישתחוו ארצה.

"God appeared to Abraham near the great trees of Mamre while he sat at the entrance to his tent in the heat of the day. Abraham looked up and saw three men standing nearby. When he saw them, he hurried from the entrance of his tent to meet them and bowed low to the ground."

Our sages say that God came to visit Abraham after he had circumcised himself and he was sick, to see how he was doing. Abraham was sitting at the entrance to his tent, apparently waiting for someone to pass by, so that he might invite him into his house. For this reason God decided to send him three visitors and—as the Torah tells us—when Abraham saw them coming, he ran to them and asked them to come in for a rest, and to eat and drink with him.

According to the Talmud , our sages asked who these three visitors were, and the answer is: the first one was the archangel Michael, who came to tell Sarah that she was going to have a son; the second was the angel Raphael, who came to heal Abraham from his sickness; and the third visitor was Gabriel, who had been sent to destroy Sodom and Gomorrah.

When the three visitors rose to leave, Abraham walked along with them to see them on their way. Here the Torah continues to tell that God said, "Shall I hide from Abraham what I am about to do?" For at this point Abraham and Sarah had been informed about the impending birth of Isaac, but Abraham was as yet unaware of the fate that awaited the cities of Sodom and Gomorrah. God decided to tell Abraham what his angels' next mission would be, at which point Abraham argued with God, and pleaded that He should save the inhabitants "if only ten righteous men can be found there." Thus far the narrative of the Torah and the talmudic interpretation.

It is not easy to understand exactly what we are told here. At the beginning of the narrative Abraham is sick. He had circumcised himself, and apart from the fact that he was already ninety years old, the third day is always the critical day after surgery. God wanted to cheer Abraham by bringing him what were supposed to be good tidings. As regards the coming birth of Isaac, He certainly succeeded, but why should Abraham have been happy about the destruction of Sodom and Gomorrah? We know, of course, that Abraham had a very strong sense of justice, and the sinfulness of these two cities was known far and wide. At the same time Abraham was a very compassionate human being, who suffered with every fellow creature. So why should God tell him that He was going to destroy the two cities—in one of which resided his nephew Lot and his family? Even if the decision was just, and the two cities deserved their fate, we could ask whether this really was the right message for Abraham, and whether it was the right moment to tell him when he was feeling ill.

Why did God want to destroy Sodom and Gomorrah in the first place? The answer, as we can read in the Torah, is that the inhabitants were so wicked that there was no hope for improvement. The only solution was to eradicate the cities from the face of the earth. In the biblical dialogue between God and Abraham, when the latter pleads for the two doomed cities, Abraham asks whether God will "sweep away the righteous with the wicked." Abraham bargains with God, until God agrees not to destroy Sodom and Gomorrah if, instead of the original fifty, even ten righteous people were to be found among the inhabitants. The fact that even this number proved too high shows conclusively how bad they were! In fact, so notorious was their way of life that even thousands of years later the expression for an example of utter depravity is, "They behave like people from Sodom and Gomorrah."

What was it that made the population of Sodom and Gomorrah so notorious? How had they become so depraved? The Talmud, in tractate *Sanhedrin*, comments that the people of Sodom and Gomorrah had not become corrupted as a result of poverty or want. On the contrary, it was the possession of material goods that had corrupted them. Their many worldly possessions had made them greedy, so that they said: Our land is a good land, and it has everything we want. Why, therefore, should we share what we have with strangers? If everyone who wants something comes to us, and we give it to him, the result is that we will have less. The best way to prevent this from happening is to stop people from coming here. The fewer guests we have, the more there will be for us.

On the other hand, the inhabitants of Sodom and Gomorrah did not want to make laws against visiting, because this would have advertised their wickedness. Instead they made sure to behave to visitors in such a way that people were frightened and avoided coming to them. For good measure, they forbade the members of their own community to entertain visitors or give food to wayfarers.

To understand what this means, we should remember that in ancient times there were no inns or hostels; travelers could not just enter a restaurant or a hotel or motel to find a meal or a bed for the night. Only the residents of the city could entertain and lodge strangers. Maybe we could not expect them to behave like Abraham, who hurried toward wayfarers and invited them for a rest and a meal. But to forbid such hospitality and punish the "transgressors," residents and strangers alike, was the height of cruelty and wickedness. In short, the way of life of the

people of Sodom and Gomorrah corrupted the morality of the
whole region, and their sinfulness was known far and wide,
even where it concerned small things that were important for
the receiver, but did not involve any loss for the giver—such as a
bed for the night, or even information. They were people who,
to use a modern expression, would not tell a person the time of
day.

When we talk about the Jewish obligation of הכנסת אורחים
(*hachnasath orechim*), the obligation to welcome guests, we do not
just think of the assistance one person can render to another. By
helping a fellow, we also help ourselves. The more we assist
others, the more confident we ourselves will become in life,
because of the knowledge that when we need help, someone else
will in turn extend a hand to us. This is how we develop confidence and faith in society. This kind of behavior sanctifies our
existence and enobles us as human beings.

Abraham believed in God, and believed that He had created
man and everything that exists on our planet. He recognized the
fellowship of man, and because of this he felt a responsibility for
other people. This does not mean that he was able to solve
everybody's problems—or even pretended that he could solve
them—but he did develop a sensitivity for other people's suffering, and he did everything to make it easier for people in need—
even by merely showing sympathy.

This kind of attitude is as essential today as it was in Abraham's time. An individual who cannot generate this kind of
feelings for his fellow humans is not truly a friend to anybody.
There is an old chassidic tale about a rabbi who was taught what
it means to love one's neighbor by two simple Russian farmers.
On a journey to a faraway town he had alighted at an inn to
spend the night. Sitting near the fire before retiring to bed, he
happened to overhear a conversation between two farmers. The
first farmer said to the other, "Pjotr, I really love you very
much."

The other said, "I don't believe you. I know you are lying."

Somewhat irritated, the first one reacted, "How do you know, when I tell you that I like you?"

To which the first one replied, "You have no idea what I am suffering. If you really loved me, you would know. The fact that you don't shows that you do not like me."

This conversation taught the rabbi what it meant to really love someone.

King David, in his famous Psalm 145, says, עיני־כל אליך ישברו ואתה נותן־להם את־אכלם בעתו (eynei kol eleicha yeshaberu ve-atah noten lahem eth achlam be-eto), "The eyes of all look to You hopefully, and You give them food at the proper time." The psalm does not say, "You are taking care of their needs at the proper times," because there are no two people in the world whose needs are always the same or, for that matter, exactly like those of their neighbor. Everybody is an individual unto himself, and everyone has his own specific needs at every specific moment. This is why we have to remember that our obligation to help means adapting our assistance to the needs of the other person, rather than to our own. The Talmud expresses it in this way: When we give something to a needy person, we are not giving away our own property. We are giving some of the things that God has entrusted to us while we are on earth and—in so doing—enables us to share with others. In another place, the Talmud says, "If we give in the proper way, God will bless us with eleven blessings." What is "the proper way"? The answer has two aspects: first, we must give spontaneously and with goodwill, and in a pleasant manner. Second, we must give what the other person needs, and not what we consider it would be useful to give, let alone what we can spare. The more the receiver feels that his needs are taken into account, and that his opinions are important, the more his self-respect and self-confidence will be strengthened, and the more he will be encouraged to do his best and not give up.

Elsewhere the Talmud says that a man who closes his eyes for the needy is like one who worships idols. This is taken as referring to a man who, even if he gives charity, gives it mechanically without taking an interest, or without the patience to find out what the recipient really needs. It is like idol worship, because if the giver had stopped to realize that God created the other like himself, he would have listened to his problems and taken the trouble to help in a way that suited him.

The people of Sodom and Gomorrah acted in exactly the opposite way. Their philosophy was the iron fist: callousness and aggression. As far as they were concerned, if a man did not succeed, this was a sign that the Creator did not like him. He was obviously useless, and therefore might just as well disappear. The Talmud relates an example of a similar mentality from a much later time. It concerns a certain Tinneius Rufus (or "Turnus Rufus," or "Rufus ha-Rasha"—Rufus the Wicked, as he is known in rabbinic circles), a Roman governor of Judea from the time of the Bar Kochba war. He liked to ask Rabbi Akiva awkward questions such as, "If your Torah is right and God likes poor people, then why does he not support them?" Even today we can meet people who think that the world belongs to them only, and that they do not have any obligation to the shlimazzels, the weak and unfortunate, so that it is better to keep them out of sight.

Because of this, Rabbi Akiva's answer is very relevant: God created every individual with a specific potential, and it is His intention that every creature should develop to the peak of this potential—not just for his own sake, so that he can live in dignity, but for the sake of everybody who lives in this world. Some people were created intelligent, and some less intelligent; some were created healthy and strong, and some weak and dependent. This is as it should be, for if it were otherwise, the world would not be able to exist.

This was also the opinion of our father Abraham. He recognized that God had created man, and that everyone had a right to live. Proof that the opposite method could not prevail were Sodom and Gomorrah. Their inhabitants were prosperous and strong—but also selfish and cruel, and this is exactly the reason why in the end they lost everything. It would seem to me that this is what our sages meant when they concluded that the people of Sodom and Gomorrah became corrupt because their land was too good. Everything had come to them too easily, which brought them to the mistaken conclusion that only people who are strong or possess material goods are important. In this respect it is interesting to see that Abraham, whose thoughts were always turned to giving, became richer.

We may be certain that Abraham's neighbors had great misgivings about the way our patriarch acted. There were no mass communication media in Abraham's time, so that the only way to disseminate new ideas was by word of mouth. This is exactly what Abraham did, and this is one of the reasons why he opened the doors of his tent to all passersby. The people of Sodom and Gomorrah interfered with the people who passed their cities on their way to Abraham. For this reason God believed that Abraham would be pleased if He told him that these cities were going to be destroyed, since as a result the world would be more open and receptive to Abraham's ideas. Nothing of the kind happened. Abraham was not happy. He was a modest man who, as he said to God, considered himself merely "dust and ashes." He believed that he was not worth the destruction of two cities, and he fought for their survival and that of their inhabitants. In fact, we find the same idea in Psalm 104, where it says: יתמו חטאים מן־הארץ ורשעים עוד אינם ברכי נפשי את־יהוה הללויה (yitamu chata'im min ha-aretz u-resha'im od einam barchi nafshe eth ha-shem halleluyah), "...may sinners vanish from the earth and the wicked be no more. Praise God, O my soul." The Talmud comments on this verse: Not the sinners will be destroyed, but their sins. A sinner can always repent, and for this reason King David prayed that God would destroy the sins, rather than the sinner.

This also makes it clear why God was anxious to come and see Abraham, the man who never acted for himself but always for others. He wanted to know whether Abraham would welcome the news of the destruction of Sodom and Gomorrah and rejoice, as other people would have done, or whether he would react as in fact he did, refusing to accept the destruction of patently wicked people who obstructed the dissemin-ation of Abraham's ideas by any means fair and foul. The outcome of this test proved once more that Abraham, the first Jew, was not like other people, in that he refused to do anything that would destroy others for the sake of furthering his own beliefs and way of life.

Parashath Chayei Sarah

ואברהם זקן בא בימים ויהוה ברך את־אברהם בכל: ויאמר
אברהם אל־עבדו זקן ביתו המשל בכל־אשר־לו שים־נא ידך
תחת ירכי: ואשביעך ביהוה אלהי השמים ואלהי הארץ אשר
לא־תקח אשה לבני מבנות הכנעני אשר אנכי יושב בקרבו.

"Abraham was now old and well advanced in years, and
God had blessed him in every way. He said to the chief
servant in his household, the one in charge of all that he
had, 'Put your hand under my thigh. I want you to swear
by the God of heaven and the God of earth, that you will
not get a wife for my son from the daughters of the
Canaanites, among whom I am living....'"

At the beginning of this portion, called חיי שרה (*Chayei Sarah*),
the "Life of Sarah," we are told that Sarah, the wife of Abraham,
passed away at the age of 127 years, or—as the Torah puts it—"a
hundred years, and twenty years, and seven years."

We call Sarah the first mother of the Jewish nation. Incidentally, the Talmud, in tractate *Baba Batra*, explains why Sarah's
age is expressed as a summation of periods, rather than a total
number of years, as we normally do. It is a symbolic way of
saying that at whatever age—a hundred years, twenty years, or
seven years—Sarah was the same woman in terms of virtue,
beauty, wisdom, strength, purpose in life, and every other characteristic. For most people life becomes harder as the years go
by. As we grow older, we are less healthy, less strong, and more
prone to anxieties. All this in some ways affects our joy of life,

even though every age also has its compensations. For instance, a gradual diminishing of physi- cal activity is compensated by increased experience and understanding. It was the same with Sarah: at every age of her life she was able to adjust herself to the problems with which life confronted her. When she was young she enjoyed the things that young people enjoyed; when she was old, she equally enjoyed everything older people are capable of enjoying—and at no time did she complain.

After Sarah's death, Abraham was left with Isaac, who was as yet unmarried. Rashi interprets the words of the Torah, that God had blessed Abraham בכל (be-chol), "in every way," according to the numerical value of the Hebrew characters, as meaning that he had been blessed with בן (ben), "a son" (both words add up to fifty-two), and that it was now high time that Isaac should find a wife.

For Isaac to marry was uppermost in Abraham's mind, and we could ask why finding a wife for Isaac became a problem only after Sarah died. According to the tradition, Isaac was almost forty years old at the time, so why had Abraham not done something about it when he was younger and Sarah was still alive? And finally, why did Abraham not do something about it himself, instead of sending his trusted servant?

Some of our sages interpret the words that God blessed Abraham "in every way" in the sense that he had a son who was his father's look-alike. People who met Isaac commented that he was exactly like his father, not only as regards his features and stature, but also in his behavior and his ideas. Those who knew Abraham and subsequently met Isaac thought they were deal-ing with one and the same person. For a father it is a blessing to have a son like this, but at the same time it is a problem. In Abraham's days parents were accustomed to select marriage partners for their children, so the more a boy looked and acted like his father, the more critical the father might be expected to be in his choice of a daughter-in-law. In fact, Abraham wanted a daughter-in-law who looked and behaved like Sarah. Besides this, considering the tribal relationships of those days, the stronger the father's imprint on his son, the more the future wife would be forced to adjust to her parents-in-law. I assume that Abraham had lost no opportunity to look for a suitable daughter-in-law, but—as I explained above—the choice might not have been easy, particularly since, as the Torah makes clear, he refused to consider a daughter of the Canaanites, among whom they were living.

Neither should we forget that a wife is one of the Jewish family's greatest assets. The happiness and stability of the entire family depend on the wife and mother. The Hebrew name for a housewife is עקרת בית (*akereth beit*), the "anchor" of the house. Jewish history is replete with stories about the Jewish women; historical and legendary accounts of their greatness and resourcefulness can be found in Tenach and Talmud and numerous other Jewish scriptural sources. Many times Jewish women distinguished themselves when difficult or even critical decisions had to be made. On many occasions Jewish women succeeded in saving the lives of their families, or even their communities—and sometimes the life and the reputation of the Jewish people as a whole.

History shows that there have been countless situations in which our people were helpless and did not know which way to turn, after which a Jewish woman intervened, quietly, to save the day. One of the best known biblical examples is when Moses' parents were forced to entrust the basket with their newborn son to the waters of the Nile. They were certain that they had lost their child, but they had not counted on his sister Miriam. She quietly stood aside, waiting for Pharaoh's daughter to discover the basket. There is something in a woman's nature—even more so than in a man's—that makes her follow her intuition, that prevents her from losing her head in critical situations, and makes her act decisively and correctly at the right moment.

When the Jewish people stood at Mount Sinai, and they felt

helpless and lost because Moses failed to return with the Tablets, they committed one of the biggest sins in their existence by erecting the Golden Calf. The text of the Torah enables us to understand that this idol had been fashioned from gold ornaments belonging to the Children of Israel—but only the male members of the tribes, because the women refused to contribute their own gold pendants and bracelets.

Of particular interest is the conception of the Torah on the role women play in our world. The first man was called אדם, "Adam," because he was taken from the אדמה (adamah), the earth. Not Eve, however (חוה,"Chava"), because she was not only the first woman but, as the Torah explains, she was the אם כל חי (em kol chai), "the mother of every living person." How significant is this difference between their names! A man is in a sense born as adamah, as "soil" or "earth," in other words he has to be worked on and cultivated in order to become "a man." Not so a woman, who without any further preparation is ready for her role as the mother of her family and people. Our sages comment that God stressed the greatness and importance of womankind by His description in the Torah.

Two major events in the early history of our people, both of which are related in the portion *Chayei Sarah*, demonstrate this clearly. First of all there is the description in the Torah of the death of our first matriarch, Sarah, in particular Abraham's purchase of the Cave of Machpelah as a resting place for Sarah and a future burial place for his family. This is, incidentally, the first recorded Jewish purchase in the Holy Land. The second event in the same portion is Isaac's marriage to Rebecca. Both these episodes are dominated by a female personality, and both are—as emphasized by our narratives—closely related to the theme of Jewish continuity.

Sarah had died, but her place was taken by Rebecca, who in every respect followed in Sarah's footsteps. The Midrash states that as long as Sarah was alive a cloud of glory covered the doors of her tent. Her doors were wide open for everyone who wanted

hospitality. There was a blessing on everything she did. The
lamp of happiness burned the entire week "from Shabbath eve
to Shabbath eve." The moment Sarah died, all this came to a
halt, but once Rebecca had become Isaac's wife, and she proved
to behave in the way Sarah had behaved, everything came
back—both the cloud of glory and the light inside the house. The
mefareshim, the Jewish biblical and talmudic expositors, explain
the words, Isaac brought Rebecca into the tent of his mother
Sarah, as meaning that at that moment Isaac saw *she became like his
mother*—and then he loved her.

In this case, the Torah tells us that Isaac first married
Rebecca, and that only then he loved her. We usually expect love
to precede marriage, but far more important as far as the Jewish
tradition is concerned is that love continues after marriage, as it
did in the case of Isaac and Rebecca. The modern world tends to
stress romance before marriage, whereas the Torah's way of life
places the main emphasis on lifelong devotion and affection
after marriage. We believe in the sanctity of the obligations that
we undertake during the wedding ceremony, as expressed in the
vow כדת משה וישראל . . . הרי את מקודשת לי (*hare ath mekudesheth li . . . ke-dath
Moshe ve-Israel*), "You are consecrated to me... according to the
tradition of Moses and Israel." The Torah expects mutual care
and devotion—more than romance—from the Jewish marriage
partners after they are married.

There is one more point worth mentioning in this portion,
namely the death of Abraham. The Torah relates that Abraham
died "at a good old age, an old man and full of years." The Torah
mentions only the bare facts. Only after the *shivah*—the seven-
day period of mourning—was over, could the realization break
through that the giant Abraham was gone for good.

The great Abraham, who had shaken heaven and earth, the
man who had changed the face of his society and brought God
and the world together, was dead. There were many people who
said to themselves: Now that he is gone, we can return to our old
way of life. For instance, the Torah tells us that the Philistines

took the opportunity to block the wells that Abraham had dug. This incident could easily be taken also in the figurative sense, as an effort to blot out the teachings of Abraham. It was a great challenge for his son Isaac. The Torah says ויהי אחרי מות אברהם ויברך אלהים את-יצחק (va-yehe acharei mot avraham va-yevarech ha-shem eth yitz-chak), "After Abraham's death God blessed his son Isaac." Isaac was great, but not a giant like his father, and he needed God's blessing in order to have the strength to pursue his father's ways and teachings.

We may say that God blessed Isaac because he was willing to accept his father's teachings and walk in Abraham's footsteps. The giant was gone, and a "lesser mortal" had to assume his responsibilities. This is how it was then—and how it still is today. As long as the Abrahams are with us, we can shift all problems upon them, but eventually there comes a time when the Isaacs have to take over and carry the banner. The lesser people must accept the challenges of the day.

This is what the Torah wants to tell us in this portion. Every period produces the leaders it requires. Not all of them will be giants, and some will be better than others, but when called upon they will find the strength and the inspiration to fulfill this responsibility.

Parashath Toledoth

ואלה תולדות יצחק בן־אברהם אברהם הוליד את־יצחק.

"This is the account of Abraham's son Isaac. Abraham became the father of Isaac."

There is an interesting duplication in this verse. The portion opens with the mention of Isaac being the son of Abraham. Immediately thereafter the Torah repeats that "Abraham became the father of Isaac."

Our sages explain that the Torah wants to repeat this message because it seems that in Abraham's time people joked about Isaac's birth. After all, Abraham and Sarah had been married many years, without having had any children, and for this reason certain cynics hinted that he was the son of King Abimelech. However, God shaped Isaac's features exactly like those of Abraham, and thus everyone had to agree that Abraham was indeed the physical father of Isaac. For this reason the Torah states *as a fact* that Abraham fathered Isaac.

There is yet another midrash , according to which Isaac was like his father not only physically but also in character and behavior. This explanation is much more difficult to understand, for when we read their life stories in the Torah, we must conclude that if ever a father and a son were different, it was Abraham and Isaac.

Abraham was an active and dynamic, even revolutionary, personality. He challenged the basic religious and ethical premises of his day. He knocked down the idols, in every sense of the word. He was honest and possessed an unparalleled sense of justice—so much so that he even questioned God's judgment when he learned that Sodom and Gomorrah were about to be destroyed. The Torah also tells that when his nephew Lot was taken prisoner near Sodom, Abraham quickly got together an army and pursued Lot's captors till "north of Damascus." He succeeded in freeing Lot and all his possessions. In other words, there was nothing sedentary or passive about Abraham; he was a man of action!

Isaac, on the other hand, was a far more passive individual. The Torah says that he "sat among the tents" and there are numerous examples in the Torah attesting to his far more dispassionate nature. The most striking instance is no doubt Isaac's wordless submission to the עקדה (akedah), when he allowed himself to be bound upon the altar that his father had built at God's command—without having the least indication that in the end his sacrifice would not be carried out! Similarly, Isaac accepted without comment or protest the wife that his father's chief servant Eliezer chose for him. Later on in his life, when the Philistines filled in the wells that his father Abraham had dug, Isaac simply retreated and dug other ones without fighting to reclaim his existing possessions. Perhaps this submissiveness was another reason why Isaac preferred Esau, who was a man of action, even though he used his energy for the wrong purposes.

Jacob, Isaac's younger son, was quiet and studious like his father, before circumstances forced a change. However, it was this disposition, and his general good nature, that caused him to become one of our three patriarchs, whose character traits Jews have tried to emulate ever since.

The truth is that just as the world needs impetuous men—men with a stormy, adventurous character, men "who move mountains," revolutinaries and radicals—the world also needs people who reflect, people of constancy who go about their work quietly and with devotion, almost passively.

The world needs consolidators no less than builders. We can observe the same differences in the characters of contemporary fathers and sons as between Abraham and Isaac, or between Isaac and Jacob. Each of them had his specific role to play; each had his appointed task in bridging the generations and carrying the Jewish people forward. If sometimes we wonder about our own significance, we can only conclude that merely our role as a link between past and future generations is enough to merit us a place in the chronology of mankind. Even if we do not aspire to change the world, or even if we do nothing, we still have our purpose, and someone else would not do as well in our place. Our role in bridging the generations alone justifies our existence.

In effect, the world can have too many adventurers, revolutionaries, or reformers. In the final analysis it is the quiet people who move the world forward. "All generals, and no soldiers" is a well-known saying for a situation where everyone wants to give orders. It is the soldier who fights the battles and carries the heaviest burdens of the war. The fact that in their more reflective moments people realize this is proven by the homage almost all nations pay to their "unknown" soldier.

It is difficult to picture the world without giants like Abraham—but at the same time it would never exist without the Isaacs. For every Abraham, we need a thousand Isaacs. Abraham and Isaac were not the same, therefore, neither in vitality, initiative, or in temperament—and for a very good reason. Yet they were alike, because both of them believed in the same principles.

The Torah continues to tell that Esau and Jacob grew up, and that Esau became "a skillful hunter, a man of the open country, while Jacob was a quiet man, staying among the tents." One day Esau came home from one of his hunting trips, and he said to Jacob, "Quick, let me have some of that red stew! I am famished." Jacob agreed, but in return he demanded that Esau sell him his birthright in exchange for the food. And the Torah says that Esau swore an oath, and sold his birthright to Jacob.

The differences between Esau and Jacob, and their attitudes

on how to live and whether—and how—to influence the way of life of others, has been a point of discussion for centuries. Jacob and Esau represent two opposing attitudes. Esau's goal in life was to achieve and to accumulate material goods. Esau was restless, never satisfied, always on the go, always hungry and—in the end—tired. Not so Jacob. His life was devoted to studying and trying to gain an understanding of the world around him. He was a realist, satisfied with what he possessed. Jacob felt no need to achieve; he completely lacked the urge to have more than his neighbors or relatives. Many people who think like Esau believe that the Jacobs in this world cannot possibly enjoy life, but the opposite is true. People who are satisfied with what they have do not have to show off in order to prove themselves. People who are satisfied like Jacob do not have to try to make an impression. Being satisfied, they are not poor, but rich. Not being enslaved to any passions, they are free.

Let us have another look at what the Torah says: "Once... Esau came in from the open country, famished. He said to Jacob, 'Quick, let me have some of that red stew!'" The question that presents itself immediately is: What was it that forced Esau to run about all day? Why did he have to drive himself so hard, to the point of being short-tempered and impatient? We should not forget that his father Isaac was a wealthy man. We can only conclude that Esau was not complaining about physical discomfort, but that he was mentally and spiritually fatigued. I believe that the answer is very simple: Esau was dissatisfied because he did not have any purpose in life. Physical satisfaction is important up to a point, but an individual who lacks spiritual nourishment will become hungry just the same. The Torah says לא על הלחם לבדו יחיה האדם (lo al ha-lechem levado yichyeh ha-adam), "Man does not live by bread alone." Physical stimuli alone are a poor diet, and sooner or later they will result in spiritual malnutrition.

Our forefathers, all the generations of rabbis and scholars, led busy lives, and they enjoyed every minute of it. They had large families, they were poor most of the time, and they certainly did not have luxuries. All the hours of the day and—often—the night were gainfully employed for the good of their communities.

Esau came home from the field short-tempered, hungry, and tired because he was disappointed with life. No doubt he had often mocked his brother for just sitting around and letting his life slip by, while he himself had plenty of excitement and all the food he wanted. But then a day arrived when he had to admit that his system had broken down, and he was fed up. "Give me something of what you have," he said to Jacob. It was only a simple lentil stew, but seeing how much Jacob enjoyed it made it look even more desirable.

Jacob said in return, "You admit that your way of life is bankrupt. Therefore I want you to give me your birthright, so that in the future people will accept my teaching and my way of life." In ancient times the firstborn was the authority and guide, and his example was followed by the entire family. Esau's preparedness to surrender his birthright was an admission that he had failed as an example, by not exercising his right to show others how they should live.

Esau's complaint is an old one, but one that is topical even today. Too often we read in the newspapers about young people who have decided to put an end to their lives. Often they leave a note saying in so many words, "I don't blame anybody for my death, but I feel that my life does not have a purpose. I no longer know what to do, and I am bored with life." And we are sad, and we wonder, because that young person was not short of food, or clothes, or family, or prospects. What was missing wasn't anything physical or material; there was a yawning spiritual gap—a deep spiritual emptiness. Esau did not so much become old; he felt old, unlike his grandfather Abraham. Abraham overcame many difficulties in his life, but it was not those problems that aged him. Abraham became old because his body aged and he was worn out: he was finished physically—not spiritually.

King David said: קוי יי יחליפו כח (kavei ha-shem yachlifu koach), "The

hope that is with you will renew your days fresh and fruitful."
These days we are too easily inclined to look for excitement—
any form of excitement, as long as we do not have to think, and
can take our minds off our problems. We crave for immediate
physical gratification; we crave excitement, because our spirit is
empty of spiritual things. Thinking of all the things we want—
materially and today—is what makes us tired. The time has
come to give some thought to the issues of the mind: the things
that will still be important tomorrow and the day after; the
things that do not serve our own physical satisfaction, but that
will benefit our society and the generations that will come after
us.

Parashath Va-Yetze

ויצא יעקב מבאר שבע וילך חרנה: ויפגע במקום וילן שם
כי־בא השמש ויקח מאבני המקום וישם מראשתיו וישכב
במקום ההוא: ויחלום והנה סלם מצב ארצה וראשו מגיע
השמימה.

"And Jacob left Beersheva and set out for Haran. When he reached a certain place, he stopped for the night because the sun had set. Taking one of the stones there, he put it under his head and lay down to sleep. He had a dream in which he saw a stairway resting on the earth, with its top reaching to heaven...."

Jacob was a dreamer. He had a dream of keeping his descendants together, and thus laying the foundation for the Jewish nation. He dreamed of the future in which God would spread his descendants "like the dust of the earth—to the west and to the east, to the north and to the south," as He had promised to Abraham. Jacob had a lot of ideals, wonderful ideals. Every age has its dreamers; some want to improve the human condition, others dream about social improvement, and still others of fame or national greatness. Similarly, every age has its writers, poets, philosophers, and prophets who try to convince their fellows that if only they would follow their inspiration, certain problems would be solved in an almost miraculous way.

Not surprisingly, it generally takes but a short time for these ideals to go awry; not only do they fail to bring a solution, but usually they create additional difficulties, conflicts, and even bloodshed. They cause problems we were completely unaware of when we dreamed our wonderful dream. Some of the most

46

fervent and idealistic dreams have brought the greatest grief to the world. All wars are cruel, but civil wars—fought for the purpose of national or social emancipation or rehabilitation— are the most cruel of all. The cruelty with which people fight their own flesh and blood exceeds that with which they fight strangers, as the French and Russian revolutions, the American and Spanish civil wars, or the war in Cambodia have taught us.

Our sages say that humanity seldom likes the look of its achievements. Why should this be? Our rabbis explain that this is because, in the process, we invariably hurt people who stand in the way of the intended "new order." The moment that the achievement of our goal involves the destruction of others, nothing good will come of it. This is the meaning of the dream our patriarch Jacob dreamed during the first night of his journey from Beersheva to Haran, where Isaac had told him to find a wife among his mother's kinfolk and build a new life.

What was this dream? That the top of a ladder placed upon the earth reached the heavens. Our sages interpret this as meaning that if you want to achieve an elevated goal in life, so spiritual and high that you feel you have reached the heavens, then you should never forget that the foot of the ladder must stay on the earth. You cannot "storm the heavens" in one big leap, never caring about what happens on the way. In fact, you have to reach your goal step by step, and from time to time you must look around you, to see whether you did not leave something broken on the way—whether in the course of your progress no other people have been trampled underfoot.

In short, not just the goal is important, but how you reach it. It should be a good goal, and the way you go about achieving it should be clean and pure. Our patriarch Jacob understood what the dream told him. When he awoke he said אכן יש יהוה במקום הזה ואנכי לא ידעתי (achen yesh ha-shem ba makom ha-zeh, ve-anochi lo yadati), "Surely God is in this place, and I was not aware of it." And he was afraid and said, "How awesome is this place. This is none other than the House of God; this is the gate of heaven."

There is an old midrashic legend about the place where Jacob spent this first night of his journey. The Torah reveals that it was a city called Luz. According to the Midrash , Luz was a special city. The מלאך המות (*malach ha-mavet*), the "Angel of Death," never visited there, which meant that its inhabitants could live forever. People who were tired of life left the city, and the moment they were outside they died—like everyone else in the world. The interesting part is that—according to this legend— when Jacob entered the city, it turned out to be a ghost town; there was not a single living soul around. Jacob became afraid, and he decided to call the place בית־אל (*Beth El*), the House of God.

Why did he choose this name? To understand it, we should ask what it was in Luz that made people want to die, when most people dream about living forever. Ever since man was created, he has been aware that one day he must die. As a result, people have done everything in their power to prolong life, or even try to achieve immortality.

Of course we know that this is a futile target, and that no one has ever succeeded in warding off the inevitable. Yet people try, if only that they may enjoy the fruits of their work, rather than leave them to other people who have not earned them, or maybe do not deserve them. Already in old civilizations people searched for ways to continue their existence—both in this world, and in the afterlife. They refused to accept the thought of being totally obliterated, and they wanted at least something to remain on earth, to remind future generations of who and what they had been.

Everyone who is familiar with the ancient Egyptians knows that their leaders built impressive pyramids and vast under-ground tombs, all of which were richly furnished and lined with portraits and paintings on which the deeds of the deceased were recorded. In many of these tombs so-called "Books of the Dead" have been found, containing all manner of advice for the deceased on his journey to the other world. The furnishings and jewelry, and even foodstuffs, were intended to sustain the deceased in the afterlife. Many of the Egyptian leaders asked that all their property and valuables be buried with them. Apparently they believed that they would need them, or that others would not be able to put them to good use. However this may be, we realize today that the vast majority did not succeed in perpetuating their memory. Except for a very few who distinguished themselves through their deeds—and a few others whose remnants proved to have archaeological or curiosity value—they disappeared or were forgotten. Most of their tombs were plundered or destroyed, and with this they, too, vanished from history and from human memory.

According to the legend, Luz was the only city in the world where people never died. Its residents could live forever—if they wanted. So the question is why Jacob found a ghost town. It looks as though even Luz did not solve the problems of life, and that the inhabitants' difficulties were more powerful than their will to live. The Midrash states that the old people became tired of life and voluntarily left the city to die. Isn't this surprising?

We can only conclude that eternal life, merely for the sake of living—without a purpose—cannot be called life. Life without purpose is a grind, and utterly senseless and boring. For, as the Torah says: לא על הלחם לבדו יחיה האדם (lo al ha-lechem levado yichyeh ha-adam), "Man does not live by bread alone." This was the reason why the people of Luz did not want to live forever, even if physically this would have been possible. One after another the remaining inhabitants chose death, and when Jacob came he did not find a living soul.

Only when one has a purpose in life—meaning that he lives the way God asks of him—will he have something to live for. Ironically, although eventually he must die, it is this kind of life that makes him immortal! Moses said to the Jewish people: ואתם הדבקים ליהוה אלהיכם (ve-atem ha-devekim la-shem eloheichem), "If you cleave to God, you will find your purpose in life." Many people think that having a building, a street, or an organization named after them will cause them to be remembered. However, it is not their name that is important, but their legacy: what they achieved for society or for their people. If not, people may remember their name, but nobody will know who the person behind the name actually was.

I once asked passersby in Nordau Boulevard, one of the main boulevards in North Tel Aviv, whether they knew who Max Nordau had been; when he lived, what he did, and what his teachings and ideas were. Nobody knew. The reality of every day teaches us that people are easily forgotten; only their ideas and deeds live on.

This explains why Jacob, after he realized that the inhabitants of Luz had departed to die outside, despite the fact that they could have enjoyed eternal life, called the deserted place "Beth-El," to signify that only a city whose inhabitants have a purpose in life, and who have dedicated themselves to God, will have the desire to remain alive.

One of our great kabbalistic leaders wrote that our entire life in this world does not measure up to one meal given to a hungry person. A name alone does not bestow eternity. Not the individual but his good deeds are remembered. Our sages of the Talmud and Midrash have commented that in order to know the kind of society we live in, we should look at how this society deals with its poor and sick. In the Talmud , in volume *Kedushin*, Rabbi Issa Ben Yehuda quotes the Torah, where it is written מפני שיבה תקום (*mipne shivah takum*), "You shall rise for old age." Our sages add הכל במשמע (*ha-kol be-mishma*), "and this includes everyone"—whether the person concerned is rich or poor, strong or weak, a scholar or a fool. Whenever a person's age renders him incapable of looking after himself, it is your duty to help him.

Our patriarch Jacob learned that there can be no eternity in the houses that we build, for the city of Luz proved to be deserted. The only place where there is eternity is in the House of God; there we shall find an answer to all our questions.

Parashath Va-Yishlach

וישלח יעקב מלאכים לפניו אל־עשו אחיו ארצה שעיר שדה
אדום. ויצו אתם לאמר כה תאמרון לאדני לעשו כה אמר עבדך
יעקב עם־לבן גרתי ואחר עד־עתה.

"Jacob sent messengers ahead of him to his brother Esau in
the land of Seir, the country of Edom. He instructed them:
'This is what you are to say to my master Esau: "Your
servant Jacob says, I have been staying with Laban and
have remained there till now."'"

Jacob spent twenty years working for his father-in-law,
Laban, until God told him to go back to the land of his fathers
and to his relatives. There he was going to meet his brother
Esau, whom he had not seen since he had tricked his father into
giving him the blessing that belonged to Esau, Isaac's firstborn
son. The relationship between the two brothers was therefore
not the best, and for this reason Jacob sent a messenger ahead of
him, to make sure that Esau would receive him with goodwill.

In the Midrash Rabbi Pinchas says, "Five times David prayed,
asking God to help the Jewish people, and God answered, 'No
matter how many times you ask, I will not do what you want.
Only when the poor are robbed and the very poor are crying,
will I get up to take action.'" So to see, it almost looks as if God
likes people to be poor—particularly when we read the following comment by Rabbi Yose. Rabbi Yose said that God did not
find a better way for the Jewish people to exist other than in

poverty and in pain. Anyone reading these words cannot help being puzzled. Why should Jews have to be poor or suffer? Don't they deserve a decent life without poverty and pain?

Why, in fact, did Jacob, who "sat among the tents" studying, as the saying goes "with Shem and Eber"—in other words, learning the right way to live—see his life as one big misery? So much so that he had to leave his father's home to go to his uncle Laban. He slept under the stars, and he was so afraid that he made a vow, saying, "If God will be with me and will watch over me on this journey I am taking, and will give me food to eat and clothes to wear so that I return safely to my father's house, then God will be my God." Although he came from a well-to-do family, he set out quite alone and penniless, and he was not even sure that he would have food to eat.

It is a fact that many people, when they have everything prepared for them, sooner or later lose their sense of perspective. When everything is too easy, we no longer appreciate the good things in life, and in extreme cases even lose control of our actions and our behavior toward our surroundings. There is a well-known verse in the Torah, warning the Jewish people that וישמן ישורון ויבעט . . . ויטש אלוה עשהו וינבל צור ישעתו (va-yishman yeshurun va-yiv'at . . . va-yitosh eloha asahu va-yenabel tzur yesheato), "Yeshurun grew fat and kicked; . . . he abandoned the God who made him, and rejected the Rock his Savior." People begin to kick at others, and even at themselves, when they have too much.

We know, therefore, that a surfeit of luxury and comfort can be morally debilitating. However, suffering and poverty are the other extreme, and similarly prevent people from living a dignified, human life. In the Talmud—in tractate Eruvin—our sages say: Poverty causes people to lose control and to abandon morals. Again, therefore, we come back to the question why the Jewish existence should depend on poverty and pain.

It looks as if Rabbi Yose intended to say the following: In the same way that we can measure every physical thing by its weight, its length, or its volume, we are capable of measuring the spiritual qualities and the character of a human being by the way he lives when he is poor or suffers. There is a wonderful saying from the sages, according to which a man can be recognized בכוסו, בכיסו ובכעסו (be-coso, be-cieso u-ve-ca'aso), in his cups, in his pocket, and in his anger; in other words: when he is drunk, when he is forced to spend money, and when he is angry. Some people react favorably under the influence of drink, or other material or psychological forms of stress, whereas others completely lose control of themselves and reveal themselves at their worst. Some of our sages say that we can even recognize a man by the way he enjoys himself.

What goes for individuals applies also—on a larger scale—to nations. In the same way as it is difficult to know an individual intimately when he is prosperous and has everything going for him, we cannot really know the character of a nation in times of peace or prosperity. There is a big difference between the collective mentality and behavior of a people who enjoy peace and economic prosperity, and their mentality and behavior when they are threatened or are passing through a period of depression. War, for instance, brings out both the best and the worst in a nation. Our experiences prior to and during the Second World War taught us that it was impossible to predict national behavior. Civilized nations, which had made important contributions to the evolution of spiritual and ethical ideals, surrendered to wicked ideologies and leaders. Even the Allied nations proved to remain seriously deficient in the support they gave the Jewish people in their hour of need.

However, everything that applies to nations in general also applies to the Jewish people—as not only the Tenach but Jewish history teach us over and over again. What our sages want to tell us, therefore, is that the best way to get to know and appreciate the Jewish people is to look at them under adverse circumstances, in other words, when they are persecuted and under stress. Only then can you see what kind of people they really are, and what they are capable of doing. Some of the greatest feats of the

Jewish people were performed in times of great distress. Our greatest spiritual literature, after Tenach, was created following the destruction of the Temple, when the Jewish people were defeated, persecuted, and dispersed. In exile the Jews showed their devotion to their spiritual sources. The Talmud was composed and finished in Babylon. This is what made one of our sages say יאה עניותה לישראל (*yaeh aniuta le-yisrael*), "We can see the beauty of Israel when they are down and defeated." This is something specific to the Jewish people: other nations and cultures produced their greatest works during periods of cultural prosperity, whereas during their years of decline their cultures were also dormant.

Let us not misunderstand each other; Jews do not enjoy being poor any more than other people. But through poverty, under stress and pressure, we can learn to appreciate the beauty of the Jewish character and the Jewish soul. This is what Rabbi Yose meant: God did not find a better method of measuring the Jewish character other than during the times when the nation was in pain and suffered.

Every nation has its writers and poets who celebrate the lives of their leaders and heroes, and sing about the deeds they performed for their people. Yet no people have done so in quite the same way as the *B'nai Israel*. When, for instance, the Jews describe the deeds of Rabbi Akiva, they do not praise him as a supporter of Bar Kochba in his fight against the Romans. Jewish tradition and literature praise him first and foremost for his great love of the Jewish people. Rabbi Akiva is praised for what he taught his pupils: "What is written in the Torah, namely that we shall love our neighbors like ourselves, is the fundamental principle of the Torah." Not mentioned are his heroism and martyrdom, but the fact that he established a place where thousands of students learned and developed a knowledge of the principles of *Torath Yisrael*.

King David was a great fighter for the Jewish people, but he is chiefly remembered as the author of the Psalms. The same applies to the countless Jewish sages: in many cases we have only the sketchiest information about their private lives, but after hundreds of years we are still studying their words, and we believe that if we continue in the ways they taught, we will survive for centuries to come.

As the Torah tells, Jacob was the man who did everything in order to keep himself and his family intact, and to prevent them from being influenced by their surroundings. The Torah tells that Jacob instructed his servants to say to Esau: עם־לבן גרתי (*im Laban garti*), "I have been staying with Laban." The numerical value of the Hebrew word *garti* is exactly 613, as a result of which this verse is also interpreted as meaning, "I lived with Laban, but I observed the 613 *mitzvoth.*"

Physically, on the other hand, Jacob was not a fighting type. When he heard that his brother Esau was coming with 400 people, and he was afraid they might attack him, he decided to split his family and flocks into two camps. His reasoning was that if Esau destroyed one camp, the second one would survive. The most interesting aspect is that Jacob himself joined neither of the camps, but remained alone. In his distress he prayed, "O God of my father Abraham, God of my father Isaac.... Save me, I pray, from the hand of my brother Esau, for I am afraid that he will come and attack me, and also the mothers with their children."

That night an unknown man attacked Jacob and wrestled with him until dawn. The result of this epic duel was not only the change of Jacob's name to *Israel*, but that—as the Torah puts it in this portion—he became a man "capable of meeting men and the world, and to emerge victorious."

What was it that caused this remarkable turnabout? The Rashbam explains that Jacob was a man who had become accustomed to running away, because he was afraid to face reality. He gives examples: while still living at home, Jacob became afraid of Esau's anger, but rather than face him, he ran away. He also was afraid when he took his family and flocks and ran away from

Laban, in the same way that he now was afraid of his renewed meeting with Esau.

Neither was Jacob accustomed to protest—let alone rebel—when he believed himself to have been unfairly treated. He customarily accepted situations as being inevitable. This was the case when Laban deceived him about Rachel and, after seven years of hard work, he discovered that he had been given Leah instead. Jacob did of course receive Rachel as well, but only after he had promised to work another seven years. Despite the fact that Jacob, through hard and dedicated work, had made Laban a prosperous man, Laban continually shortchanged Jacob when it came to paying him a decent wage. Yet Jacob did not confront Laban, but continued to work for him and to accept the ever-changing conditions Laban imposed upon him.

Finally, when Laban's sons complained that everything Jacob owned was in fact stolen from their father, Jacob again did not stay to face up to their accusations but collected his belongings and decamped. No wonder that Laban, who pursued and over-took him, could rightly say to Jacob, "Why did you run off secretly and deceive me?"

It was during this last journey, when he was returning to Eretz Israel , that the news of Esau's approach reached him. Afraid of his brother, Jacob decided to repeat the old pattern and again flee. However, during the night a man—in fact the angel of God—confronted him and forced him to fight. The angel did not let go of him; even if Jacob had wanted to run away, this time he couldn't! They struggled all night until—when dawn had nearly broken—the angel hobbled him by damaging Jacob's thigh muscle. From now on he would never try to run away. This was how Jacob learned to fight. He had become a new man, a new personality, and this explains why his name was changed from Jacob to *Israel*. The minute the new Israel realized that he no longer had a choice but must stand up and fight for his survival, he asked the angel for a blessing, to give him strength when on future occasions he would have to prove himself.

This stubbornness and power of endurance that the angel taught Jacob is what enabled our forefathers—Israel's successors—to survive in countries that insisted on imposing their beliefs upon the Jews. In the midst of pagan cultures the Jews proclaimed the idea of a single God, without compromising or ever letting up. In a world governed by the worship of power, the ancient Jews worshiped righteousness. The Jew was unique, because he refused to conform to the pagan majority's rules, and was willing to accept the consequences of being different. The Jew did not try to escape his destiny; he did not renounce his God—on the contrary, he walked his separate way with his head held upright.

The Torah wants to teach us that trying to escape life's difficulties does not solve our problems; it only postpones the day of reckoning. Ultimately man has to face up to his responsibilities. Ultimately he must learn that, however severe, they can be borne by human shoulders. As the angel said to Jacob: לא יעקב יאמר עוד שמך כי אם־ישראל כי־שרית עם־אלהים ועם־אנשים ותוכל (lo ya'akov ye'amer od shimcha ki im-yisrael, ki sarita im-elohiem ve-im-anashim va-tuchal), "Your name will no longer be Jacob, but Israel, because you have struggled with God and with men and have over-come." Israel shall be your name, and it will remind you to be strong, and to stand up for your ideals—and never to run away.

Parashath Va-Yeshev

וישב יעקב בארץ מגורי אביו בארץ כנען: אלה תלדות יעקב
יוסף בן־שבע־עשרה שנה היה רעה את־אחיו בצאן והוא נער
את־בני בלהה ואת־בני זלפה נשי אביו ויבא יוסף את־דבתם רעה
אל־אביהם: וישראל אהב את־יוסף מכל־בניו כי־בן־זקנים הוא
לו.

"Jacob lived in the land where his father had stayed, the
land of Canaan. This is the account of Jacob. Joseph, a
young man of seventeen, was tending the flocks with his
brothers, the sons of Bilhah and the sons of Zilpah, his
father's wives, and he brought their father a bad report
about them. Now Israel loved Joseph more than any of his
other sons, because he had been born to him in his old
age...."

The Torah tells that Jacob lived in Canaan, and that his
beloved son Joseph, who was at that time seventeen years old,
"was a shepherd with his brothers in Shechem." A little further
on the Torah says, however, that Jacob said to Joseph, "As you
know, your brothers are shepherds in Shechem. Come, I am
going to send you to them."

One of the questions the *mefareshim*—the interpreters of our
Scriptures—ask is, How do we understand that, when the
Torah says that Joseph "was a shepherd with his brothers," he in
fact wasn't there, and apparently did not even know where to
find them, for—as the Torah says—"a man found him wander-

58

ing around in the fields." It looks as if he went to join his brothers for the first time, which would contradict the introductory statement that Joseph was helping to tend his brothers' flocks.

A second question the interpreters ask is why Jacob loved Joseph more than all his other children. According to the Torah, it was because he was the son of his old age. However, there was only a small age difference between Joseph and Leah's sons Issachar and Zevulon. If, on the other hand, "son of his old age" meant the youngest child, then Benjamin should have been the favorite.

This seemingly simple passage from the Torah prompts still more questions. Jacob was a very intelligent person. Why, then, did he not realize that favoring one child over another was bound to create jealousy and ill-will, if not hatred, between the children? Had he not himself suffered in his younger years from the fact that his father preferred his brother Esau?

Yet another question is why the brothers hated Joseph, rather than their father. After all, it was Jacob who spoiled Joseph. Admittedly, Joseph was not a very tactful person. The Targum Onkelos interprets the words כי־בן־זקנים הוא (*ki ben zekunim hu*) as כי בר־חכים הוא (*ki bar-chakim hu*) rather than the "youngest," Joseph was the "cleverest" of Jacob's children, and this is why Jacob loved him. But if he was indeed so clever, we may well ask why Joseph insisted on telling his brothers his dreams. For they were no ordinary dreams; what in fact he told them was that after their father's death he, Joseph, would be their leader. Wasn't this a sure recipe for trouble, in a society where the firstborn was traditionally the leader and the successor?

A final question comes to mind: Jacob must have known that there was bad blood between Joseph and his brothers. Why, then, did he ask the boy to go all by himself? Given the distances involved, Joseph's youth and inexperience, as well as his strained relations with his brothers, it looked like asking for trouble.

We can only conclude that the situation within the family must on more than one occasion have been a subject for discussion between Jacob and his children, and that the problem wasn't just one of jealousy. There must have been a more profound difference, a difference of views about the future of the house of Jacob. The Talmud , in *masecheth Berachoth*, writes נאמר כי אין מראין לו לאדם בחלומו אלא מהרהורי לבו (*ne'emar ki ein mar'in lo le-adam be-chalomo ele me-herhorei libo*), meaning that dreams do not come from nothing; that they are not mere fantasies, but the product of conscious or unconscious thoughts that surface in a person's sleep. In other words, Joseph's dreams must have expressed his thinking and views about the future of the *B'nai Ya'acov*.

Earlier we referred to the fact that Jacob, too, had suffered from the fact that his father preferred Esau. There are, in fact, many parallels in the earlier experiences of the two. Both were the favorite of only one of their parents. Both were forced to leave their parental home because of fundamental differences with their brothers. In both cases the other brothers came close to killing the object of their hatred—with one difference. Whereas Esau was indeed a bad sort, Joseph's brothers and their families were not bad. This even raises the question how virtuous people like them came to hate their brother to such an extent that they considered killing him. The fact that in the end they sold him as a slave does not make the situation any better, for the fate of a slave could be worse than being killed.

As we have said earlier, there must have been some very vigorous and open discussions about the future between Jacob and his sons, the main question being who among the brothers would be sufficiently strong, wise, and influential to be able to keep the tribes together. Neither was this a hypothetical question about some distant future; immediately after Jacob's death the fate of all the coming generations, and of the Jewish nation in the making, would be at stake. If after Jacob's death his family had been dispersed, there would not have been a Jewish nation!

We should not forget that the tribe of Jacob had experienced some bad examples from its immediate forefathers. Abraham had two sons, Ishmael and Isaac. Following Abraham's death, each one had gone his own way. The same thing had happened in the case of their father Jacob and their uncle Esau. These two had not succeeded in building a coherent tribal family, to the extent that Esau had gone to live in a different country altogether—in Seir, the country of Edom.

Yet another important aspect must be taken into account, namely that we are talking about a pastoral society, about shepherds who moved about with their flocks. Such a society is vitally dependent upon sufficient land on which it can move. As the tribal family—and thus the size of its flocks—continues to expand, both people and animals need more food and more water. In such a situation, the moment there was a lack of solidarity and fraternal feeling between such shepherd families, they separated; one family went left, the other right, until they had put sufficient distance between themselves. This is exactly what happened in the case of Abraham and Lot. Esau's children were similarly divided: as the Torah puts it, everyone was an אלוף (aluf), a "chief" unto himself.

Finally, if we take into account that—according to God's revelation to Abraham—Jacob's children knew that they would one day migrate to a foreign land, we may be sure that Jacob and his sons worried about the future, and about what they should do to avoid danger to the future nation.

The problem in this patriarchal society was therefore to decide which of the twelve sons would prove to be the strongest and the most capable and influential, to prevent the tribes from falling apart. Experience has shown that building a nation and keeping it together requires three things: (1) common beliefs, (2) a common national bond, and (3) economic interdependence. A society possessing these three characteristics has a good chance of consolidating into a nation. In the absence of these conditions, there is little hope that it will survive for any length of time. Neither does a geographical name, or even a language, make a nation. North America and Canada talk the same language, but their mentalities and the aspirations of their peoples are very different.

Belgium and Switzerland, on the other hand, developed into unified nations despite the absence of a common language, whereas Hungary and Finland are striking examples of countries that are ethnically and linguistically related, but nevertheless developed into geographically separate nations. Their peoples were at one time united, but they separated because their habits and values were different. Realizing this will also help us to understand the problem that faced Jacob and his children.

Earlier I said that there was no immediate cause for worry while Jacob was alive, because of the strong influence he exercised on his children. For example, even when Joseph was in Egypt, far away from home, he did not dare succumb to Potiphar's wife, out of fear of what his father would think. The Torah says: ויהי כיום הזה ויבא הביתה לעשות מלאכתו (ve-yehi ba-yom ha-zeh va-yavo ha-baytah la-asoth melachto), "One day he went into the house to do his work." Our sages differ in the interpretation of this sentence. One version holds to the literal meaning, in other words that Joseph entered the house to attend to his household duties. Another version, however, interprets it as meaning that Joseph intended to yield to Potiphar's wife, but that a vision of his father's face appeared before him, so that he did not yield to the temptation. This is how strong Jacob's influence must have been, and therefore, as long as Jacob was alive, there was no fear that the tribes would separate.

However, what would happen after Jacob's death? Jacob believed that it was Joseph who, in the end, would turn out to be the strongest and most influential of the brothers, because he was the בר־חכים (bar-chakim), the smart one. This was why Joseph dreamed that he would be fit to be the leader. The other sons did not agree that Joseph was more suitable than they. Yet they could not criticize their father, so their only solution was to neutralize Joseph instead.

According to the Torah, the brothers "could not talk peaceably to Joseph," because they were afraid that in an open discussion Joseph and Jacob would convince them that Joseph should be the leader, a situation that, in their opinion, would lead to disunity and strife. From this, too, we may deduce that the brothers' enmity was not a question of jealousy about their father's affection, but a more serious problem about the unity of the tribes and the establishment of the Jewish nation that was promised to Abraham.

We do see, however, what dire consequences a lack of communication can have. In fact, we have this very problem today, within families as well as between nations. As long as people keep talking to each other, there is a chance of agreement. But the moment people stop communicating, all manner of discord, including violence, oppression, and war, may result.

Parashath Mi-Ketz

ויהי מקץ שנתים ימים ופרעה חלם והנה עמד על־היאר: והנה
מן־היאר עלת שבע פרות יפות מראה ובריאת בשר ותרעינה
באחו: והנה שבע פרות אחרות עלות אחריהן מן־היאר רעות
מראה ודקות בשר ותעמדנה אצל הפרות על־שפת היאר:
ותאכלנה הפרות רעות המראה ורקת הבשר את שבע הפרות יפת
המראה והבריאת וייקץ פרעה.

"When two full years had passed, Pharaoh had a dream: he
was standing by the Nile, when out of the river there came
up seven cows, sleek and fat, and they grazed among the
reeds. After them, seven other cows, ugly and gaunt, came
up out of the Nile and stood beside those on the riverbank.
And the cows that were ugly and gaunt ate up the seven
sleek, fat cows. Then Pharaoh woke up."

When the incident related at the beginning of this *parashah*
took place, Joseph was still being held in prison on the false
charge of Potiphar's wife.

According to the Talmud, two full years had passed since the
day he should have been released, but—as the Torah relates—
Pharaoh's chief cup-bearer, a fellow prisoner whose release
Joseph had predicted, "had forgotten him."

Pharaoh's dream about the seven fat and the seven gaunt
cows was followed by a similar dream about seven healthy ears
of corn and seven thin and scorched ears of corn. Pharaoh was
troubled, and he consulted his magicians, but no one was able to
interpret his dreams in a way that he could accept.

At that moment the chief cupbearer remembered Joseph, and how he had explained his dream and that of the baker while in prison. Joseph was quickly sent for and brought to Pharaoh. What was Joseph's interpretation? He told Pharaoh that God had shown him what He was about to do. Both dreams meant the same, namely that there would come seven years of great abundance, followed by seven years of famine.

Joseph did more than that, however. He told Pharaoh what to do, in order to prevent the Egyptian population from going hungry. One-fifth part of the harvests of the coming abundant years had to be set aside as a reserve for the lean years that were to follow. In this way, there would be a continuous and sufficient supply of food in Egypt for years to come.

A simple and elegant solution, indeed. In fact, we all know that what happened in Pharaoh's days is still happening all over the world, and in all spheres of life. Years of prosperity, copious harvests, high prices, and full employment are invariably followed by years of recession and unemployment. Periods of vigor and health alternate with periods of sickness and depression. This "cyclical" phenomenon, sometimes referred to as "the swing of the pendulum," is a characteristic part of our existence. Pharaoh's dream was therefore representative of a very common human experience. An explanation of this phenomenon, however, is not so easy—and to prevent it is even more difficult, if not impossible. The prevention of economic ups and downs is the task of the economist, but practice seems to show that there are as many solutions as there are economists.

Neither are the Jewish people exempt from such cyclical swings. Jewish history provides ample proof that periods of power and economic and cultural flourishing have been followed by lengthy periods of depression and defeat—and vice versa . Many times in our history the situation of the Jewish people appeared catastrophic. People asked themselves: will this be the end? And then things turned around again.

The same applies to the more recent history of the State of

Israel. For a number of years Israel and Israelis were almost universally admired. Yet, when on Yom Kippur Israel was treacherously attacked, hardly a democratic nation was prepared to extend even indirect assistance to a country that was fighting for its very survival. Israel won, but soon afterwards the United Nations passed a resolution declaring Zionism to be a form of racism!

Joseph, the *bar-chakim*, the smart one, interpreted Pharaoh's dreams by telling him that God had shown him what was about to happen to Egypt and the surrounding countries. In addition, he advised Pharaoh to look for a discerning and wise man who could be placed in charge of the collection and storage of food throughout the land of Egypt. It did not take long for Pharaoh to realize that Joseph, a man who not only could predict but also offered intelligent solutions, and possessed both wisdom and foresight, was the ideal person to assume this responsibility.

Parashath Mi-Ketz is always read around Chanukkah time. According to our *parshanim* the events behind the Chanukkah festival also contain a lesson for present-day generations. In the Talmud, in *masechtah Shabbath*, our sages ask why the festival is called חנכה, Chanukkah. They answer that in Hebrew the word Chanukkah can be read as two words: *chanu*, "they rested, and כה (*kaf heh*—the Hebrew for twenty-five, meaning the twenty-fifth of the month of Kislev)." These eight days of Chanukkah are regarded as such a happy time for the Jewish people that no eulogies are given, nor is anyone allowed to fast.

Actually, we might ask what the happiness was all about, for the circumstances that led up to Chanukkah were far from auspicious. The Greeks, who occupied Eretz Israel during the second century before the Common Era, had broken into the Temple of Jerusalem and profaned it. Alien, heathen rites were conducted at the altar, and even the oil for the big temple candelabra had been profaned. The Jewish people were oppressed and despondent. There seemed to be almost no hope—until they rose in revolt under the leadership of the

Maccabees and defeated the Greeks. The Temple was cleansed and rededicated. The big candelabra had to be relit—but no pure oil was available. Only one small jar with the seal of the high priest was discovered. This oil, meant for one day only, burned for eight days, sufficiently long to enable the priests to prepare fresh oil.

It looks as if the sages of the Talmud wanted to explain why the eight days of Chanukkah were established as a holiday for all Jewish generations. They wanted every future Jewish generation to light an additional candle each night to commemorate the Maccabean victory over the Greeks.

However, even this explanation leaves some questions unanswered. What kind of victory did the Jews achieve—military or otherwise? The really great miracle that happened appears to have been that a small band of partisans could succeed in raising a revolt that vanquished a large and powerful army, the most powerful army that existed in this part of the world at that time. The Maccabees, named after the leader of the revolt, lived in the small village of Modi'in and were after all farmers, rather than soldiers. They were not organized in any way, and theirs was an entirely spontaneous revolt. Why, then, is this victory not somehow commemorated in our Chanukkah rituals?

In the Chanukkah prayers על הנסים ועל התשועות ועל הנפלאות (al ha-nisim ve-al ha-teshu'oth ve-al ha-nifla'oth), "on account of the miracles, the deliverances, and the wonders," it is mentioned that רבים נפלו בידי מעטים (rabim naflu bi'yedei me'atim), "many fell at the hands of a few." If anything was a miracle worth remembering and celebrating, it was the defeat of a multitude by a few, the defeat of a strong army by a small, unorganized band of rebels. Why, therefore, is there not something on Chanukkah that symbolizes this great military victory? If this miracle had not happened, the Jewish people might very well not exist today.

A second question concerns the celebration on Chanukkah of the miracle of the oil. In every Jewish home around the world

candles are lit during the eight days of Chanukkah to commemorate this miracle. But why was it so important to relight the
Temple candelabra immediately? Why was it not possible to
wait eight days until fresh oil had been prepared? Was it so
urgent that God had to change the way of nature by making one
small cruse of pure oil, which normally would have lasted one
day, sufficient for eight days?

To understand all this, we must explain the background of
the Maccabee revolt. The Seleucid Greek kingdom of Syria,
which (together with the Ptolemaic Greek kingdom of Egypt)
had succeeded the Roman Empire, was the strongest power of
its time. In fact, it was not only a kingdom but a civilization. The
original Greeks were a small nation, but when the Roman
Empire was already on the decline, they had produced the conqueror Alexander the Great, whose power extended throughout much of the then known world. Alexander's empire was
populated by descendants of many nations and religions, who
had been granted citizen's rights in the Greek empire, provided
they adopted the belief in the Greek god Zeus. In so doing, these
populations adopted alien customs and, in the process, lost their
own way of life and separate identities. Rather than deport
indigenous populations, Alexander the Great's empire spread
by way of conquest and assimilation. This was what was meant
by Hellenism: Greek culture, implanted onto foreign soil.

The same process was taking place in Eretz Israel. A great
part of the Jewish people who lived in Eretz Israel agreed to
accept the alien Hellenist culture and its pagan gods. They saw it
as a way of ensuring their physical survival. The Greeks were
cruel oppressors who presented the occupied nations with a
simple choice: assimilate or be killed.

We can understand why so many people in Eretz Israel
decided to accept this condition and were prepared to become
Hellenized. What they did not realize was that their choice also
represented a form of national genocide, and that the Hellenists
aimed at the spiritual elimination of the Jewish people. If the

Hellenist plan had succeeded, not a single Jew would have survived as a Jew.

That this did not happen is due to the Maccabees, who entered the battle for Jewish survival, even though at the time they had almost no prospect of succeeding. The assimilation with the Hellenist Greek culture was spreading rapidly. Even in a little town like Modi'in, most of the citizens were becoming Hellenized. They even built an altar to Zeus to sacrifice an animal. At this critical moment Mattityahu ha-Cohen arose, drew his sword, and killed the man who wanted to make a sacrifice. The die was cast. With this act of an individual, the cry for revolution was raised in the entire country. If until that time the population had believed that most people agreed with the assimilators, they now realized that this was not the case. The fire spread, fighting started, and the population battled and disarmed the Greek soldiers. Any weakness in armament was made good by their will to survive; any lack of organization was compensated by their seriousness of spirit, and the conviction that *Torath Moshe* guided their lives and would grant them victory.

Here, by the way, we see that quantity is not always the decisive factor. Often quality is far more important. At the rededication of the Temple, the priests did not look for a great quantity of oil, but for oil of the required pure quality. After that, God saw to it that it would burn a sufficiently long time.

The Maccabees, a band of volunteers who defeated an army hundreds of times their size, and in so doing saved our Jewish civilization, also proved that it is quality of purpose that counts, rather than quantity of arms.

Only one Joseph was needed to show the Egyptians how to survive—and to secure the course of Jewish history—throughout the Egyptian exile, the Exodus, and until the giving of the Law at Mount Sinai.

In fact, it was not because the Hebrews were a big people that God chose us, but because God considered that we, among all other—often far larger and more powerful—nations had the required qualitative potential for implementing His plan with the world.

This leads us to the reason why at Chanukkah not the military or the material aspect of our survival is celebrated, but the spiritual side. This is also why there is a difference between the celebration of Chanukkah and, for instance, Purim. The feast of Esther and Mordechai commemorates the fact that a threat of physical destruction—as lethal and sure as the Holocaust—was turned away from the Jewish people. In the time of Antiochus, however, the threat was spiritual destruction. It was not a matter of physical extermination; what was at stake was our spiritual survival. This also explains why Purim is celebrated in a physical manner, with food, drink, and presents, whereas at Chanukkah we are asked to celebrate the light of the Torah that was kept burning thanks to the heroism of the Jewish people under the leadership of the Maccabees. To symbolize this miracle of the spiritual survival of the Jewish people the Maccabees lit the Temple candelabra immediately with pure oil, even though not enough of it was available.

Nothing has changed since the days of Joseph and the Maccabees. Quality of purpose is as important today as it was then. What is told in *Parashath Mi-Ketz* about Joseph, the *bar-chakim* and his wisdom, and in the story of the Maccabees and Chanukkah, which is celebrated at the same time of the Jewish year that this portion is read, teaches us that at any time a mere handful of wise, principled, and farsighted Jews are capable of changing our Jewish destiny.

Parashath Va-Yigash

ויגש אליו יהודה ויאמר בי אדני ידבר־נא עבדך דבר באזני אדני
ואל־יחר אפך בעבדך כי כמוך כפרעה.

"Then Judah went up to him and said: 'Please, my lord, let
your servant speak a word to my lord. Do not be angry
with your servant, though you are equal to Pharaoh
himself.'"

The words referred to above form a part of a dramatic
incident that happened when Jacob's children had traveled a
second time to Egypt, this time—at the express command of
their as yet unknown brother Joseph—in the company of their
youngest brother Benjamin. Joseph's drinking cup had been
found hidden in Benjamin's sack, and now Joseph threatened to
keep Benjamin behind as a slave.

Our sages infer from Judah's words that he was very angry
with Joseph for what he considered an act of treachery, and that
in protesting the brothers' innocence he had talked to Joseph in a
harsh way. Therefore he asked Joseph not to be angry, even if he
did not talk to him the way one is supposed to address a viceroy
of a powerful country. Judah bargained with Joseph—who had
in fact himself instructed his servants to hide the cup with
Benjamin—arguing that if they returned to Canaan without
Benjamin, their aged father would die. The Torah tells that at
this point Joseph was no longer able to hide his emotions, and he
asked all his attendants to leave the room. When they were

alone, he finally told his brothers that his name was Joseph, and
that he was their long-lost brother.

Quite a few questions are raised by Joseph's behavior from
the moment his brothers first arrived in Egypt in search of food.
In the first place, we wonder why Joseph did not send a message
to his father, once he had been released from prison and had
achieved an influential position in Potiphar's household. Jacob
had no idea that Joseph was in Egypt, and for all he knew his
beloved son was dead. How could Joseph let his father live in
such agonizing uncertainty?

A second question follows from the fact that Joseph, being so
close to the Egyptian ruler, must have known that the Egyptians
were not the only ones suffering from the famine. He surely
knew that there was hunger in the surrounding countries,
including Canaan. How could he fail to enquire what had happened to his own family, and whether they needed help? It is
very likely that he was angry with his brothers for having sold
him as a slave, but his father and his blood brother Benjamin
were also in Canaan. They certainly had never done him any
harm, and neither had his brothers' children and families. Why
did he not extend a helping hand?

Jewish tradition calls Joseph a saintly man: *Yoseph ha-Zadik*. Is
this how a saintly man behaves? To judge by his behavior, we
would sooner call him a cruel man. From the moment he had
discovered his brothers' identity, and he knew that they had
come to Egypt to buy food, he not only failed to help them, but
he put all kinds of obstacles in their way. He even accused them
of being thieves and spies. Why wasn't Joseph capable of over-
coming his resentment; why did he want to revenge himself at
all cost?

The third question refers to the moment when Joseph finally
made himself known to his brothers. He said, "I am Joseph! Is my
father still living?" And the Torah adds that his brothers were
not able to answer him, because they were terrified at his
presence. Why were they so afraid that they could not even

talk? For that matter, it is difficult to understand why Joseph asked them whether their father was still alive; he knew that Jacob was alive and well, for he had specifically asked them the first time they had come to Egypt, and they had answered him, "Our father is alive." So why did he ask them again?

A fourth question is why Judah became so angry with Joseph that he talked harshly to him. Judah himself had suggested that if the lost drinking cup should be found with one of the brothers, all of them would become slaves. Joseph had rejected this offer, answering that only the man who proved to be the thief would suffer. Yet, when the cup was in fact found with Benjamin, he became angry, and the question is why? A very interesting detail is also that Joseph went out of his way to embarrass Judah, when it had been Judah who had protected him from being murdered by suggesting that he be sold as a slave instead.

Rav Chai Gaon in his writing explains the relationship between Joseph and his brothers as follows: The brothers subconsciously realized that they deserved punishment for their past treatment of their brother Joseph, and for having sold him into slavery. Somehow, sometime, they expected to be punished according to the deed, and thus they reconciled themselves to the idea of having to spend the rest of their lives as slaves—even though they knew that none of them had stolen the Egyptian viceroy's silver drinking cup. But the moment Joseph made it known that he wanted only Benjamin, who had nothing to do with the entire affair, whereas the real culprits would go free, they realized that the whole thing was a put-up job, and Judah confronted Joseph, telling him that if Benjamin did not return with them, his father would die of grief.

At this point Joseph recognized the sign he had been waiting for, namely that the brothers were united in purpose and were ready to fight for their younger brother, even though he was not a son of their mother Leah, but—like Joseph—of Jacob and Rachel. From this followed a second conclusion, namely that apparently the brothers had not sold him into slavery because they hated the child of Jacob and Rachel, but because they did not like Joseph as a person; possibly even his father Jacob did not like him either!

This last conclusion requires a further explanation. Judah told Joseph that if the boy, Benjamin, did not return with them, they would not be able to face their father, since "it would bring his grey head to the grave in sorrow." If Jacob had liked Joseph, would he not have died much earlier, namely after Joseph disappeared? This is also why Joseph said, "I am Joseph! Is my father still living?" This repetition is not really a question, but a statement, by which Joseph meant to say, even though my father thinks that I am dead, he is even after all these years alive and well. This can only prove that he did not like me, but that he loves Benjamin—for if Benjamin disappears, he will die. To this argument the brothers had no answer, and it scared them. This explains why the Torah continues, "But his brothers were not able to answer him, because they were terrified at his presence."

Our rabbis comment that Joseph was mistaken in thinking that his father's remaining alive proved that he did not like Joseph. It is in the nature of a human being that one can endure hardship as long as he has not lost everything. Following Joseph's disappearance, Benjamin had remained. However, if Benjamin would also be lost, so the other children believed, Jacob would no longer have anything to live for.

We already indicated that, to put it mildly, Joseph had very little faith in his brothers. For this reason he also did not believe that they would be capable of living in Egypt and yet remain a family unit. He was afraid that in a pagan country like Egypt they would forget the ways of Abraham, Isaac, and Jacob and adopt the ethics and morals of the Egyptians. This most probably explains why he did not tell them that the powerful viceroy was in fact their brother, for the moment they would know he was so influential, they would also want to live in Egypt—not because they liked Joseph, but for the good life, and it would not take long before they and their families would have assimilated and disappeared among the surrounding population. Because of this danger to the future of the Jewish nation, Joseph tested the brothers in all kinds of ways, to see to what extent they showed a sense of solidarity. He accused them of being spies, and of stealing, to see whether this would shake their unity and cause one to defend himself at the expense of the others.

According to our narratives, there was another reason for Joseph's suspicions. For he knew that, although the brothers had come from one home, they had entered the city through different gates, almost as if they had some mischief in mind and wanted to hide themselves. So he asked them why they came so stealthily through different gates, to which the brothers answered: Your Highness is mistaken. We only came to buy food. We were twelve children of the same father. The youngest is now with our father in Canaan, and one is no more. We came separately at our father's request, because he feared that if people saw ten strong brothers together, they might be suspicious in case we had evil in mind. And our sages add the interpretation: even the brother who is missing we love today. When Joseph heard this, and saw that they were united and his fears had proved to be unfounded, he talked and said, "Come near to me, I pray you."

The message of this portion of the week is that we cannot survive as Jews if we are not united. Every Jew should say to his brother, "Come near to me. Your problem is my problem," and only then shall we be able to exist.

There is an old story about two friends who were very devoted to each other. One day one of the two was accused of killing another man. The judge found him guilty, and he was condemned to death. Before having him taken away to be executed, the judge asked, "Have you a last request before you are hanged?" The accused answered that he would like to go to his home town to settle his affairs, but that this would take at least three days. The judge agreed to give him three days, provided he could find a guarantor to take his place in case he should not return. In olden times it was not possible to go to a bank and pay bail; the guarantor had to be another person, and such people were obviously hard to find. Fortunately the man's friend came forward, saying that he would be prepared to serve as a security, and even be killed if his friend failed to return. The judge agreed, and the condemned man left. Three days passed, but he did not return. Toward the early morning of the fourth day they brought out the friend to have him hanged, but only minutes before the rope was placed around his neck, the condemned man came running, breathlessly explaining that he had been held up because of bad weather. The judge was so impressed by this act of loyalty that he stayed the execution and decided to reinvestigate the case—after which the condemned man's innocence was finally established.

The judge asked the friend what had given him the courage to stand bail under such risky conditions. His answer was, "I was certain that my friend would return in time. But even if he had not returned, I would not have minded to be killed, for my life would have been worthless anyway!" The judge said, "If two people can be so loyal to each other, I shall be happy to have friends like you; please take me as a third friend of the two of you."

Maybe the above story is intended to be a parallel to the biblical verse, ואהבת לרעך כמוך אני יהוה (ve-ahavta le-re'echa kemocha. Ani ha-shem), "Love your neighbor as yourself. I am the Lord." Nowhere else in the Torah does this sudden mention of "I am your God" appear. We may explain this as meaning that if we love our neighbor as ourself, God says that He will be the third partner to our union.

This is what Judah said to Joseph. "If Benjamin does not come back, our father's life will be worthless to him." Because of this sign of genuine concern, Joseph decided to reveal himself, and he said, "I am your brother"—in other words, I want to be a part of this loyalty and devotion.

Parashath Va-Yechi

ויחי יעקב בארץ מצרים שבע עשרה שנה ויהי ימי־יעקב שני
חייו שבע שנים וארבעים ומאת שנה.

"Jacob lived in Egypt seventeen years, and the years of his
life were a hundred and forty-seven."

The words above are the opening words of the weekly portion of *Va-Yechi*. According to the *halachah*, the writer of a *sefer
Torah* begins each *parashah* on a new line. The one exception is the
end of *Parashath Va-Yigash*, which is followed immediately by the
first words of *Parashath Va-Yechi*. It would seem, therefore, that
these two portions are purposely connected, and our sages ask
themselves what the reason could be.

One of our sages answers: because *Parashath Va-Yechi* tells us
about the passing away of Jacob, and the fact that a number of
years later Jacob's children became slaves. A slave does not
usually have time to pause or rest when he wants. Because of
this our sages decided that these two *parashoth*, which contain
the narrative of Jacob's sojourn and death in Egypt, and the
bondage of the *B'nai Israel*, should not have a pause either.

Other interpreters give another reason for this seamless
succession of the two *parashoth*, which traditionally is referred to
as סתומה (*setumah*), "closed," as opposed to the customary break
between *parashoth*, which is called פתוחה (*petuchah*), "open." They
explain that as soon as our father Jacob departed this life, the
hearts and eyes of Israel were closed—in other words, they
became dim and troubled, because of the misery of the bondage
that began to be imposed upon them, and they were no longer
able to see clearly ahead.

77

There is indeed a difference between the life of the Jewish people and that of other nations. Most peoples are more or less able to see ahead and predict what the consequences of their actions will be. If they plan their economy, they may look forward to years of prosperity; if the world goes into a recession, they can predict how it will affect their production or exports. If they are warlike, they know that sooner or later hostilities will begin, and they know what the outcome—leaving surprise circumstances aside—will be.

Jewish life, however, is impossible to predict. Our entire history is full of unexpected—and often fateful—twists and turns, both on the individual and on the national level. How many times have Jews escaped from hostile places to other countries, where they found shelter and were granted rights because they were needed at the time. There, they believed, they would finally be safe, and if someone came and warned them not to be too sure, because one day they would no longer be needed and they would be thrown out, he was considered a pessimist and a coward who insisted on seeing black clouds everywhere. But not too many years passed, and everything was again taken away from them—and the Jews passed on to their next temporary refuge.

On the individual level, the example of Joseph is also very illustrative: Joseph was sold to Egypt as a slave. Yet we see that within a short time he was placed in charge of Potiphar's household, an unusual distinction indeed. The next thing we know he was in prison—a more ironic twist of fate we can not imagine! Not only the false accusation is unusual, but also his punishment, for a slave who was found guilty of trying to seduce his mistress would surely have been put to death. Joseph spent twelve years in prison—a very long time, during which his innocence could have been established many times over. Yet, when he was finally released, it was not because he was finally found innocent or pardoned, but because the king needed him.

Now followed the most miraculous turn of events by far,

namely Joseph's appointment at the age of twenty-nine as over-seer of Pharaoh's palace and as governor of all Egypt—a respon-sibility second only in importance to that of Pharaoh himself, who was the most powerful ruler of his day. Through his cleverness Joseph saved both Egypt and the surrounding coun-tries from the results of a severe drought. Joseph became fam-ous, both in Egypt and abroad, and we can judge his popularity by the reception Pharaoh accorded his father Jacob. Not only did Pharaoh send carts to transport him and his family, but he invited the Children of Israel "to settle in the best part of the land."

Not much time passed and everything changed once more. ויקם מלך־חדש על־מצרים אשר לא־ידע את־יוסף (va-yakam melech chadash al mitzraim asher lo yada eth-Yoseph), "Then a new king, who did not know about Joseph, came to power in Egypt." Our sages say, it was not that the king did not know about Joseph, but he did not *want* to know. He enslaved and persecuted the Jews and tried to destroy them by overworking them and by killing all the new-born male children.

All this poses more questions than it is possible to answer. What had the Jews done to make them deserve this treatment? They surely were still the same Jews; we can hardly accept that people change from one generation to the next. What were the Egyptians afraid of?

The answer is that the circumstances had changed. The Jews had prospered and multiplied. The famine was finished and forgotten, and the Egyptians did not need the Jews any more. Doesn't all this sound familiar? Haven't we heard the same argument over and over again in our own century?

During all the centuries that Jewish generations existed in the East and the West, they contributed to the development of economics, medicine, philosophy, and art, to mention only some of the most important fields of human endeavor. The German chancellor Bismarck at one time commented that without the assistance the members of the Mosaic faith had rendered the

Germans during the sixteenth and seventeenth centuries, Germany could never have achieved its present strength. The British prime minister Gladstone stated in the British Parliament that England would forever be beholden to a Jew by the name of Rothschild, since Britain would never have bought the Suez canal without his initiative and assistance. And who is not aware of the pivotal Jewish contribution to the development of American commerce and industry, to banking, the media, entertainment, and other enterprises of the most varied kind? Why is it that almost 50 percent of all Nobel Prize winners are Jews? Certainly not because our nation is so numerous, or because it has ways of influencing the Nobel Prize Committee. The answer is that we are a literate and thinking culture, and that in everything we undertake we invest all the energy we possess. Of course, this argument is often turned on its head by adversaries, who claim that this only proves that Jews are bent on taking over their country—or even the world. This is said about a nation that—unlike, for instance, the churches—does not possess a single world-encompassing organization that will command the loyalty of more than a few percent of all Jews!

Where does all this hatred and prejudice originate? One day we are important, feted, and protected, the next maligned, persecuted, and accused of wanting to destroy "civilization," if not the world. Jews are accused of being capitalists, except by genuine capitalists, who call them Communists. We cannot possibly answer all these questions. This seems to be the life of our nation. We are, as the Midrash says, סתומים (setumim), "closed," "blocked," without an exit.

Among the many wonderful Biblical interpretations of our sages, we should mention their exegesis of the opening verse of the book of Exodus: ואלה שמות בני ישראל הבאים מצרימה את יעקב (ve-eleh shemoth benei yisrael ha-ba'im mitzraimah eith ya'akov), "These are the names of the sons of Israel who went to Egypt with Jacob." Note that the Hebrew text reads הבאים (ha-ba'im)—in the present tense. This is interpreted as containing a lesson for the Children of

Israel, namely that whenever Jews are living among other nations, as the Jews at one time lived in Egypt, people will always look at them as if they had only just arrived, as strangers, regardless of how many years they have already spent in the particular country.

A little further in the portion of *Va-Yechi* the Torah says: ויהי אחרי הדברים האלה ויאמר ליוסף הנה אביך חולה (*va-yehi acharei ha-devarim ha-eleh va-yomer le-yoseph hinneh avicha choleh*), "Some time later Joseph was told, 'Your father is ill.'" This did not mean that Jacob had some common illness; in fact he was very old, and he was going to die and wanted to collect his descendants around him to bless them.

Our narratives say that when Abraham was alive, people did not in fact see him become old—he remained a young-looking man. For this reason Abraham talked to God, saying: Here is an old man sitting together with his sons, and nobody really knows who is old and who is not. According to the Torah, ואברהם זקן בא בימים (*ve-avraham zaken ba ba-yamim*), "Abraham was now old and well advanced in years," which is interpreted as meaning, "his old age started to show."

But people became accustomed to seeing old people, and they did not believe that they had to prepare their affairs for the day that they too would die. So, in the same way as Abraham requested God to make his gradual aging visible, Isaac asked God that man might before he died experience some suffering. God agreed, and the Torah says, ויהי כי־זקן יצחק ותכהין עיניו (*va-yehi ki-zaken yitzchak va-tichheina eynav*), "When Isaac was old, and his eyes were so weak that he could no longer see...."

Again it did not take long before people became accustomed to suffering. So Jacob asked God to make every man before his death experience some symptoms of sickness, in order to warn him, and to give him an opportunity to settle his affairs. And the Torah informs us that ויאמר ליוסף הנה אביך חולה, "Joseph was told, 'Your father is ill.'"

So far the Midrash. We might ask why our patriarchs asked for their lives—and ours—to be made harder? How much would each of us give to stay looking young, not to suffer pain, and not to be ill? Why did they ask God to change the way of nature? It seems that our narratives want to say to us that we must always be conscious of what happens in our life; we cannot just dream and wish for bad things to go away. The only way to face life, and to survive, is to have a sense of reality. The man or woman who expects to always remain thirty or forty is getting older, whether he or she likes it or not. Thinking of riches does not help to meet daily expenses. Dreaming of success is no alternative to patiently working at a career.

This was the purpose of Abraham's request: he wanted God to make him realize that his life was temporary, and that—as King David would write—"My days are like a passing shadow and I wither away like the grass." God agreed, and said: You will be the first person whose age will show in his face.

However, after a while people became accustomed to seeing old people, and it failed to influence them. Isaac realized that a new reminder was necessary: the debilities of old age would help to preserve man's sense of reality.

Jacob noticed that people were getting used to suffering as well, and that it did not change their attitude to old age and the ever-present possibility of death. He asked God to bring sickness, as an even stronger reminder.

We must learn from this that life is not, as the expression goes, "a picnic," or a pleasure trip, but a "package deal"—a mixture of good things and bad, of pleasant and unpleasant events, of joy and pain. But even this realization is insufficient, as long as we fail to draw the proper conclusions and prepare ourselves for what fate may have in store for us. We learn to realize and appreciate good only because there is bad; we know joy only because we sometimes experience sadness and pain. This realization not only steadies us in life, it in turn enables us to help people in trouble, if only because we know that the same thing could—and maybe will—happen to us.

Parashath Shemoth

ואלה שמות בני ישראל הבאים מצרימה את יעקב איש וביתו
באו: ויקם מלך־חדש על־מצרים אשר לא־ידע את־יוסף.

"These are the names of the sons of Israel who came to
Egypt with Jacob, each came with his family; Then a new
king, who did not know Joseph, came to power in Egypt."

The Midrash asks how we should understand the duplication in the opening sentence of *Parashath Shemoth*, according to
which the "sons of Jacob"—in other words, all of Jacob's children
and their families—came to Egypt, when this statement is followed in the same sentence by the words "each came with his
family." Apparently our sages want to explain that this repetition is meant to emphasize that Jacob and his children did not
come to Egypt as individuals, but as a united family of tribes.
They did not come with different opinions, beliefs, and theories,
but as one man, under the leadership of Jacob.

The Torah continues to tell that "a new king, who did not
know Joseph, came to power in Egypt." Some of our sages say
that he was not really a new king, but the Pharaoh of Joseph's
time, who simply did not *want* to remember what Joseph had
done for him and his country. This Pharaoh decided to destroy
the Hebrews, by literally working the grown-ups to death and
killing the male Jewish children. We know, of course, that he did
not succeed, but why did he fail to destroy them? The reason is
that the Hebrews were united: איש וביתו באו (*ish ve-beito ba'u*),
meaning as much as, "Each came as part of a united family." So
far the Midrash.

The prophet Isaiah prophesied מהרסיך ומחריביך ממך יצאו (*mehara-seicha u-machareiveicha mimecha yetze'u*), "Those who laid you waste depart from you." This is often interpreted as referring also to the "enemies from within," in other words those Jews who through their lack of solidarity, or even outright cooperation with our enemies, threaten the security of the Jewish people. In other words, we can survive as long as we maintain a united front. This was the case with the Children of Israel when they went to Egypt, for "each came with his family": they were united, and there were no dissenting elements to give aid and comfort to their enemies.

There is an ancient legend, according to which the trees in the forest saw a group of woodcutters approaching to cut down the trees at the edge of the forest. Some of the younger trees began to quake with fear, upon which a big, old tree spoke up and said, "There is a lesson for you here. Look what the wood-cutters are using: iron saws with wooden handles, and steel axes with wooden shafts. When we refuse to yield our wood, the woodcutters will no longer be able to destroy us. For a saw without a wooden handle is no saw, and an ax without a wooden shaft does not exist." What is the moral of the story? As long as the Jewish people are united, and refuse to give their enemies a "handle," they will not be able to destroy us.

When God told Moses to return from Midian to Egypt, and to approach Pharaoh to tell him that he should let the Children of Israel depart, Moses replied, "Suppose I go to the Israelites and say to them, 'The God of your fathers has sent me to you,' and they ask me, 'What is His name?' Then what shall I tell them?" In answer, God said to Moses: "I AM WHO I AM. This is what you are to say to the Israelites: 'I AM has sent me to you.'"

Are we to understand from this that Moses wanted to know what God's name was? Of course not. God is not like a human being, with a name such as we are accustomed to give people. On the one hand He is everywhere, or—as we read in the Additional Service of the Shabbath: מלא כל־הארץ כבודו (*male kol ha-aretz kevodo*), "The whole earth is full of His glory." On the other hand He is incorporeal: אין לו דמות הגוף ואינו גוף (*ein lo demuth ha-guf ve-eino guf*), "He is without bodily form or substance," as the Rambam puts it. What Moses wanted, therefore, was an answer to the question: In whose name do I speak? For what purpose have I been sent to take the Israelites out of Egypt? And how can I best convince them that the coming struggle will be worthwhile? Even at this stage Moses realized that taking the Children of Israel out of slavery, to make them face a hard and uncertain future, was insufficient if they did not at the same time have a purpose, as well as a strong confidence and belief. What was the use of their struggle, if afterwards they would not survive?

Ever since the end of World War II we have seen many nations being liberated from colonial rule or slavery, but unfortunately in many cases this did not mean that they became free—free from oppression and free from material want. Political independence in itself is not sufficient. We only have to look at countries such as Cuba, Cambodia, Vietnam, Uganda, Ethiopia, and Biafra to realize that many nations are at present suffering more under the oppression of their own people than ever before under colonial domination. Literally millions of people have been killed—and are being killed—in the most cruel ways, for one reason only: they did not shed their slavery, they just changed their taskmasters. The only difference is that, whereas before they were enslaved by strangers, they are now enslaved and exploited by their own kin.

This is what Moses, the inspired leader, did not want to happen to the Jewish people, and he asked God: What moral system will You instruct me to teach the Children of Israel, to prevent them from being oppressed by their own leaders? God answered, "After you have brought the people out of Egypt, you will take them to worship God on this mountain." This mountain—Mount Sinai—was where God was going to give the Children of Israel the Torah, which would stipulate their rights and duties—but also those of their leaders. And obviously, once the people had a Supreme law, under which they would all have equal rights, they would no longer have to be afraid of being abused by their own leaders.

Unlike most human legislation, the Torah that God gave the Children of Israel on Mount Sinai did not represent any temporal—or temporary—party, faction, or ideology that, however logical or attractive it may have looked at the time, was bound to lose its luster because it was unable to withstand the changing circumstances. One look around us in the real world is sufficient to convince us how every new "truth" that is invented takes only a few years to be proven wrong; how every new principle or ideology—in fact any idea the human mind can dream up—soon either fades or becomes corrupted. Communism, supposedly the ultimate social ideology that was going to introduce a righteous New World, was implemented at the cost of millions of human lives. And what did it achieve. Justice? Abundant food supplies? Material welfare? We know that the Soviet Union is even today deficient in all these and other fields. Most other systems or "isms" suffer from the fact that they do not solve problems but only create new ones. Even the socialist welfare state seems to have become a victim of its success, with growing numbers of young people taking recourse to hooliganism, petty crime, drug abuse, and other forms of permissiveness as a reaction to more money and less work. It looks as if for every problem we solve, two new ones present themselves, often from an entirely unexpected and unpredictable direction.

In other words, with all our human knowledge and wisdom, we do not have people who are able to foresee the needs and wishes of even the next generation—let alone to predict the "shape of things to come." We scarcely have an idea what the world will look like fifty years or a century from now. We don't even begin to understand *how* to approach the problems that our children and grandchildren will have to face. What will they need; how will they think; what will their dreams and aspirations be? In the meantime, we have forgotten many of the ideas that were so important to us that we insisted on forcing through their application. Some—like Communism—exist in name but are unrecognizable in practice.

All this leads, of course, to a comparison with the Torah; how different is the situation with the teaching of Moses. It is 3300 years ago that Moses received the Torah on Mount Sinai, and since that time this Jewish עץ חיים (*etz chaim*), or "Tree of Life," did not change and was not forgotten. How is this possible? The reason is that the Torah was not a mere idea or fad, but that it represents a way of life. The Jewish "Tree of Life" is rooted in creation itself, and this explains why future generations will be able to live by it, in the same way it has supported past generations. Moses asked God, "Suppose I go to the Israelites and say to them, 'The God of your fathers has sent me to you,' and they ask me, 'What is His name?' Then what shall I tell them?" What Moses meant was, How can I assure them that this idea is not going to be a flash in the pan? God's answer was: "Tell them that I AM, the God of your fathers, sent you; that the same God who created the heavens and the earth, who watches over everything, and who made this world on the basis of mercy and compassion, is sending you, Moses, to the Children of Israel." God wanted this message to be taken to the Children of Israel as the first step toward their redemption—and that of the entire world.

The redemption of the Jews from Egypt was the fundamental formative event in our history—and a crucial event in world history. For the first time an embryonic but as yet enslaved nation liberated itself, and in the process proved that it could be truly free if it adopted a "constitution" representing a way of life in which people would not be looking for their own benefit only. God instructed Moses to tell the Children of Israel that if they wanted to avoid being enslaved to their own people—as today, thousands of years later, is still the case with other nations—he had to remind them that "the God of your forefathers sent you to them." Those who would lead the new nation following their departure from Egypt would behave like the descendants of Abraham, Isaac, and Jacob, and they would preserve the values of the patriarchs.

King David said צדקתך צדק לעולם ותורתך אמת (tzidkatcha tzedek le-olam ve-toratcha emeth), "Your righteousness is everlasting and your Law is true." Ever since the beginning of human civilization, nations have tried to formulate and improve codes of justice; every generation revised and expanded its existing laws, and believed that as a result life would become better. But we see that in effect nothing has changed; new and different problems and situations keep on cropping up, forcing us to abandon old laws and write new ones. Only the Torah has remained unchanged: תורתך עומדת לעולם (toratcha omedeth le'olam), "Your Law will remain forever." Torath Moshe has preserved the Jewish ethical way of life ever since the moment it was received on Mount Sinai.

This fact may explain why Judaism has throughout history faced such violent opposition from other civilizations trying to find their own lasting legal codes. Every nation was familiar with the Torah, and the Western world even adopted the Jewish Bible as the foundation stone of its own faith. This means that not a single nation has been able to avoid comparing its deeds with the commandments of the Torah, as given to Moses. The Torah was—and still is—a mirror in which people see their own deeds reflected. This confrontation with the Torah way of life, which the Jewish people accepted and are trying to implement with varying degrees of success, is often disturbing; people don't like the picture that looks back at them from the mirror. And what is easier in such a case than to break the mirror— rather than change one's behavior! Throughout history the Jewish people have, through their Torah, been a mirror to the conscience of the nations. And since the image reflected by the mirror failed to please, they have hated the Jews instead.

The portion of *Shemoth* contains the first story about anti-

Semitism: it even uses some of the arguments that have been voiced throughout history by people who fear to compete with hard-working strangers in their midst. "Look," Pharaoh said to his people, "the Israelites have become much too numerous for us. Come, we must deal shrewdly with them, or they will become even more numerous...." There is a hint here of the *Protocols of the Elders of Zion*: the Jews were suspected of wanting to take over the country and even the (then known) world! What was Pharaoh's solution? Let's work those that are already grown up to death, and kill their male children!

The same hatred and prejudice have continued in every century and every generation. During the reign of King Xerxes, when part of the Jewish nation lived in exile in Persia, it was Haman, the king's grand vizier, who incited the king by saying, "There is a certain people dispersed and scattered among the peoples in all the provinces of your kingdom whose customs are different from those of all other people and who do not obey the king's laws.... If it pleases the king, let a decree be issued to destroy them."

What is it that causes such intense hatred? Some would conclude that if only the Jews had ceased being "different," and if had would have abandoned their traditions, the hatred would have stopped, but recent experience has once more given the lie to this assertion. The greatest pogrom in living history was directed against a fiercely nationalistic, assimilated German Jewry. Anti-Semitism persists in Poland—a nation in which today only a handful of Jews are left! Our tradition has it that this hatred of the Jews is ordained, and it was Balaam who said in his famous prophecy in the Book of Numbers: הן־עם לבדד ישכן ובגוים לא יתחשב (*hen am le-vadad yishkon u-va-goyim lo yitchashev*), "I see people who live apart and do not consider themselves one of the nations."

In this portion of the week the Torah tells how Moses had to flee from Egypt after it had become known that he was a Jew. He fled to Midian, and one of his first acts was to rescue the

daughters of Jethro, who were being bothered by some shepherds. When their father asked them who it was that came to
their rescue, they answered, "An Egyptian rescued us from the
shepherds." However, they must have seen from the way
Moses was dressed that he was not an Egyptian, and a simple
question would have established his identity. So we assume that
they realized he was Jewish.

It was fortunate that Moses did a good thing; if he had
misbehaved, they might have said, "It was a Jew." As Albert
Einstein once said, "If my theory of relativity proves to be right,
France will call me a citizen of the world, and the Germans will
claim me as one of theirs; but if it is proven wrong, the French
will call me a German, and the Germans a Jew."

As long as we understand what happened when the Children
of Israel lived in Egypt, more than three thousand years ago, we
shall also understand how our people should be guided today.

Parashath Va-Era

וידבר משה לפני יהוה לאמר הן־בני־ישראל לא־שמעו אלי
ואיך ישמעני פרעה ואני ערל שפתים.

"But Moses said to God, 'If the Israelites will not listen to me, why would Pharaoh listen to me, since I speak with faltering lips?'"

God said to Moses, "Go, tell Pharaoh king of Egypt to let the Israelites go out of this country." But Moses answered, "If the Israelites will not listen to me, why would Pharaoh listen to me?" Already at this stage of the biblical narrative two things are clear, namely that the Children of Israel did not want to listen to Moses, and that Moses was lacking in self-confidence that he would be able to encourage and convince them.

According to the Midrash, God's response to Moses was, "How sorry I am for those who are gone and cannot be replaced"—meaning, how I do regret that your forefathers Abraham, Isaac, and Jacob are no longer alive, so that I could send them on this mission that I have asked you to perform. I promised your forefather Abraham that his son Isaac would one day have children, who would establish a new nation. Yet, when I told him to take his son to Mount Moriah, and to be prepared to sacrifice him, he never hesitated or objected. He did not even ask *how* My request could be reconciled with My promise to him. And look: the moment I send you on your first mission on behalf of the Children of Israel, you begin to ask Me all kinds of questions, and you complain למה הרעות (lamah hera'ota), why do You worsen their condition?

91

In this connection we must refer to the Talmud Yerushalmi, which, in the volume *Sanhedrin*, comments on the fact that God had *told* Moses that Pharaoh would not agree to let the Jewish people leave Egypt. In other words, Moses knew what kind of difficulties would be in store for him, and in this light it is not so surprising that he was trying to get out of his mission, and in fact begged God: "Plase send someone else to do it."

In light of the above, it is difficult to understand why God was so disappointed with Moses, since He himself had warned him that He would harden Pharaoh's heart, and that the latter was going to put all kinds of obstructions in his way. The Torah also makes it clear that when Moses, who was a very bad speaker, actually went to Pharaoh, the situation of the Children of Israel became worse instead of better. Why was God disappointed that Moses did not behave like the patriarchs, by accepting without questions what God asked him to do? And what was the use of sending Moses, who lacked the confidence that he would be able to achieve the purpose?

Before discussing the answers, we should ask another question altogether—why did God harden Pharaoh's heart in the first place? Jewish tradition holds that every human being is capable of choosing between good and evil. Even assuming that Pharaoh was not a righteous man, the plagues that were visited upon the Egyptian people would sooner or later have caused him to change his mind and let the Jews go. But God did not give Pharaoh a chance; He suspended his free will. Why did God force Pharaoh to be evil, causing both the Egyptian people and the Children of Israel to suffer?

The enslaved Hebrews were sorely oppressed. Their cup of bitterness was already filled to the brim, but God worsened their condition as a result of Moses' demand that Pharaoh should let them depart from Egypt. Is it surprising that Moses cried out, "God, why have you brought more trouble upon this people than they had before? Is this why you sent me—to cause them even more suffering?" It almost looks as if God decided to play games with Pharaoh at the expense of the Jewish people. And when Moses complained, God—instead of sympathizing with him—put him down by saying, "How sorry I am for those who are gone and cannot be replaced."

There are many such questions in the history of the Jewish people that were not understood at the time they were first asked. In many cases it took years, if not generations or centuries, for it to become clear what God intended. Referring to these obscure passages in the Torah, the prophet says: הנסתרות לד' אלקינו והנגלות לנו ולבננו (ha-nistarot le-shem elokeinu ve-ha-neg'lot lanu u-le-vaneinu), "That what we do not understand, God will reveal (later) to us and to our children."

One very pertinent example of such a problem is God's instruction to the Jewish people to "destroy Amalek." People have often wondered how the same God who gave numerous commandments about compassion for all forms of life could tell his people to "attack the Amalekites and totally destroy everything that belongs to them; to put to death men and women, children and infants, cattle and sheep, camels and donkeys." The Torah even repeats, "You shall blot out the memory of Amalek from under the heaven," adding for emphasis, "Do not forget!" Why this deliberate cruelty? The answer is that the Torah does not merely refer to the historical Amalekite people, who have long ceased to exist. The Torah talks about enemies who attack a weak and unprotected people without any provocation, like the Amalekites, who "attacked the worn out Children of Israel from behind, who cut off the weak ones who were straggling behind, and who had no fear of God"—in other words, people who were so utterly lacking in human conscience that they just wanted to kill. The Israelites were not threatening the Amalekite country; instead, the Amalekites pursued the Israelites through the desert with the sole purpose of destroy- ing them.

For a long time we forgot the meaning of this reference to the Amalekites, until in our own generation we were reminded—but too late—that there exist situations, created by nations and ideas, in which the Jewish people must choose between destroying or being destroyed. Many countries have had their Hitlers, and they and their ilk have been responsible for the greatest traumas in the history of the Jewish people. It is to them, and the ideologies they represent, that the Torah refers when it says: Remember the Amalekites! You have no choice; either you destroy them, or they will destroy you. With them you should have no compassion; with them you do not compromise.

It is interesting that, despite the enslavement of the Children of Israel, and Moses' conflict with Pharaoh, the commandment about the Amalekites does not apply to the Egyptian people. The Egyptians simply wanted to keep the Israelites as slaves; all nations in those days had slaves, but it so happened that God did not agree, since He had other plans for the Jewish people. So we had to fight to get out of our Egyptian slavery. Our conflict with the Amalekites was—and is—of an entirely different nature. Here we are talking about שנאת חינם (sin'at chinam), causeless hatred. Normal problems, arising from clashes of interest or differences of opinion, can be discussed and solved. With causeless hatred, however, there does not even exist a basis for a discussion; the only solution is to disable the enemy!

The previous discussion makes it clear that also in another sense Pharaoh was not responsible for the obstacles he placed in the way of the Jews; as we explained, God forced his hand and prevented him from giving in to their demands. The question is why, and the answer is connected with the fact that the Children of Israel, despite their bondage and hardships, did not really want to leave Egypt. If God had not hardened Pharaoh's heart and—even more important—if God had let Pharaoh give in too quickly, they would not have listened to Moses and would have stayed in Egypt.

It is a very human trait that people value only the things that are difficult to obtain; the harder they have to struggle, the more desirable something becomes in their eyes. God simply prevented Pharaoh from being liberal, and until the bitter end, with Egypt devastated and its population reduced and hungry, the more plagues God sent, the more stubborn Pharaoh became; and the more stubborn he became, the more the Children of Israel protested, and the more they wanted to leave. In hindsight, all that Pharaoh need have done—had he been free to do so—was to ease the situation a little, and a thousand persons like Moses could not have dragged the Children of Israel from the "fleshpots of Egypt."

This situation, too, has its parallels in history, the most recent ones having occurred in living memory. After the end of World War II, when the full horror of the Holocaust began to dawn, the world realized that a large part of the Jewish people had been exterminated under the most unbelievable and bestial circumstances. Yet, there were survivors, a hundred thousand of them homeless or living in camps, without anywhere to go—except of course Eretz Israel, the "Promised Land" of the Jews. President Truman appealed to Great Britain to make available 100,000 immigration certificates to allow these survivors to go to Palestine. But a modern pharaoh, a British foreign minister by the name of Ernest Bevin, refused. I firmly believe that God hardened his heart. In his memoirs, President Truman wrote an interesting comment to the effect that if Bevin—who probably was the most influential person in the postwar British cabinet—had agreed, it is very doubtful whether the Jewish state would have come into being. Instead, his refusal helped to turn the Jewish problem into an international issue of the first order, and the resulting political pressures eventually swayed (just) enough countries to agree to the establishment of a Jewish state. By this time the Jewish nation had also awakened, and many more Jews immigrated to Eretz Israel than European refugees only.

The second and related recent example is the Arabs' stubborn refusal to agree to the establishment of a Jewish state—

even a "bi-national" state in which Jews would constitute a sizeable part of the population. However, here too God hardened the hearts of their leaders, and eventually they were confronted with an official proposal for the partition of Palestine. If the Arab leaders had accepted the partition plan, Israelis might now be living in a Jewish state consisting of no more than the central coastal plain and the arid Negev.

When talking about Arab intransigence, we must also mention the Six-Day War. The world begged Nasser not to blockade the Straits of Tiran and dismiss the United Nations peacekeeping forces. It almost looks as if the Supreme Being intervened personally and decided to harden Nasser's heart. When war broke out, the entire world was certain that Israel would be defeated and that the Arab threat "to throw the Jews into the sea" would be realized. However, the unexpected happened, and within a few hours the Egyptian air force was destroyed and its army defeated.

At this point the war should have been finished, but it almost seemed as if a Divine Hand wanted the Jews to recapture Jerusalem and create a situation leading to defensible borders. Even before it had become clear that Egypt had lost the war, the Israeli government implored King Hussein of Jordan not to open hostilities; in exchange, Israel promised to leave Jordan alone. But history did repeat itself; Hussein did not listen, enabling Israel to regain historical trritories.

Almost the same thing happened with Syria—with the result that Israel occupied the strategic Golan Heights, from which the Syrian army had been shelling Israeli settlements for almost twenty years. Let us imagine the catastrophe that would have happened if on Yom Kippur of the year 1973 the Syrians had started the war from their original positions at the Jordan river!

God said to Moses: I am hardening the heart of Pharaoh for a reason, so why do you doubt and complain? Why don't you think of your forefathers, and believe and accept My word as they did? How sorry I am for those who are gone and cannot be replaced.

After God had visited the Egyptians with nine plagues—blood, frogs, gnats, flies, the death of their livestock, boils, hail, locusts, and darkness—He said to Moses, "I will bring one more plague on Pharaoh and on Egypt. After that, he will let you go from here.... *At* midnight I will go throughout Egypt. Every firstborn son in Egypt will die, from the firstborn son of Pharaoh, who sits on the throne, to the firstborn son of the slave girl, who is at her hand mill." The previous plagues had almost ruined Egypt, but the plague of the firstborn was the worst. We should realize that in the ancient civilizations the oldest son, apart from becoming the head of the family, was expected to dedicate himself to government service; the firstborn sons stood at the head of the civil service and the army, and their death left the country virtually leaderless.

Our sages connect Moses' complaint that the Children of Israel refused to listen to him with his statement in the name of God further on in the same portion about the death of the Egyptian firstborn: כחצת הלילה אני יוצא בתוך מצרים: ומת כל בכור בארץ מצרים (*ka-chatzot ha-lailah ani yotze be-toch mitzra'im. u-met kol-bechor ba-aretz mitzra'im*...), "About midnight I will go throughout Egypt. Every firstborn son in Egypt will die."

What could this connection be? We should note that Moses, when he talked to Pharaoh, used the words "about midnight," and not "at midnight," as God had wanted him to say. God obviously knew exactly at what time He would smite the firstborn of the Egyptians, so why did Moses say "approximately at midnight" and not "at midnight"? As indicated above, the answer to this question is connected with Moses' lack of confidence in his powers of persuasion. In fact, he was afraid that the Children of Israel would not depart immediately after the slaying of the firstborn. Nine times earlier Moses had demanded that Pharaoh let them go—and the Children of Israel had not left. According to our sages, if this time again they would fail to leave at the exact moment Moses had announced, the Egyptians—so Moses thought—would call him a liar, and his credibility would be compromised forever.

Our interpreters explain that the quandary of our great leader Moses expresses the tragedy of the Jewish nation till this very day, namely their indecision to recognize the right moment to pack up and go. See how carefully Moses had prepared the Children of Israel for the Exodus. He even told them to ask their Egyptian neighbors for articles of silver and gold, which they would need in the course of their journey. He had taught them how to prepare the Passover sacrifice, and told them to count the days till Passover—not in the customary way, but for the very first time according to their own Jewish calendar. (Nissan is the first Jewish month, and the counting of this month is the first commandment that God communicated to the Jewish people.)

Then came the last plague, which, Moses was convinced, would break Pharaoh's resistance once and for all. The Egyptians were totally demoralized. The effects of the plague were being felt throughout the country, and Pharaoh's servants even rebuked him, by saying: הטרם תדע כי אבדה מצרים (ha-terem teda ki avdah mitzra'im), "Do you not yet realize that Egypt is ruined?" Let these people go, so that they may worship their God!

According to the aggadah, Pharaoh gave orders to release the Children of Israel, but apparently there were no longer people to give orders to. Everyone had gone to look after his own home and family. So Pharaoh had no choice but to travel personally to Goshen to order the Children of Israel out of his country. Upon his arrival there, he believed that he would find the Hebrews all packed and ready to go—and in a very revengeful mood because of their treatment at the hands of the Egyptians. But everything was quiet, and he wondered what was happening. Maybe he had taken the wrong way, and this place was not Goshen, where the Hebrews were living. Again according to the aggadah, he knocked at one of the houses and asked whether the people who lived there were members of the Hebrew tribes. "Yes," was the answer, "but please do not disturb our sleep." Pharaoh was surprised. How was it possible that a nation that had been clamoring to be freed, and according to its own declared intention was about to pack up and leave, was in fact sleeping?

This is exactly what Moses was afraid of. He knew his people better than anybody else, and he realized that they were not at all anxious to go. This makes it even clearer why he said "*approximately* midnight" to Pharaoh, although God had told him to say "*at* midnight." The Torah tells us that, when finally the hour struck that they should leave, the Hebrews were not prepared and, instead of leaving of their own accord, the Torah says that גרשו ממצרים ולא יכלו להתמהמה וגם צידה לא עשו להם (*garshu me-mitzra'im ve-lo yachlu lehitmamehah ve-gam tzedah lo asu lahem*), "... they were driven out of Egypt and did not have time to prepare food for themselves." In other words, instead of leaving of their free will, they were thrown out!

The Jews in Egypt were in danger of assimilation, and God decided that the time had come for them to leave. Given their opposition to departing of their own free will, God saw to it that they were driven out. There is a lesson here that, to judge by the events of our recent history, the Jewish people have as yet found difficult to absorb. God's message is clear, however, and I pray that we shall never have to witness another repeat.

Parashath Bo

החודש הזה לכם ראש חדשים ראשון הוא לכם לחדשי השנה.

"This month is to be for you the first month, the first month of your year."

The above commandment is the very first that was given to the Jewish people—even while they were still in Egypt. According to a midrash in the name of Rabbi Levi, these words from the Torah about the first Jewish month are connected with one of the later commandments, which stipulates that "you shall be holy, because I, your God, am holy." Of course the question immediately arises, what could a commandment about a calendar and a commandment about holiness have in common? Would a calendar be able to make the Jewish people holier?

According to the Midrash, when God said, "You shall be holy," He meant that He wanted the Jewish people to be devoted to Him with their bodies and with their material goods. In fact, Moses expressed this idea in very similar terms when Pharaoh asked him whom he wanted to take with him into the desert to worship God, and he answered: "We will go with our young and old, with our sons and daughters, and with our flocks and herds, because we are to celebrate a festival to God." Our interpreters point out that Pharaoh wanted to let only the men leave; he did not believe that the Children of Israel would attach any importance to the worship of women or children. But Moses insisted: We are going together! Only when we can take the old and the young, our sons and our daughters, can we celebrate our festival.

100

Although we know, of course, which festival Moses had in mind, and on which date the Passover sacrifice had to be brought, these facts do not bring us much closer to the connection between the commandment regarding the month and the holiness of the Jewish people. To understand this, we must go back into Jewish history.

When the Jewish people arrived in Eretz Israel their history was, as it were, beginning anew. They were strangers in a land occupied by all kinds of people. They conquered many of these peoples, but it would take four-hundred years before King David subdued the last opposition. During these years history was made, but the surprising thing is that we do not know a single date of any Jewish conquest or victory. There is hardly a nation in the world that does not commemorate its revolutions or victories over its enemies. The French have Bastille Day, the Americans the 4th of July, and even the modern State of Israel celebrates its Independence Day. In the Bible, however, there is no hint about when particular victories occurred, or when our leaders occupied a particular city; we do not even know when David captured Jerusalem, although the Tenach relates countless other occurrences in minute detail.

In much the same way the Jewish people do not commemorate the birthdays or the deaths of even their greatest leaders, and even if we were in the habit of erecting statues, I do not think anyone of us could imagine any Jewish authority, no matter where, erecting a statue of Moses or King Solomon in the center of a public square! To the extent that we do commemorate historical events, it is our defeats, like the destruction of the Temple, or the capture of Jerusalem by the Persians and the Romans.

There is one seeming exception, namely Chanukkah, which falls on *Kav He be-Kislev*, the twenty-fifth day of the month of Kislev, when the Jewish people rested after the Maccabees had defeated their enemies. But even in this case, what we celebrate is not a military victory or an act of revenge, but a miracle: the miracle that our *spiritual* existence was saved, and that the designs of our pagan enemies to abolish Torah service and destroy the Jewish faith were defeated. This is why the festival is not marked by anything even remotely reminding us of our military victory, but with the light of a candle, to symbolize our spiritual salvation.

We Jews are indeed a strange people. We differ from other nations not only in our way of life, or because of the fact that we adhere to ethics and morality derived from the Torah, but in our entire way of thinking. Whereas all other nations feel they can sit back and celebrate their past glories, symbolize their historical achievements, immortalize their national heroes, and incorporate the celebration of their successes into their national inheritance, the Jewish people are taught that they must continue to fight for their existence. This also explains why our "holidays" are not festive celebrations, but first and foremost occasions to remember and reflect: lessons that we are supposed to learn from—and with reason, for we Jews are the only people who cannot take our existence for granted, but are continually called upon to explain and justify ourselves.

Some might think that the above is purely a result of historical circumstances, but in fact the Jewish condition is very much a part of God's plan—so much so that the Torah precedes six occasions by the word זכור (*zechor*)—"remember." Some of them commemorate crucial events in our history, whereas the others remind us how we should behave to ensure the survival of our nation.

They are:

1. Remember the day you came out of Egypt;
2. Remember the Shabbath, to make it holy;
3. Remember the things your eyes saw in the desert, and tell your children what you saw the day you stood before God at Mount Sinai;
4. Remember how you provoked God in the desert;

5. Remember what God did to Miriam on the way, after you had come out of Egypt;

6. Remember what Amalek did to you on your way out of Egypt, and destroy his memory from under the heavens; do not forget!

What is the common denominator of these six commandments, and why do they form the basis of Jewish survival? Earlier we explained that the Jewish worldview is different from that of other nations. We do not celebrate our victories, or the destruction of an enemy. We fight for our existence and survival each and every day, but if we succeed, we do not set aside a special day to commemorate it. Our tradition warns us: בנפול אויבך אל תשמח (be-nefol oyvecha al tismach), "Do not rejoice at the downfall of your enemy." According to Jewish philosophy, a hero is not necessarily someone who wins a war, but someone who conquers *himself*. In the words of our sages: איזהו גיבור הכובש את יצרו (eize gibor ha-kovesh eth-yetzro), a hero is he who controls himself—and who therefore, by his example, can teach others to live the right way. Even so, in the Jewish tradition, heroes—of any kind—are not put on a pedestal. The Torah does not praise Moses for having overcome Pharaoh. God never praised, let alone rewarded, Moses for his strength of character, which enabled him to withstand the hardships the Jewish people inflicted on him during the forty years of wandering in the desert. The only—but possibly most valuable—praise for Moses is the sentence in the Torah: משה ענו מכל אדם (moshe anav me-kol adam), "Moses was the humblest of men." He taught the Jewish people through his personal example that nobody, however great or important he is, has the right to feel himself above his fellowmen.

Summarizing the above, we can say that the most important thing is not *when* something happened, or who was the victor. The Torah says: אין מוקדם או מאוחר בתורה (ein mukdam o me'uchar ba-torah), "There is no first or last in the Torah." And as regards heroes, the Jewish view is that fame is not in the first place a matter of courage, but of character. What is important is not a leader's show of strength, but how he behaved at a given critical moment. Taking everything together, not the year or the hour are important, but *how* something was done.

King Solomon said, "What once happened, may happen again, and what once was done, may be done again." The episode of Cain and Abel at the very beginning of human history can recur. The problems facing every new generation are not new. The animal that lives inside us all is not dead. In some it sleeps, in others it has been tamed, and in still others it has merely changed its spots. The instinct, however, is still there, and this is why we have every reason to value a person who has learned to control his animal side.

All our knowledge, and the techniques that have enriched the world notwithstanding, one thing has as yet eluded us: peace of mind. This is why the six commandments that we are told to remember are so essential. They touch upon certain fundamental aspects of our existence. They are not merely historical memories, but they remind us how certain things should be done—or *not* done.

The first event to remember is the Exodus from Egypt, representing our yearning—and that of mankind in general— for physical freedom.

The second commandment to remember concerns the Shabbath. Its importance for the existence of our nation cannot be expressed better than in the saying of our rabbis: "More than the Jewish nation has kept the Shabbath, the Shabbath has kept the Jewish nation."

The third event we are commanded to remember is how we received the Torah at Mount Sinai. The giving of the Torah was the quintessential event in our history, without which the Jewish nation and, for that matter, Judaism, would not have existed.

The fourth thing we are told to remember is how the Children of Israel provoked God with their complaints. Admittedly,

their situation seemed on many occasions insecure and threatening, and their long sojourn in the desert put both their physical and spiritual endurance to a severe test. At the same time,
they had God's promise that everything would turn out well in
the end, and—maybe equally important—these trials strengthened them, and prepared them for their entry into the Promised Land. Life is like this, and it has always been like this. Even
God's promise to Abraham, that his descendants would take
possession of Eretz Israel, is followed almost directly by the
sentence, "Know for certain that your descendants will be
strangers in a country not their own, and they will be enslaved
and ill-treated." God promised Abraham and his descendants
ownership of Eretz Israel, but not that they would *live* there
forever. To receive something is often easy; to *keep* it, and to
remain worthy of it, usually requires great effort and sacrifice.
The poet Nahum Alterman expressed the same idea in one of his
famous poems about the rebirth of the State of Israel, saying
that it would not be handed to the Jewish people on "a silver
platter"—in other words, that its establishment and survival
would entail a long and intensive struggle.

In light of the above, there can be no doubt that the constant
infighting and complaints of the Children of Israel only placed
their survival at risk. It is impossible to maintain the fabric of a
nation or a society if everybody complains and at critical
moments displays a lack of solidarity. This is also why the Torah
says in this portion: החודש הזה לכם ראש חדשים (*ha-chodesh ha-ze lachem
rosh chadashim*), "This month is to be for you the first month,"
meaning that during the month in which the Children of Israel
departed from Egypt, they started a new way of life. The Midrash says, "The very minute you accepted the Torah, you
became the master of your future, and of your time, and from
that moment on you yourself had to decide what would happen
to you."

The fifth event, reminding us of Miriam's gossip about
Moses, seems strangely out of context compared with the pre-

vious four. Yet it is not, and a closer look makes us realize that it is connected with the previous commandment. The Jewish people were entirely on their own, without a friend in the world. They had to depend—as has been the case ever since—entirely upon themselves. Even so they could hold out, provided that they remained united and refrained from backbiting and criticizing each other. If even ordinary members of a society can be a disruptive influence when they gossip about each other, how much more can a nation be divided when its leaders are disunited in public. Miriam was loved by the Jewish people; she had inspired them on many occasions, and her example counted. This explains why her criticism in particular was so damaging— and why God made her an example, so that future generations would remember not to indulge in divisive gossip.

The sixth event, finally, connected with "Amalek," the archetypical enemy of the Jewish people, derives its importance from the fact that our physical survival depends on it.

The Exodus and the assembly of the Jewish people at Mount Sinai were watersheds in the history of mankind. Even so we now understand why the essential thing was not when these— or other—events took place, but the fact *that* they took place. We count the approach of these festivals on our calendar, not just to fix their location in time, but in order to prepare ourselves for their approach. This, by the way, is also one of the reasons why the Jewish people do not follow the solar calendar, as was the custom with most agricultural nations, but count the Jewish year according to the phases of the moon. The Jews, too, used to be farmers, and of course the seasons were important from an agricultural and economic point of view. But it was not just the material and practical aspects that made us what we are, but the spiritual side and our distinctive way of life. This is why the midrashic interpretation says החודש הזה לכם (*ha-chodesh ha-ze lachem*), meaning, "This month is *yours*." A slave does not have his own time; his time belongs to his master. The Torah wants to say: From now on you will be a free nation. You yourself will decide when to rest and when to work. From now on you are counting the days to prepare yourselves for the receiving of the Torah, and the Torah will make you a holy nation.

The Torah wants us to remember, but not merely the historical details: who did what and to whom, or when. This is why we do not commemorate generals and rulers. Our remembrance has to do with what makes us different—an עם סגולה, a "separate—and special—nation." This separateness gives us a potential for being "other" and better, not because we are born better, or because we are intellectually or morally superior, but because it grants us a priviliged opportunity to remember. This is the connection between the Jewish calendar and holiness: Remember your past, and this will make you holy.

Parashath Be-Shalach

ויבאו מרתה ולא יכלו לשתות מים ממרה כי מרים הם על־כן
קרא־שמה מרה: וילנו העם על־משה לאמר מה־נשתה: ויצעק
אל־יהוה ויורהו יהוה עץ וישלך אל־המים וימתקו המים שם
שם לו חק ומשפט ושם נסהו.

"When they came to Marah, they could not drink its water,
because it was bitter. That is why the place is called Marah.
So the people grumbled against Moses, saying, 'What are
we to drink?' Then Moses cried out to God, and God
showed him a piece of wood. He threw it into the water,
and the water became sweet. There God made a decree and
a law for them, and there he tested them."

In its commentary on the biblical verse in this *parashah*—
according to which God gave the Israelites חק ומשפט (*chok ve-
mishpat*), "a decree and a law"—the Talmud, in *masechtah Sanhedrin*,
writes that in effect God gave them two commandments. The
two commandments in question are the laws of the Shabbath
and the commandment of the Red Heifer.

Our biblical interpreters ask themselves what exactly happened in Marah that forced Moses to give the Children of Israel
two commandments barely a week after they had left Egypt. In
another six weeks they were to receive the Torah at Sinai. Why
the hurry? Why was it impossible to wait another few weeks
and give them 612 *mitzvoth* all at once? (One *mitzvah*, the commandment ordaining the Children of Israel to begin counting
the Jewish months, was by necessity given in Egypt, because the
Pesach sacrifice had to take place on the fourteenth day of this
month; apart from this, God wanted to symbolize the Israelites'

newly found freedom by the inauguration of their own calendar.)

One explanation given by our biblical interpreters is that God wanted to show His people the kind of *mitzvoth* they could expect to receive. For there are two kinds of *mitzvoth* in the Torah: the first kind consists of the ones we can understand logically, whereas the second kind appears to have no logical reason. The Shabbath is an example of an understandable *mitzvah*. People who work also have to rest. As against this, the complicated instructions about the Red Heifer, whose ashes were intended for the purification of people who had been defiled by a corpse, were almost impossible to understand, and they certainly could not be explained logically. As such these two *mitzvoth* are indeed excellent illustrations of the kinds of commandments the Jews could expect to receive. Even so, this does not explain why they had to be given at this particular moment, and why it was so difficult to wait another six weeks until the entire Torah was given on Mount Sinai.

We can only conclude that God must have had a specific reason for wanting to give some of the commandments almost immediately following the crossing of the Red Sea.

It is a known fact that every individual is born hungry: hungry for food, hungry for possessions, and hungry for achievement. It is our basic human nature not to be satisfied with what comes to us by itself, but constantly to try to improve our condition. Something in our nature urges us on. Obviously this is how God wants it; we were given a creative impulse in order to improve our existence and that of the world. If we would simply sit still and vegetate, the world would soon grind to a halt and die out.

However, our ambitions can easily carry us too far. All people have a desire for progress, but whereas good people like to give of themselves for the benefit of their fellows, others exploit their ambitions mainly for selfish purposes—for self-aggrandizement, fame, or money. The first category of individuals, however busy they are, will feel spiritual satisfaction and peace of mind; the second category will be continually restless, dissatisfied, and in the end embittered. Unselfish people are rarely embittered, because their actions carry their own reward.

Here lies the connnection with this portion of the week. Only three days earlier the Children of Israel had been miraculously saved when they crossed the Red Sea. They had passed through the middle of the sea on dry land, but their enemies were drowned. Not only were the Children of Israel alive, but they had found a lot of booty. Apparently the Egyptian horses were adorned with gold and silver ornaments, studded with precious stones. The Egyptian soldiers and horses had washed ashore, and the Jews had busily started stripping them of their valuables. According to the tradition, they were so busy with this ביזת הים (bizath ha-yam), the collection of spoils from the sea, that they did not want to move on. In fact, Moses had to force them to leave the place that a day earlier they would have fled in panic.

Everyone would expect the Children of Israel to be happy, because only a week earlier they had been slaves and had suddenly seen their enemies drown. They had survived, and their enemies were dead. More than that; tradition has it that they collected more silver and gold at the shores of the Red Sea than they ever believed they would possess. To have so much loot just for the picking is exhilarating; an experience like this makes people drunk with happiness. Yet, instead of being happy and grateful, they became embittered and rebellious. The Torah says that when they arrived at Marah, they could not drink the water because it was bitter. However, our sages comment that the water tasted bitter because they were bitter, and that to a bitter person everything tastes bitter. The absence of a purpose, or of discipline or obligations, makes one bitter. It is said that the ancient Greek philosopher Socrates was only 45 years old when he commented to his students, "I feel very old. I am mentally empty, so much so that I do not know what I am living for."

Let us compare this with Moses, about whom the Torah writes that at the age of 120 לא כהתה עינו ולא־נח לחו (*lo kahatah eiyno ve-lo nas leicho*), "his eyes were not weak nor his strength gone." The Midrash comments that Moses, when he was asked why he looked so healthy and young, answered, צורי חי (*tzuri chai*), "I feel young because I feel God inside me."

Property, silver and gold, stocks and bonds, don't necessarily make one satisfied. Here lies the difference between the person who pursues ethical purposes and the materialist, who lives for himself and according to his own beliefs. Individuals whose actions are guided by an unconditional belief in God and His ethical commandments will feel confident, and derive a great deal of satisfaction from their achievements. The opposite will be the case with people who lack this confidence in God and the ethics of His commandments, and who therefore engage in an endless pursuit of material possessions, only to discover that there is no limit to having, and that satisfaction—and happiness—continue to elude them.

Why were the Children of Israel so embittered? The answer is that they were physically free, but spiritually devoid of purpose. The Torah tells that Moses made their water sweet by throwing into the water a tree that God had shown him. Rabbi Eliezer says that Moses threw into the water the עץ החיים (*etz ha chaim*), the "Tree of Life," in other words the Torah. God there and then gave the Children of Israel two of the *mitzvoth* to give them a purpose. It could not wait; they were purposeless, dissatisfied, bitter, and rebellious. Once they had a purpose, they would no longer be embittered. The Torah says: אם־שמוע תשמע לקול יהוה אלהיך והישר בעיניו תעשה ושמרת כל־חקיו כל־המחלה אשר־שמתי במצרים לא־אשים עליך כי אני יהוה רפאך meaning: "If you listen carefully to the voice of God and do what is right in His eyes, if you pay attention to his commands and keep all his decrees, I will not bring on you any of the diseases that I brought on the Egyptians, for I am the God who heals you."

Rabbi Moses Maimonides—the Rambam—was physician to

the court of the Egyptian Sultan al-Fadil in Cairo. It is told that after a while the Sultan told him, "I do not need your services any more, for I am never sick, and I am paying you for nothing." Maimonides answered, "With all respect, Your Eminence, I think that this only proves how much you need me. The task of a good physician is to see to it that his patients do not get sick." Surprised, the Sultan asked, "Where did you learn such wisdom?" Maimonides answered, "From our Torah, Your Eminence, where God promised the Jewish people not to bring sicknesses upon them, because—as He says in the Torah—'I am the God who heals you.' There I learned that the best doctor is the one who prevents sickness."

This portion of the Torah continues to tell how the Children of Israel journeyed in the desert. This was by no means an easy matter. After all, they had no maps, and neither were there any roads or signposts. The Torah tells, however, that God was their guide, for: ויהוה הלך לפניהם יומם בעמוד ענן לנחתם הדרך ולילה בעמוד אש להאיר להם ללכת יומם ולילה (va-ha-shem holech lif'neihem yomam ba-amud anan la-n'chotam ha-derech ve-lailah ba-amud esh le-ha'ir lahem lalecheth yomam va-lailah), "By day God went ahead of them in a pillar of cloud to guide them on their way and by night in a pillar of fire, to give them light, so that they could travel by day or night."

Note the fundamental difference between the function of the pillar of cloud, which guided the Children of Israel, and the pillar of fire, which only lit their path. During the day, even when they could see, they were nevertheless guided by the pillar of cloud, to keep them from losing their way—both physically and spiritually. At night, however, when the surroundings were steeped in darkness, the Children of Israel apparently did not need guidance—only a light to prevent them from stumbling off the track they were following.

Our sages comment that this is the nature of the Jewish people: When it is dark, and they are surrounded by darkness, the Jewish people know where to go. They automatically stay on the right track. They know where to go and what to do; they do not lose their way and their identity. When, on the other hand, it is light—in other words when they have a clear view and they are free to go where they want—they need guidance in order not to lose their way. It is in the free, enlightened, and liberal societies that assimilation takes its heaviest toll. It is in these societies that the Jews most need the Torah, to protect their identity and to ensure that they will remain an עם סגולה (am segulah)—a special, and a treasured people.

Parashath Jethro

וידבר אלהים את כל־הדברים האלה לאמר: אנכי אלהיך אשר הוצאתיך מארץ מצרים מבית עבדים: לא־יהיה לך אלהים אחרים על־פני.

"And God spoke all these words: 'I am the God who brought you out of Egypt, out of the land of slavery. You shall have no other gods before me.'"

With these words from the weekly portion of *Jethro*, the Jewish people—and through them the entire world—were asked to embrace the concept of the one God. Even today the world has many different faiths, some monotheistic and others polytheistic, similar to the old pagan religions. To some people the distinctions between one religion and another may appear superficial, but they are very fundamental indeed.

A closer look at our own Jewish philosophy shows how substantial is the difference between the Jewish belief in God and that of other faiths. These differences are not merely quantitative, or related to questions such as the nature of God, or the manner in which He intervenes in our lives, and whether He does so directly or through intermediaries. We are talking about the entire concept of God.

To begin with, Judaism is not a religion, in the sense of a belief in a Divine Being who asks to be worshiped in return for favors of whatever kind. Judaism is a way of life: a philosophy about the way people must behave in order to be worthy of their Creator, in whose image they were made. We believe that God is the symbol of good, and that all he asks from his creatures is to emulate Him. Our sages tell us that in the same way as ד׳ אל רחום וחנון (ha-shem el rachum va-chanun), "God is a compassionate and merciful God," we too must be compassionate and merciful. In the Jewish view we are far more dependent upon God for all our needs than He needs our worship, and the only reason God wants to tell us about Himself is to enable us to be like Him.

This concept of compassion is not easily accepted by other religions. The fact is that people are not usually taught to cultivate unselfishness or compassion. Most societies are not guided by their attitude toward the weak and helpless (which is what mercy and compassion are all about), but by strength, in the form of power and achievement. People like activist and militant or even aggressive behavior, and they admire supermen and heroes. They are ashamed of people who are weak and have to depend on the assistance of others. Unfortunately, as long as people keep on being educated to admire strength and cruelty, and have contempt for the weak, we will live in a world of bloodshed—regardless of whether we are talking about individuals or nations.

The Jewish "hero," by comparison, is an antihero, probably best personified by Charlie Chaplin's little tramp, and dozens of other, kindred "shlimazzels," who accept that everything in this world is temporary and relative, and who sooner suffer indignity than inflict it on somebody else.

From this follows another distinction, namely the Jewish view of the value of the individual. According to our Jewish philosophy, people must be accepted as they are. Our sages state that we have an absolute obligation toward every human being, regardless of whether he is strong or weak, smart or foolish, old or young, because whoever he is, or whatever he does, he was created in the image of God. The famous Gaon of Vilna is said to have remarked that if a follower of another faith were to come to him, as the Gentile came to Hillel, and ask him for a short definition of Judaism, he would answer, "Judaism is fighting against aggressors." Judaism means helping people who are oppressed and persecuted. The Talmud says in the name of Rabbi Channa that the biblical verse, והאלהים יבקש את־נרדף (ve-ha-shem yevakesh eth-nirdaf), "God seeks out the persecuted," means that even a guilty person will find God on his side the moment people persecute (rather than prosecute) him.

If this seems self-evident to the average Jew, we should remind him that as recently as the nineteenth century the opposite way of thinking found formal expression in the "superman" theory of the philosopher Friedrich Nietzsche. Following his death from insanity his "will to power" influenced generations of artists, writers, and psychologists—as well as madmen like Hitler. Nietzsche professed a form of "heroic nihilism," including the need for the "death of God," in order that the superman might arise. Although apparently sympathetic to the Jews as such, his writings claim that Jewish religious morality is the product of a people who are themselves physically and mentally weak, in other words, who have the mentality and souls of slaves. Obviously, individuals or nations who are strong have no reason to teach compassion for one's fellowman, because they can take justice into their own hands; only slaves need compassion. They want to—in fact have to—arouse feelings of compassion in their fellowmen because it is the only way they can survive. This, in essence, is what Nietzsche said, and most of us have witnessed how, in our twentieth century, this ethics was carried to its logical—and fatal—conclusion.

We Jews have never been able to admire the hero or superman, and never in our long history have we accorded him a special place. We believe that every individual in this world has the same rights — not because we are a nation of cowards, or a nation of slaves, but because this is what the Torah teaches us. A world without compassion, a world in which people do not help each other, simply is not worth living in. If I feel that I do not have to assist a fellow human being in need, then why should anybody help me if ever my turn should come to be dependent? This mentality, multiplied a millionfold, would mean that nobody has any rights, that every person is a hostage to fortune, and that—ultimately—nobody can ever be sure of his life.

In an earlier book I mentioned a comment by our sages, according to which every person has three obligations. The first is his obligation to God; the recognition that there is a Creator and Supreme Ruler, without whom one would be responsible to no one else, and could do absolutely any-thing he wanted. The result would be pure chaos. The second is his obligation to his fellowman and to his society. It was the seventeenth-century English poet John Donne who wrote the famous lines: "No man is an Island, entire of Itself; every man is a piece of the Continent, a part of the main."

The third obligation is man's responsibility to himself. Here, again, we have a characteristic difference between Judaism and many other faiths. Judaism does not want us to suffer for the sake of suffering. A society cannot be successful when the individuals of which it is composed do not look after themselves. The Torah commands us ואהבת לרעך כמוך (ve-ahavta le-re'echa kemo-cha), "Love your fellowman like yourself"—in other words, we are obliged to love our neighbor, but we must *first* love ourselves, because one who does not like himself is simply unable to look after his fellowman. The Torah enjoins us time and again to enjoy all the permitted things that the world has to offer, so much so that a person who purposely abstains from what is permitted in life is considered a sinner. Other religions consider abstention a sign of holiness, and in many communities physical pursuits and material enjoyment are frowned upon.

The Jewish view is exactly the opposite: the world was created to serve man. One of the best examples is related to the rules concerning the Shabbath. Jews are forbidden to work on the Shabbath, according to the biblical injunction זכור את יום השבת לקדשו ... ויום השביעי שבת ליהוה אלהיך לא־תעשה כל־מלאכה (zechor eth yom ha-shabbath le-kadsho... ve-yom ha-shevi'i shabbath la-shem eloheicha lo *ta'aseh kol melachah*), "Remember the Day of Rest, to keep it holy... the seventh day is a Shabbath to God. On it you shall not do any work." Our sages comment that "keeping it holy" covers all our activities. Not only are we asked to abstain from work, but everything we do must have its own character and rhythm: when we talk on the Shabbath, we shall talk more softly; when we walk on the Shabbath, we shall walk slowly. From this it follows that the Shabbath permeates all our activities on this day.

That is, as long as we are well, and there is no emergency. For at that point health and well-being become the paramount factors, which override the commandments about the Shabbath. *Halachah* even goes so far as to call somebody a murderer when he refuses to break the commandments about the Shabbath rest in order to assist in a life-saving situation. There is a story about one of our great rabbis who on the Shabbath came upon a seriously ill patient, but discovered that nobody was prepared to make hot water needed for tending to the patient. He concluded that he had no choice but to "desecrate" the day of rest. Not only did the rabbi break the Shabbath, but he pronounced a blessing, because he had been privileged to perform this *mitzvah*.

The Talmud gives many examples of the way the Torah makes us aware of the importance of human life. One of our sages comments, "When it is written בראשית ברא אלהים (*be-reshit bara elohim*), 'In the beginning God created...,' this means that we are expected to live and to build, and to enjoy everything that God has permitted us. God 'only' removed the chaos; *our* task is to establish orderly life on earth."

Given the importance of human life, we can also understand why the Torah commands us in no less than four places not to take revenge. This might seem an impossible task, unless we learn to see the person who hurts or abuses us as a part of ourself. Our sages give the following explanation: Say that you were holding a knife or an ax in one hand, and suddenly the knife or the ax would slip and cut the other hand. Would you revenge yourself on your hand? Of course not, because that hand is a part of yourself. The same thing applies to our fellow-man: as long as we regard him as a part of ourselves—in other words, as a part of the same creation to which we belong—we cannot compensate for our own suffering by inflicting suffering on somebody else. And unless, and until, we learn this, the cycle of violence will continue.

Oppression, persecutions, and pogroms are a direct result of this lack of recognition of the other as our equal, and a lack of a sense of responsibility for helping to promote this equality. Too many people lack confidence in themselves; they distrust the world as it was created and regard it as an inherently wicked place. This "other-worldliness" has, ever since the ancient Essenes and the early Christian hermits, caused many to run away from society out of disgust with other people's sinfulness, and for fear of being infected themselves. Those who took this easy way out may have avoided exposure to violence and sin, but they certainly lost out in terms of challenges, in creativity, and in fulfilling God's purpose with His world—not to speak of human company, happiness, and laughter.

The ancient Greeks so valued their state that they placed its interest above that of the individual. Because of this, they educated their youngsters to sacrifice their lives in the service of the state. When a boy was seven years old, he was taken away from his family to be educated in a state institution. Here he remained until he was seventeen years old, to be taught the martial arts, love of country, and a spirit of sacrifice; individual needs were not taken into account. Even in our time many aspects of this "classical" example were adopted in Russia, and subsequently in Germany and—at this very moment—in countries such as Iraq, Syria, Libya, and Iran. Lack of respect for the individual and human values is one of the main reasons why civilizations like the Greek disappeared, despite their (in terms of those days) high cultural and technological development. If individuality is denied, it will finally wither and die. And since a nation is a collection of individuals, the moment we rob people of their individuality, there can be no nation either.

Within the Jewish nation the individual occupies a very important place. We only have to look at the Torah, which in its continual emphasis on individuals—and not Jews only—is a veritable charter of human rights. That is what our sages said: God laid down a condition for His creation, namely that someone had to accept His Torah. The Jewish people accepted it, and as long as they will undertake to uphold it, the world will exist; if not, it will ultimately be destroyed.

Parashath Mishpatim

ואלה המשפטים אשר תשים לפניהם: כי תקנה עבד עברי שש
שנים יעבד ובשביעית יצא לחפשי חנם.

"These are the laws you are to set before them: If you buy a
Hebrew servant, he is to serve you for six years. But in the
seventh year he shall go free, without paying anything."

According to our rabbis, the Torah wants to teach us that the
most important thing for a Jew is a harmonious relationship
with his fellowmen. Thus they interpret the words אשר תשים
לפניהם (asher tasim lefaneihem), "which you are to set before them,"
which appear in the introduction to this parashah, as meaning
that the importance of the commandments relating to man and
his fellows supersedes that of all the other mitzvoth.

Some of the interpreters of the Torah ask why this first
example of the numerous mitzvoth concerning the relations
between man and his fellow deals with slaves. Why slaves, and
not thieves, or robbers, or—for that matter—relationships
between close relatives such as parents and children? Some of
the interpreters point out the fact that the preceding portion of
the week, Parashath Jethro, dealt with the Ten Commandments.
And the first of these commandments reads, אנכי יהוה אלהיך אשר
הוצאתכם מארץ מצרים מבית עבדים (anochi ha-shem eloheicha asher hotzeticha
me-eretz mitzra'im mi-beit avadim), "I am your God who brought you
out of Egypt, out of the land of slavery." Isn't it significant that
here, too, slavery is mentioned? This significance is increased
even further when we realize that the Torah recalls no less than

forty-two times that we—the Jews—were slaves in Egypt, thus warning us that, having experienced the hardships and iniquities of slavery ourselves, we should never enslave others.

The lesson of this portion of the week, called משפטים (mishpatim), meaning "Laws," is therefore that the first law of human relationships is that no Jew, or any other human being, shall ever be enslaved for life. To a society in which bondage—of enemies and prisoners of war, but also of tribal kinsmen who had fallen into debt—was accepted practice, the Torah prescribed a radical departure to a more humane and moral relationship between people by stating that no Jewish slave should be kept for more than six years. More than that, if the *shemittah* year occurred during these six years, the slave had to be freed earlier, even if his bondage had only just begun. Also if the master refused the slave proper food, or imposed tasks upon him that hurt his dignity, even by saying "put on my shoes," or if he insulted or beat him, the Beth Din would immediately free the slave. No wonder, therefore, that our sages commented that if a Jew acquired a Jewish slave, he in fact acquired a master over himself.

Now we understand why the parashah begins with the words ואלה (ve-eleh), "and these," rather than merely אלה (eleh), "these." Our interpreters explain that, in effect, this law about the relationship between man and his fellow refers back to the previous *parashah*, that of the Ten Commandments.

Our rabbis have stressed time and again how much these commandments have contributed to the existence and survival of world civilization. Yet, looking around us in the present-day world, we also see how far we still have to go to implement this important contribution of the Torah. We have only to look at how governments and societies are struggling to prevent crime, to the extent that the strictest punishments are implemented to punish offenses such as robbery, rape, and murder—including life imprisonment and death sentences by hanging or the electric chair.

Most criminal codes are aimed at instilling fear in criminals, in the hope that this will have a preventive effect. In their zeal to prevent crime, some legal systems even go so far as to overlook the necessity of incontrovertible proof of guilt, as long as the effect is to frighten potential lawbreakers. The consequences can be terrible, in particular when we are dealing with life sentences or, even worse, capital punishment, for if the accused should subsequently be found innocent, the sentence can no longer be undone. Justice then becomes injustice.

One case out of thousands of similar cases that comes to mind is that of an accused rapist in the United States who was condemned to life imprisonment. After he had served five years of his sentence, the real culprit was caught. The man was released, but in the meantime he had lost his job, his wife had divorced him, and his children were estranged and did not want to know their father. He sued the government for compensation, but even if his claim was recognized, it would have helped him very little. But at least this particular individual survived to tell the tale. Numerous cases are known in the judicial histories of countries meting out death sentences—in addition to the many others that will forever remain unknown—where the only redress has been a posthumous reprieve!

The moral of all this is that all the writing, talking, moralizing, and punishing does not seem to bring us nearer to a solution of the problem of crime prevention. However stringent the laws and their application are, the question is whether they really help us to prevent crime. Is the situation improving as a result? Have all these strict punitive measures brought down the crime rate?

The opposite seems to be the case. There is not one country that can claim to have succeeded in eliminating crime, or even in reducing the amount of crime. In most cases, if one kind of crime is reduced, other kinds increase. Robbery, murder, and all other kinds of crime form a part of our everyday existence. The prisons are so full that we cannot find place for new inmates.

Judicial establishments everywhere are looking for additional budgets—not to rehabilitate, but to build new prisons. Rehabilitation efforts, insofar as they are undertaken, seem to be swamped by the rising crime wave. We are living in a society where it is becoming increasingly difficult to walk the streets at night, and even at home we surround ourselves with all kinds of electronic and mechanical protection gadgets, alarm systems, guards, and so forth. More and more we accept this as a part of our everyday lives. And meanwhile the police are powerless, and the judges are overworked. What would happen without the existing judiciary and public law-and-order apparatus is altogether too frightening to contemplate. Corruption, violence, and vigilantism would take over, and total anarchy would be the result: man would eat man. Our society would not survive.

How surprising is it, therefore, to learn how a few thousand years ago the Jewish inhabitants of Eretz Israel lived undisturbed and unafraid in their towns and villages. We know, of course, how people used to go up to Jerusalem on their annual holiday pilgrimages, and it is a well-documented fact that they left their homes unguarded, and that on their return they found everything intact. Yet there were no policemen to guard against thieves.

The Midrash relates an episode about two women who left their homes in Galilee to go up to Jerusalem. Following their return, one of the women saw the other looking for something. She asked her friend, "Are you missing something?" The other answered, "For one minute I thought I was missing a new pot, but now I remember that I lent it to my sister." The Midrash ends this story by saying that, as far as is known, nobody ever complained about losing property during his absence from home. It simply did not enter people's heads to take something that belonged to somebody else.

Even more surprising is that violent crimes, including murders, were not more common in those days, particularly if we know how extremely difficult it was to convict a murderer. For example, in accordance with Jewish law, the Beth Din would refuse to convict a man for murder unless two witnesses had been present at the time, *and* they had first warned him to desist from committing the deed.

The Talmud relates how on one occasion one of our sages saw a man chasing another man, who took refuge in a cave. The pursuer entered the cave, and after a while came out with a blood-stained knife. The sage went in to see, and saw that the other man had been killed. Confronting the murderer, he said, "There are only two possibilities. Either I killed the man, or you did. Alas, what can I do to you, since I do not have a second witness. But you will receive your punishment from God." The story relates that eventually the man was bitten by a snake and died. This also shows how impartial justice was, since even the testimony of a spiritual leader of the Jewish people was not considered more convincing than that of an ordinary man.

Even after all the above conditions had been met, there remained a great moral reluctance on the part of the Sanhedrin to mete out death sentences, so much so that—as stated in our talmudic literature—a Sanhedrin that pronounced a death sentence once in 70 years was called a "killer Sanhedrin."

A second example concerned theft. Even today there are societies that punish thieves by amputating the hand or arm of the culprit. Not so in Eretz Israel of old. If someone was apprehended for stealing something, he simply had to return double what he had taken; he forfeited whatever he had stolen, in addition to which he was expected to recompense the victim with the value of the stolen object or goods.

We could go on giving examples, such as the institution of the ערי מקלט (*arei miklat*), the "cities of refuge," where people who were convicted of manslaughter—in other words those who had committed an accidental murder—could continue to live a normal life with their families. At the same time, they were not allowed to mix with people from other cities; the purpose of the sentence was not to take revenge, but to prevent the guilty from harming society again.

In the light of such apparent leniency, why weren't the streets of Eretz Israel filled with murderers and thieves? Apparently people had very little reason to be afraid of the courts, which created an added incentive for trespassing against the law. How can we explain that the Jewish society was so quiet and peaceful?

Again we could ask why in the modern society severe punishments do not deter, and why the lenient system of punishments in the Jewish society of old succeeded in preserving the peace? The answer can be found in the *mechilta* of *Parashath Jethro*, which explains that the Ten Commandments which God gave to the Jewish people on Mount Sinai are written on two tablets. Why two tablets? Because the contents of every commandment on the first tablet is related to the contents of the commandment next to it on the second tablet. In fact, the *mechilta* reveals the essence of Jewish existence. For example: next to "I am your God..." on the first tablet is written "You shall not murder" on the second tablet. This means that only a society based on the belief in God will not have murder. Similarly, he who breaks the Shabbath bears false witness, as it were denying that God created the world in six days, and that He rested on the seventh. This explanation of the *mechilta* reveals the essence of Judaism. The Ten Commandments show the relationship between man and his beliefs, on the one hand, and man and his fellow, on the other.

Modern society attempts to legislate capital crime out of existence through deterrent punishments such as life imprisonment or execution—but to no avail. In fact, nothing will help to prevent murder and bloodshed, except a belief in God. Not until we learn to respect the value of individual property and life, for the sole reason that we recognize that our fellow-men are created in the image of God, can we succeed in raising our moral and ethical standards, both individually and collectively. No legal codes, no punishments will help to prevent crime. As long as individuals feel that only strength or money counts, as long as they fail to respect values, as long as they lack יראת שמים (*yirath shamaim*), the "fear of God," all our lives will be in jeopardy. This, in fact, was the situation at the time of the Great Flood. Primitive society failed to respect the Creation: first the value of human life was reduced to that of an animal, and since animals may be killed, murder resulted.

ויאמר אלהים לנח קץ־כל בשר בא לפני כי־מלאה הארץ חמס מפניהם (*va-yomer ha-shem le-noach ketz kol-basar ba lefanai ki mal'ah ha-aretz chamas mip-'neihem*), "So God said to Noah, 'I am going to put an end to all people, for the earth is filled with violence because of them.'" This is how the Torah describes it.

If we want a society without cruelty and injustice, a society without incarceration, amputations, electric chairs, and gallows, we shall have to return to the belief in God and His commandments. No library full of law books and statutes, and no amount of learned treatises on crime and punishment, express the essence of it all as briefly, clearly, and convincingly as the Ten Commandments. And thus, only when we adhere once more to these elementary rules shall we be able to return to a society as it existed in the early days of Eretz Israel, when people could move about freely and without fear, because they accepted the laws of the Torah as a natural part of their daily way of life.

Parashath Terumah

וידבר יהוה אל־משה לאמר: דבר אל־בני ישראל ויקחו־לי
תרומה מאת כל־איש אשר ידבנו לבו תקחו את־תרומתי.

"God said to Moses, 'Tell the Israelites to bring Me an
offering. You are to receive the offering for Me from each
man whose heart prompts him to give.'"

The Midrash comments that there appears to be a contradiction between the words "tell the Israelites to bring Me an
offering," and "receive the offering from each man whose heart
prompts him to give." On one hand the Jewish people are
instructed to give, whether they like it or not, but on the other
they need to do so only "when their heart is willing"—in other
words, voluntarily.

Some of our sages interpret this as meaning that even
though it is a Jewish obligation to set aside part of our income
for charitable purposes, the donor should never forget that he
himself is the first to benefit. It is a fact that nobody is really
impoverished by setting aside some of his earnings, whereas the
act of giving is both a rewarding and an enriching experience—
enriching also in the sense that it changes the personality, and
helps to make the donor another person. The Torah says, עשר
תעשר (aser te'aser), "You shall bring a tithe," and our sages of the
Talmud, with a slight variation, interpret this as עשר בשביל שתתעשר
(aser bishvil she-tit'asher), "Give, and enrich yourself." In the same
way, some of our interpreters read the word li in ויקחו לי תרומה
(ve-yikchu li terumah) as referring not to God but to the donor
himself as the real beneficiary of the donation.

128

We might conclude therefore that God does not in fact force us to take offerings, but that He appeals to our heart and our feelings, rather than to our brain, when relating to our duties to Him and our fellowmen. Thus it cannot be a coincidence that the *Shema Yisrael*, which the observant Jew recites three times a day, is immediately followed by the words, ואהבת את יהוה אלהיך בכל-לבבך ובכל-נפשך ובכל-מאדך (*ve-ahavta eth ha-shem eloheicha be-chol-levavecha u-ve-chol-nafshecha u-ve-chol-me'odeicha*), "You shall love God with all your heart and with all your soul and with all your strength." Also in this central commandment the Torah talks about our heart and our soul, rather than about our intellect.

Does this, in fact, mean that Judaism is an emotional faith, which has to appeal to our hearts in order to arouse feelings of compassion and mercy for our fellowmen? Not quite, for in another place in the Torah it is written, ודע את יהוה אלהיך (*ve-da eth ha-shem eloheicha*), "You must know God." The only way to "know God" and understand Him is to use our intellect.

In order to solve this apparent contradiction, we should look for a moment at the functioning of our heart and our brain, and compare not only the role both play in our lives, but also how they have developed throughout the ages. One look at the changes that have taken place in our environment even during the last few centuries is sufficient to make us realize the tremendous development of our human mental facilities. We enjoy unheard-of comforts, more and more people die at a ripe old age instead of as the result of sickness or epidemics, and the once exhausting working day is steadily becoming shorter. And that is not all; the more we achieve, the more we realize that this is only the beginning. In fields such as computers and automation—to mention only two examples—we are standing on the threshold of technical breakthroughs whose complexity can be grasped only by a new generation of highly trained specialists. We are dealing here with profound conceptual changes, which mean that even the most intelligent members of the older generation have the greatest difficulty in keeping up with the developments. In this sense we can talk of a definite evolution of the human brain.

The strange thing is that the same cannot really be said about our emotions and our feelings, and—as a result—of human ethics and morality. In many ways we are still as brutal, thoughtless, and egoistical as thousands of years ago. The story of Cain's fratricide at the very beginning of the Book of Genesis is reenacted daily. Jealousy, greed, and intolerance still cause individuals and countries to try to destroy each other. In the area of human emotions, nothing seems to have changed— except that we are now able to harness superior technical facilities for the purpose of murdering and destroying on a vastly larger and more efficient scale than before. No, the human character still has a long way to go!

In light of this we can understand why the Torah has to appeal to our heart, and all that it symbolizes, in order to arouse its mercy and compassion, and thus, slowly and imperceptibly, change our personality. We must learn not to regard our fellow-men as outsiders but as an integral part of ourselves. What each and every one of us has to learn is to accept giving, not as a burden and a duty, but as a response to an intuitive feeling for the needs of the other. It does not help us to say that this is idealistic or impractical, since society as a whole does not practice these rules either. The only way in which the Torah will eventually succeed in changing the world is by changing individuals.

Despite the above, some people might ask why it should not have been possible to bring some of the more practical uses of the intellect to bear on the improvement of ethics and morality. Wouldn't logic and understanding be a more powerful motivator for doing good than emotion? The problem is that our brain is so intensely engaged in the never-ending pursuit of material improvements that the more sensitive issues usually take a backseat. As a result, our intellect can hardly be relied upon to be a stabilizing influence on the emotions of the heart.

In this context we cannot help wondering why God imposed upon us this slow evolution, which continuously confronts us with new frontiers and therefore turns the achievement of a more perfect world into a "moving target." Why did God not reveal to us the secrets of nature and the process of creation in more detail, rather than present us with a vague and general conceptual phrase, such as: "In the beginning God created the heavens and the earth"? The answer is connected to the evolution of the human mind. Let us imagine that only a hundred years ago someone had confronted the then living generation with Einstein's theory of relativity. Only a handful of people would—maybe—have understood it, for the very same reason that only a few members of our present generation are capable of grasping the concept of an expanding universe, or the mystery of the millions of faraway galaxies, whose existence is known, even though not a single scientist has seen them.

In Psalm 19, we read: השמים מספרים כבוד־אל ומעשה ידיו מגיד הרקיע: יום ליום יביע אומר ולילה לילה יחוה־דעת (ha-shamayim mesaperim kevod el u-ma'aseh yadav: yom le-yom yavia omer ve-lailah lailah yechaveh da'ath), "The heavens declare the glory of God; the skies proclaim the work of His hands. Day after day they pour forth speech; night after night they display knowledge." Nature itself is teaching us, and in the course of time it will help us to understand the greatness of God.

Even so, although Jewish tradition has always encouraged scientific research, the Torah does not depend on human knowledge or scientific theories, but on the dissemination of moral values throughout the world. Our views of nature change with the expansion of our knowledge; morality, however, remains unchanged. The Torah is not interested in nature as such, but only in human nature: our human character. The Torah aims at changing our moral behavior. This does not mean that we should not be interested in worldly things. On the contrary, our narratives explain in a beautiful way that man was created with a strong ambition. Without ambition he would not have been able to develop the world. But ambition also has a negative side; negative, in that it encourages the יצר הרע (*yetzer ha-ra*), our less desirable impulses such as lust and greed, and the morality of the Torah is the only way to change the animal side in ourselves.

Immediately following the opening words of *Parashath Terumah*, the Torah says, ועשו לי מקדש ושכנתי בתוכם (*ve-asu li mikdash ve-shachanti be-tocham*), "Then have them make a Sanctuary for Me, and I will dwell among them." Notice that the text does not read, "I will dwell in it" (in other words in the Sanctuary), but "I will dwell among them"—among the Jewish people and in the hearts of men. If we build a sanctuary for God in our own hearts, evil will disappear, for it will have no place to exist.

We have our schools and universities to develop our intellect and teach our younger generation the latest techniques and scientific methods. There is only one place, however, where we can learn to develop our feelings and to forswear jealousy and cruelty towards our neighbor, recognizing that—like us—he was created in God's image.

This, then, is the meaning of the words, "You are to receive the offering for Me from each man whose heart prompts him to give." We are expected to "take the Torah to ourselves," for then our hearts will be changed, and we shall be capable of giving, unselfishly and voluntarily—not for our own greater glory, but for the benefit of our fellowmen. This is the highest and noblest form of giving, because it helps to establish God's Sanctuary among ourselves.

Parashath Tetzaveh

ואתה תצוה את־בני ישראל ויקחו אליך שמן זית זך כתית
למאור להעלת נר תמיד.

"Command the Israelites to bring you clear oil of pressed
olives for the light, so that the lamps may be kept burning."

In most cases, when he transmitted commandments to the
Jewish people, God talked to Moses, telling him to talk to the
Jewish people and give them this or that commandment. The
interpreters of the Torah ask themselves why in this portion of
the week, when it comes to the candelabrum in the Tabernacle,
Moses' name is not mentioned at all. What can be the reason?
Immediately afterwards, however, we read the sentence: ואתה
הקרב אליך את־אהרן אחיך ואת־בניו אתו מתוך בני ישראל לכהנו־לי (ve-atah hekrev
aleicha eth aharon achicha ve-eth banav eto me-toch benei yisrael le-kahano-
li), "Have Aaron your brother brought to you from among the
Israelites, so that he may serve me as a priest." The Torah
continues to describe how God asks Moses to consult the
"skilled men who have wisdom in such matters," so that they
will make Aaron and his sons special priestly garments, orna-
mented with gold, silver, and precious stones. The instructions
are very detailed; in fact, for every task in the Sanctuary there
had to be special garments that were to be changed depending
upon the task to be performed. (Once a year, however—on *Yom
Ha-Kippurim*—when the high priest entered the Holy of Holies in
the Temple, he wore a plain white everyday garment.)

It is clear that in this part of the Torah it is Aaron, rather than Moses, who takes pride of place. In most places in the Torah, Moses is mentioned before Aaron, but there are others where Aaron is mentioned before Moses. Our sages explain that the Torah wants to emphasize that both were equal, but different; that each one had his own particular tasks and responsibilities in leading the Jewish people. This is why the Torah tells Moses, "Have Aaron your brother brought to you from among the Israelites, so that he may serve me as a priest."

A closer look will show us how the tasks of these two great leaders of the Jewish people differed. When God needed someone to tell the Children of Israel that they would have to leave Egypt, He chose Moses. When He needed an emissary to transmit the Torah and the Commandments at Mount Sinai, He chose Moses. In other words, every time God wanted to communicate with the Jewish people, He turned to Moses. But when it was a matter of the Jewish people communicating with God, either through sacrifices or through prayer, He chose Aaron, "so that he may serve me as a priest."

The really interesting question is why God did not choose Moses for this task as well. The answer is that Moses and Aaron were two entirely different characters, and because of this their allotted tasks and responsibilities were also different.

Moses really loved his people with his whole heart and soul, and he was literally ready to lay down his life for them. He was even prepared to disappear into anonymity to save the Jewish people, for after the Israelites had committed the sin of the Golden Calf, he prayed to God: "Please forgive their sin—but if not, then blot me out of the Book You have written." In other words, he asked God to erase his name, so that it would not even appear in the Torah. About Moses' loyalty and sacrificial spirit there can be no doubt!

However, Moses also was a disciplinarian; he was not close to the people, and he was feared rather than admired. In a sense Moses was an extremist, and he did not yield one hair's breadth on any point of principle. Moses could be quite hard, as we see from the way he ordered death for those who were guilty of making the Golden Calf. Neither did he relent in his punishment of the spies who brought such negative reports following their exploration of Canaan. He fought Korach and his band of agitators until the earth swallowed them. Clearly, Moses was not an easy person, but only a man like him was able to deal with a "stiff-necked"—to use the words of the Torah—and undisciplined people like the Israelites, and implement the observance of God's word by the Jewish people in practice and theory.

Aaron was cut of a different cloth altogether! He was a far more reflective and kind-hearted type of man. He was soft-spoken, he hated to give orders, and he had a pleasant way of talking to people. Like Moses, Aaron loved his people. However, if we draw a comparison, we could say that whereas Moses acted like a father—strict and demanding—Aaron behaved like a mother—tolerant and forgiving, and therefore unable to see wrong in her children. Even when the Israelites approached Aaron to build the Golden Calf he went along with them, because he did not believe that they would stray from God's ways, and neither did he have the desire or the moral strength to oppose them.

Let us take the episode of Korach: when Korach, one of Moses' and Aaron's close relatives, revolted against their leadership, Moses punished the rebels with a plague, but Aaron protected them. The Torah describes how, after the plague had already started, Aaron took his censer with incense in it and ran into the midst of the assembly. "He stood between the living and the dead, and the plague stopped." This was the task of Aaron, to be on the side of the weak and suffering, even when they were guilty or wrong.

Moses was well aware of Aaron's forgiving love for his people. Yet, when God informed him that Aaron would receive the priesthood instead of him—meaning that when the Jewish people wanted to talk to God, they would do it through Aaron— he was badly hurt. He worried that God had found him unfit to represent the Israelites in their hour of need. However, God answered him, "I know that your heart is full of love for your people, but your obligation is to teach them the Torah, and guide them in its ethics. For this, your eyes and ears have to be continually open, so that you see what they are doing. It is your task "to tell my people their offenses, and the Children of Jacob their sins," and this your brother Aaron is not capable of doing.

The priesthood, on the other hand, which meant representing the Jewish people before God through sacrifices and prayers, was exactly the kind of responsibility for which Aaron was suitable. In legal terms, we could say that Moses was like a judge, who implements the law that is handed down by the highest authority, whereas Aaron was like the defense attorney who, even when it looks as if his client is guilty, will continue to stay by his side and plead for him. Moses saw his people's weaknesses too clearly to be able to do this, and this explains why their missions were different.

This brings us to another question, as topical today as it was in the days of Moses and Aaron, namely how a leader should behave. Should he behave like Moses, rigorous and strict, or like Aaron, soft-hearted and prepared to overlook failures? Hillel, one of our most illustrious sages, teaches us in *Pirke Avoth*, the "Ethics of the Fathers": "Be of the disciples of Aaron, loving peace and pursuing peace, loving your fellow creatures and bringing them near to the Torah." We could ask why he went into such detail, instead of simply saying, "Be like Aaron," just as in another quote in *Pirke Avoth*, which states briefly: "Be humble like Hillel."

The answer is that a present leader of the Jewish people cannot always pursue peace—not if he sees that this would result in injustice to others, or the trampling of morals and ethics. There will come a point where he has to stand up and fight. A leader has to know when he can go in the ways of Aaron, and when not. With Moses at his side, Aaron could afford to be soft-hearted, but if he had been alone, the situation would have been entirely different. Therefore other words of Moses apply today: צדק צדק תרדף (tzedek tzedek tirdof), "Justice, justice you shall pursue," and the modern leader has to know that justice does not come by itself, but that it has to be fought for. When Moses saw that one Jew was beating another, he confronted the evildoer and said, "Why are you hitting your fellow Hebrew?" He did not overlook the offense, and neither did he pacify the attacker. King David says in the Psalms, "Turn from evil and do good; seek peace and pursue it." The interpreters of our Scriptures also take this as meaning that often it is not sufficient to simply promote peace and justice, but that both have to be actively fought for.

All that has been said before explains why, when God wanted to talk to the Jewish people, he talked through Moses—and it was Moses' responsibility to see to it that God's words were implemented. However, when the people wanted to communicate with God—either through prayers or sacrifices—or when there were problems between man and wife, between neighbors, or between relatives, they needed a man who was close to them, like Aaron. Now we can understand why Moses' name is not mentioned in connection with the *mitzvah* of the lighting of the candelabrum. The lighting of the candelabrum was a ritual closely connected with the people coming to the Sanctuary to plead for their needs, and this was a task allotted to Aaron.

Another important question concerns the need for special priestly garments for Aaron and his sons. The Torah says, "Make sacred garments for your brother Aaron, to give him dignity and honor." In the days of old, the priests who served in heathen temples were so revered, and so closely identified with the sacrifices they offered, that they themselves became subjects of veneration.

There is a fundamental difference, however, between the Jewish priesthood and that of the ancient pagan civilizations. The priesthoods of Egypt and Mesopotamia, to mention only some examples, in addition to controlling the temple services greatly influenced the political and legal affairs of their countries. Priests could elevate or depose kings, ministers, and religious dignitaries, and often they controlled the country's economy and tax system, and even the country's fortunes in peace or war.

In complete contradiction to this, the priests in Israel had no divine status, nor were they allowed to overrule the king or interfere in political matters. They were servants of God and, apart from their priestly functions and prerogatives, they were like any other Israelite. In fact, the only time the high priest could exercise his special status was during the Temple services, and for this he had to be attired in his priestly garments.

This does not mean that there never were conflicts between kings and priests. As the history of the Jewish nation unfolded, the priests gradually began to regard themselves responsible, not only for the spiritual welfare of the nation, but for its temporal salvation as well.

The same applies to the relations between the priesthood and the prophets of Israel. Successive prophets in different periods had different views of the way in which the priestly responsibilities were to be carried out. Thus it could happen that Isaiah and Jeremiah strongly supported the priesthood, whereas Amos and Hosea were bitterly critical of the way the priestly functions were exercised in their time. Eventually, however, it became accepted that the priesthood was a specialized type of service, aimed at assisting the people through the priestly relationship to God, as expressed through sacrifices and prayers. In all other respects, the priests were not a priviliged class.

In the course of time the Jewish nation came more and more under the influence of the Sanhedrin, the rabbinical court, rather than that of the priests. The ultimate development of Jewish philosophy was the replacement of the Temple services and the sacrifices with the rule of the Torah, as expounded by the rabbis. The Torah and the Commandments became the measure of the Jewish people's relationship to God and to each other.

The Torah makes it clear that the priests did not possess special power or wisdom. They were regarded as knowledgeable people, but in all other respects they were merely a religious instrument—a medium for assisting the Jewish people to communicate with God. The high priest of old could not enforce any of his own opinions. We read, however, that he wore the *urim ve-tummim*, the "breastpiece of decision," in whose sparkling stones he could read judgments on the fate of the Twelve Tribes.

The priestly function was inherited, but its performance and privileges were entirely dependent upon the personal conduct of the incumbent. A priest who was defiled, either physically or spiritually, or who in any other way failed to live up to the required standards of the priesthood, lost all his privileges of office.

Parashath Ki Tissa

וידבר יהוה אל־משה לאמור: כי תשא את־ראש בני־ישראל
לפקדיהם ונתנו איש כפר נפשו ליהוה בפקד אתם ולא־יהיה
בהם נגף בפקד אתם: זה יתנו כל־העבר על־הפקודים מחצית
השקל בשקל הקדש.

"Then God said to Moses, 'When you take a census of the
Children of Israel to count them, each one must pay God a
ransom for his life at the time he is counted. Then no
plague will come on them when you number them. Each
one who crosses over to those already counted is to give a
half shekel, according to the sanctuary shekel....'"

According to the Talmud, *masecheth Baba Batra*, Rabbi Avihu
said that Moses asked God how he could raise the spirit of the
Jewish people. God answered, "You will raise their spirit if you
count them, by making every one of them contribute half a
shekel." In the Midrash , Rabbi Yochanan ben Zakkai said to his
disciples, "My dear children, how do we understand the words
of the Torah, צדקה תרומם גוי וחסד לאומים חטאת (*tzedakah teromem goy
ve-chesed le'umim chata'ath*), 'Mercy and charity raise the spirit of
the [Jewish] people, whereas the charity of the other nations can
cause them to sin.'"

Rabbi Eliezer's answer to this last question was, "When the
Jewish people give charity, they do it to help themselves and
others, and this raises their morale, as it is written in the Torah:
ומי כעמך ישראל גוי אחד בארץ (*ve-me ke-amcha yisrael goy echad ba-aretz*),
which means as much as "Who can find a nation like the Jewish
nation in their land?" The same charity and righteousness of

other nations can cause them to sin, because—according to the Midrash—they do it not only for charity, but for the purpose of self-aggrandizement and gaining prestige.

In order to understand the above statements, we should first ask some questions. First, why did God tell Moses not to count the Jews by means of a head count, but through the shekel? When we ask people to each donate a coin or any other object, and then count the coins or the objects, is this not counting?

Even more puzzling is the talmudic commentary in *Baba Batra*, from which we understand that counting was expected to raise the spirit of the Jewish people. What is the connection between counting and raising someone's spirit?

Finally, there is the puzzling statement to the effect that Jewish charity brings happiness, whereas other people's charity not only lacks righteousness but even causes sin.

Taking the second question first, we can readily understand how counting can boost a people's spirit once we realize that, in the most general sense, counting is an aid toward judging a certain strength. In order to try to judge the outcome of a war, one of the most important things is to know the relative strengths of the warring sides; how many soldiers do they have, how many tanks, and how many fighter planes or bombers?

However, we do not only evaluate quantities, but quality as well. One tank is more effective than a single soldier. There are differences even between soldiers, depending on their training and the kind of weapons they bear.

In a similar way we add up income and expenses—in other words we count—when we want to know whether we have enough money to finish the month. Here, too, the quality of the money is important; in times of inflation big denominations may be worth very little! Neither do we simply add bills or coins of different denominations. Bank tellers, or cashiers in supermarkets, put different bills and coins into separate compartments. So we understand that counting is very important, both for the individual and for nations.

The example of the bills and coins in separate compartments contains a lead to the explanation of the first question, namely why God told Moses not to count the Jews by means of a head count, but through the shekel. The Jews who had to be counted were equal and yet not equal. They belonged to different tribes, there were leaders and followers, young ones and old ones, and strong ones and weaker ones. In this particular instance, for God's purpose, all the Children of Israel were equal. God's commandment to Moses to count all the people together, through the expedient of asking everyone to donate half a shekel—not more and not less—was intended to show that all of them were of equal value. Now we see why counting was so important, as well as why God asked Moses to count through the shekel. Counting in itself means taking note of a person; counting together, by a common yardstick like the shekel, emphasizes that every individual Jew was as important as the next. It is evident that this must have raised the spirit and morale of the people.

This brings us to the third question, namely why the charity of the [non-Jewish] nations should cause sin. The answer is connected with the nature and the manner of the act of giving. When people care for each other, and see to it that they render their assistance timely and in the right way, then we can talk of real and effective charity. It is on this point that the Jewish people are expected to be different from the other nations. This is why Rabbi Yochanan asked his pupils how they should understand the verse that "mercy and charity raise the spirit of the [Jewish] people, whereas the charity of the other nations can cause them to sin."

Rabbi Eliezer answered that the difference lies in the way people give their charity, and that charity as commanded by the Torah is a blessing for the nation. The Midrash adds that the charity and righteousness of other nations are a sin because their contributions are not given for charity's sake, but for the purpose of self-aggrandizement and gaining prestige.

To understand this in the right way, we should realize that there exist many different kinds of charity. Maimonides, for one, mentions eight kinds, which are listed below in the reverse order of their importance:

Lowest on the scale is charity that is given with a bad face. A better, but by no means ideal, form of charity is that which is given without emotion: the giver does his duty, but the problem behind his giving does not touch him. In the third lowest place comes the donor who gives only when he is asked to give. The fourth place from below is occupied by one who does not wait until he is asked, but gives spontaneously as soon as he realizes that there is a need. The fourth place from the top goes to the donor who gives without knowing for whom or what he is giving, although the receiver knows from whom the contribution originates. Third from the top is the giver who knows for whom he has given, whereas the receiver does not know from whom the contribution originated. The almost ideal form of charity is where neither the giver nor the receiver know each other. This is what in Hebrew is called מתן בסתר (*matan be-seter*), a "hidden donation."

In all the previous cases we have been talking about situations in which there existed an immediate need. It stands to reason that much acute distress can be alleviated this way. However, the problem is that it does not solve the basic problem, and that the same person continues to be dependent, and may soon be in need again. The highest level of צדקה (*tzedakah*), the ideal form of Jewish charity—and the one at the top of Maimonides' list—is therefore when we are helping someone to help himself. There is a well-known saying, according to which when we give a person a fish, we are giving him a meal, whereas if we give him a fishing rod, we are giving him a livelihood! Clearly, this is the perfect way to support and strengthen the receiver in such a way that he will not need help tomorrow or the day after.

The foregoing not only shows that there are many types of

charity, but also helps us to classify charitable acts according to merit. Let us compare what the Torah asks with what is actually happening in our present-day society, as reflected by, for instance, national insurance benefits, welfare services, and the activities of voluntary organizations. Why does society help? Largely out of compassion for its weaker elements—but not only out of compassion. For example, most governments are also interested in maintaining peace and quiet in the country, or to put on a progressive face, to demonstrate to the outside world how good or progressive they are.

Why does the Torah not agree with charity out of compassion? Because it turns the receiving party into "a case," a *nebbich*, an inferior being. Charity out of compassion lowers society's esteem for the recipient, as well as his self-esteem. The Torah tells the Jew: don't merely have compassion, don't merely help in a way that puts people down by, for instance, asking them to fill in countless forms. Two well-known examples in the Torah are the injunction to the farmer to leave a corner of his field uncut, and the command to refrain from picking up the stalks that have fallen off the sheaves. These examples are representative of a "natural" form of charity, that is designed not to lower the receiver's morale or self-esteem.

When we help, we must do so because the other person has the same right to a decent existence as ourselves. This kind of help involves more than "crisis intervention"—last-minute attempts to prevent distress. Apart from this, the proper approach to charity avoids the risk of causing jealousy and resentment, or even hatred, on the part of the needy against their benefactors. My own experience has taught me that children in charity-dependent families run a serious risk of growing up with a chip on their shoulder, and that sooner or later they may take out their resentment on society.

How wonderful are the words of our sages, for instance the famous saying by Rabbi Tarfun, המציל נפש אחד מישראל כאלו הציל עולם כולו (*hamatsil nefesh achad me-yisrael, ke'ilu hitzil olam kulo*), which may be interpreted as, "He who helps a person in the right way, as it were prevents the destruction of the entire world!"

Often we hear people say that it is not their job to worry about their fellow citizens: "That is the duty of the authorities!" How completely wrong they are! What is at stake here is a fundamental concept of צדקה (tzedakah)—charity—in the broadest sense of the word. Jewish tradition claims that "the establishment" is not capable of providing for the individual in the way he needs. Why do we call a person an "individual"? Because that is exactly what he is: an "individual." There is no second person exactly like him, or in exactly his circumstances, and from this it follows that his needs are also individual. Every person "needs" in a different way. In ancient times, when important personages went on a journey, a runner went out in front of them to clear the way by informing the populace who was passing. So relative, according to Jewish tradition, are the needs of the individual, that in the above case they included providing the personage with a runner if he became needy, simply because he was accustomed to this kind of service! Even though it was considered a luxury, society was obliged to provide it to him, since for him it was as essential as bread.

More and more enlightened governments realize that they are not required—nor, for that matter, able—to supply blanket welfare services. Their solution is, therefore, to subsidize voluntary, private charitable initiatives of the most diverse kinds. The voluntary organizations are able to render the necessary individualized services to identifiable groups with whom they are intimately acquainted.

King David said, אשרי משכיל אל דל (ashrei maskil el dal), "Fortunate is the man who helps the needy in an intelligent way." Why should we need intelligence to help? Are not a good heart and an open hand sufficient? The answer is that what is needed is an understanding of the kind of need and its solution, knowledge of how to talk to the needy person, as well as patience to see the initiative through to the end.

Parashath Ki Tissa teaches us how to count individuals, while demonstrating that it is not important whether they are rich or poor, scholars or simpletons, smart or dumb. Only when we know how to count people as if they are all equally important will we know that we have one nation.

Now we understand the meaning of the dialogue between Rabbi Yochanan ben Zakkai and his students, and the answer of Rabbi Eliezer. Of course it is good to give charity, but we also have to know *how* to give, to prevent that what is intended as a good deed from turning into a sin.

Parashath Va-Yakhel

ויקהל משה את־כל־עדת בני ישראל ויאמר אליהם אלה הדברים
אשר־צוה יהוה לעשת אתם: ששת ימים תעשה מלאכה וביום
השביעי יהיה לכם קדש שבת שבתון ליהוה כל־העשה בו
מלאכה יומת: לא־תבערו אש בכל משבתיכם ביום השבת.

"Moses assembled the whole Israelite community and said
to them: 'These are the things God has commanded you to
do: For six days, work is to be done, but the seventh day
shall be your holy day, a Sabbath of rest to God. Whoever
does any work on it, must be put to death. Do not light a
fire in any of your dwellings on the Sabbath day.'"

The portion of *Va-Yakhel* opens with a commandment about
the Shabbath and lighting fire, immediately followed by a series
of commandments about the building of the Tabernacle.

A closer look at the above-quoted paragraph immediately
raises several questions. To begin, this commandment about the
Shabbath seems out of place in a portion dealing entirely with
the instructions for building the Tabernacle and the allocation
of the tasks involved among the Israelites—quite apart from the
fact that the Shabbath commandment had already been given
earlier in *Parashath Jethro*.

Second, when the Torah is so explicit about forbidding us to
do *any* work on the Shabbath, why does it emphasize that we
may not light a fire? Wasn't making a fire considered work? Or
was lighting fires included in the Shabbath work prohibition,

but did it for some reason deserve extra emphasis in the context of the building of the Sanctuary?

A third question is why Moses had to assemble the whole Israelite community to give them these commandments. Why did Moses not pass them on in the same way as all the other commandments, namely—according to our traditional view— first to Aaron, then to Aaron's children, then to the heads of the tribes, and finally to the elders of the people—four times in all?

According to the Talmud , God said to Moses, "I have a good gift in My treasure house, called the Shabbath." In our narratives the question is asked why this gift was so important, and the answer is: Because more than Israel has preserved the Shabbath, the Shabbath has helped to preserve Israel. Indeed, few people would disagree that the Shabbath, apart from all its other beneficial aspects, has been one of the outstanding unifying factors in the history of the Jewish people.

The entire concept of the Shabbath, and its central place in Jewish thought and ritual, is extremely interesting. For instance, on one hand the Torah warns in the most rigorous terms against the desecration of the day of rest, even to the point of threatening transgressors with capital punishment. But at the same time we are *commanded* to break the Shabbath if our uncompromising observance should place someone's life at risk. According to *halachah*, the person who places Shabbath observance above saving a life is called a criminal, and his behavior is counted as worse than that of the ordinary Shabbath desecrator. Our tradition even prescribes that the person who breaks the Shabbath for the purpose of saving life is supposed to thank God for the privilege. It once happened in a small village in Eastern Europe that the wife of a poor man went into labor on the Shabbath. None of the neighbors dared light a fire to boil water. Fortunately word reached the rabbi, who sped to the house where the baby was about to be born, quickly lit a fire under a large pail of water, and then pronounced the blessing,

"Blessed art Thou, O God, King of the Universe, who... commanded us to desecrate the Shabbath in order to save life."

Maybe, then, it was the crucial role of the Shabbath in Jewish life that made Moses decide to assemble the entire Israelite community, even though the commandment as such had already been given earlier. But this doesn't answer another question, namely why this repetition of the Shabbath commandment appears in a portion dealing with the building of the Sanctuary. According to our sages, God intentionally reminded the Israelites of the prohibition of Shabbath work at this point to emphasize that even an undertaking as important as the building of the Sanctuary did not imply permission to desecrate the Shabbath.

We should remember that we are talking here about a point in time not long after the incident of the Golden Calf. The Ramban (Rabbi Moses ben Nachman) says that Moses gathered the entire community—including the women and children—to tell the Israelites that God had forgiven them, that they were now permitted to build the Sanctuary, and that God would once again dwell among them as if nothing had happened. The Ramban adds, however, that God wanted to emphasize that the Israelites were not to desecrate the Shabbath for building the Sanctuary—and that, in order to stress the difference between the Shabbath and other holidays, they were not to make fire even for cooking food.

There is still another connection between the Shabbath and the Sanctuary. Earlier we mentioned the role of the Shabbath in keeping the Jewish people together. Exactly the same can be said of the Sanctuary, which from the earliest times has occupied a central place in Jewish community life—first as the Tabernacle, then as the Temple, and still later in the form of the *Beth ha-Midrash* and the synagogue. There can be no denying that the synagogue has played a crucial role in Jewish survival for more than two thousand years—not only because we prayed there,

but also as the focus of all aspects of Jewish religious and
community life. There was not a village or town with a Jewish
population anywhere in the Diaspora that did not have one or
more synagogues. Of course the Jewish residents prayed and
studied there, but no less important was the fact that the
synagogue—regardless whether it was a *shul* or a *shtiebel*—was
the place where every family came with its joys and its sorrows:
here the newly born children were brought for the *brith milah* or
name giving, here fathers brought their sons for their *bar mitzvah*, mothers their daughters for the *chuppah*, and here mourners
came to say *Kaddish* in the company of their fellow congregants.
Everyone shared his fortunes and misfortunes with his brothers and sisters. This is what kept the Jewish people together, and
in this joint and united observance lies a parallel with the
Shabbath.

From this follows yet another reason why Moses assembled
the Israelites to instruct them about the building of the Sanctuary. The Torah says at this point, זה הדבר אשר־צוה יהוה לאמר: קחו מאתכם
תרומה ליהוה כל נדיב לבו יביאה את תרומת יהוה (*zeh ha-davar asher tzivah ha-shem
le-emor: kechu me-itchem terumah la-shem kol nediv libo yevi'eha eth teru-
math ha-shem*), "This is what God has commanded: From what
you have, take an offering for God. Everyone who is willing is to
bring to God an offering...." God wanted to impress upon the
Israelites how important was the contribution that was being
demanded of each of them, given the fact that the Sanctuary
would, in turn, help to keep them together in exactly the way as
the Shabbath was doing.

As an interesting sidelight, the Torah informs us that the
women among the Israelites apparently understood this, for
they reacted with such an outpouring of precious jewelry that
Moses was forced to call a halt to their giving. According to our
sages it was in fact the righteousness of the Israelite women
that caused the redemption of the Children of Israel, and the
interpreters asked how their generosity could have affected the
redemption—meaning the Exodus from Egypt—which as we

realize had taken place several months before the events recorded in this *parashah*.

The seventh-century sage Rabbi Chai Gaon comments that the righteousness referred to here does not concern the jewelry the women donated for building the Sanctuary, but an event during the final years in Egypt. According to Jewish history, the situation of the Children of Israel during their last 50 years in bondage was so desperate that they doubted whether the next generation would survive. As a result the men decided that no more Jewish children should be born, and they moved out into the fields, leaving their wives behind in Goshen. When the women realized what was happening, they revolted; there was no doubt in their minds that there was a future for the Jewish people. Our narratives give a moving description of how the women decided to make the men change their minds, how they carefully groomed themselves, to make themselves look desirable, and how in the end the men came back, and life continued as before. This is what our sages meant when they say that it was the righteousness of the Israelite women that caused the redemption, and thereby safeguarded the future of the Jewish nation.

According to our tradition, this revolt was headed by Miriam, a daughter of Amram and Yocheved (who also became the mother of Moses). We might say, therefore, that indirectly, thanks to Miriam, the Children of Israel gained their most illustrious leader and liberator.

Returning to our previous argument, we see that the righteousness of the Jewish women was not manifest only in their overgenerous contributions to the construction of the Sanctuary. In fact, these same women who donated so much for the Sanctuary had only recently refused to give their gold for erecting the Golden Calf! Neither did their contribution to the survival of the Jewish people end here. Also in our later history, when the Jewish nation lived in the *galuth*—in times when the situation looked hopeless and the men despaired—their courage and fortitude, and their belief in the Jewish destiny, on more than one occasion saved their families and the nation.

We might see here yet another reason why Moses assembled the entire Israelite community, including—and particularly—the women, to hear his commandments, because Moses knew that the women could be relied upon, and thus were essential for the Jewish destiny.

Parashath Pekudei

וירא משה את־כל־המלאכה והנה עשו אתה כאשר צוה יהוה כן
עשו ויברך אתם משה.

"Moses inspected the work and saw that they had done it
just as God had commanded. So Moses blessed them."

After the Israelites had completed both the Sanctuary and its
furnishings, and the sacred garments for Aaron and his sons,
they took them to Moses for inspection. Moses saw that everything had been done exactly as God had commanded, and he
blessed them.

It would seem strange that Moses should bless the Jewish
people. There is no precedent for this anywhere in the Torah,
for blessing did not belong to Moses' special responsibilities; this
was the task of the *kohanim*. The Midrash explains that what
Moses said to them was in fact, "May it be the will *of God* that His
presence rests upon the work of your hands." Even then we
might ask why Moses should want to invoke a blessing on the
activities of the Israelites. They had already shown what they
were capable of, and they had performed their collective task
with energy and goodwill. Why invoke a blessing on what they
were doing, when they had already successfully completed the
work?

Taking into account that every word in the Torah has a
meaning, there must be a lesson in these words. The answer to
the question will become clear once we realize that neither
individuals nor nations can succeed in anything they

undertake—regardless whether the task is of a spiritual or a material nature—unless two factors are present: capability and motivation. Some people possess manifest skills for one thing or another, whereas others seem to be completely impractical. As against this, there are those who do not appear to be particularly handy or intelligent but who succeed nevertheless in what they undertake, since what they lack in skill is made up by a stubborn desire and perseverance. Examples of both types can be seen everywhere around us. It also follows from this that people who combine both characteristics, ability *and* willpower, should be almost certain to succeed.

The question could be asked, however, which characteristic is preferable: ability or willpower? I believe that people who possess skills, but lack willpower or a desire to succeed, will by necessity remain nonachievers. Those, on the other hand, who are short on skills, but who possess a strong drive to succeed, have an excellent chance of achieving their purpose. A good example is a comment in our narratives about how people only seldom die for want of food. Extreme circumstances excluded, people can always find a way to secure food, for the simple reason that survival is one of the human's most powerful and fundamental instincts. As against this, many people die the moment they lack motivation, or no longer have the will to fight for their existence.

The Torah tells that when Jacob fled from Esau, leaving everything behind, he prayed that God would give him food to eat and clothes to wear. Why didn't he simply ask for bread and clothing? The Torah indicates that Jacob realized that having food and clothing would not help him, unless he had the capability to eat, and the will and the strength to dress. In the Psalms we read, "Once the soul abhors all manner of food, we draw near to the gates of death." If we do not maintain an unconditional desire to live, we die before we are dead.

In short, between skill and willpower, both of which belong to the most fundamental factors determining our existence, willpower should be considered the most important. In the *Ashrei*, a section of the Psalms introduced into our daily prayers by the Rabbis of the Great Assembly during the third or second century B.C.E., we find the verse, פותח את־ידך ומשביע לכל־חי רצון (*poteach eth-yadeicha u-masbia le-khol chai ratzon*), "You [meaning God] open Your hand, and satisfy the desire of every living thing." There is an interesting *halachic* custom, according to which the person who recites the entire *Ashrei* prayer without the proper intent nevertheless does not have to repeat it. But if he fails to concentrate on the words *poteach eth-yadeicha u-masbia le-khol chai ratzon*, he must once again start from the beginning. The reason is that we regard this verse not only as an expression of gratitude for all the material things God enables us to have, but also as a prayer for *ratzon*, the desire to live—in other words the will to perform and achieve, which is the key to our existence and survival.

Summarizing, we must realize that our physical as well as mental well-being depends on willpower. Without it, people cannot achieve anything. The great inventor Thomas Alva Edison, in answer to a question, admitted that he had always possessed a very strong urge to achieve. "I never despaired," he explained, "but instead I stubbornly pushed on until my experiments were eventually crowned with success." To him, of course, we owe the maxim, "genius is one percent inspiration and ninety-nine percent perspiration."

People are often deterred from undertaking something difficult—and we ourselves are no exception to this—because we try to convince ourselves that the effort is bound to end in failure. Indeed, nobody can expect us to go out and fight windmills like Don Quixote. There is a difference, however, between difficult and impossible. The Talmud tells that Rabbi Akiva, possibly the greatest Jewish scholar of all time, was until the age of forty illiterate. Then he fell in love with Rachel, the daughter of a rich Jerusalemite, who promised that she would marry him if he became a scholar. Akiva left Jerusalem, and when he returned twelve years later, he had established a yeshivah and collected 24,000 disciples.

Another example is Rabbi Eliyahu, a seventeenth-century Lithuanian rabbi who has since become famous as the "Vilner Gaon." Gaon means "genius," and indeed there have been few rabbis ever since the time of the Talmud who were as learned in all kinds of subjects, both religious and secular, as the Gaon of Vilna. When anyone commented on his knowledge, he modestly replied, "I am not a genius, and I have had to work and study very hard to learn all that I know. But I am a Vilner "—a play on words, since *Vilner* ("from the city of Vilna") sounds exactly like the Yiddish *will nur*: "if only you want it."

Now we understand what Moses meant with his blessing. He wished that God's Divine Presence would always be near the Jewish people, the way it had been when they were busy building the Sanctuary, so that in future ages they would always have not only the inspiration but also the desire and the willpower to succeed.

Parashath Va-Yikra

ויקרא אל־משה וידבר יהוה אליו מאהל מועד לאמר : דבר אל־
בני ישראל ואמרת אלהם אדם כי־יקריב מכם קרבן ליהוה מן־
הבהמה מן־הבקר ומן־הצאן תקריבו את קרבנכם.

"God called to Moses and spoke to him from the Tent of
Meeting. He said, 'Speak to the Israelites and say to them:
"When any of you brings an offering to God, bring as an
offering an animal from either the herd or the flock."'"

God instructed Moses to tell the Israelites that if they
brought a sacrifice, they should offer an animal. Then the Torah
continues to add details to the effect that the sacrifice could be
an animal from the herd—in this case a bull—or from the flock,
meaning a goat or a sheep. We might ask why, after using the
word *behemah*, which in itself already includes all (kosher) animals, it was necessary to add information on specific animals?

The Midrash explains that the Torah wants to emphasize
that any kind of animal could be sacrificed because, contrary to
human creatures, their spirit disappears after the animal is dead.
This would seem to contradict the idea that is expressed in
Koheleth (the Book of Ecclesiastes) where it says: ומותר אדם מן
הבהמה אין, כמות זה כן כמות זה (ve-mutar adam min ha-behemah ayin; ke-moth
zeh ken ke-moth zeh), meaning that what happens to animals also
happens to human life. Similar to the way animals live and die,
so—Koheleth appears to say—people are also born and also die
without leaving a trace. Superficially it would seem as if all are
the same. The Torah, however, states that there exists a funda-

157

mental difference between humans and animals. Let us try to understand this difference—or rather these differences.

To begin, the Torah stresses that, unlike what happens to animals, the human spirit continues to exist after death. Our great Rabbis say that when they began to read and interpret ויקרא (Va-Yikra), the Book of Leviticus, which is the third book of the Torah, they first summarized the contents of the first two books בראשית (Be-Reshith), Genesis, and שמות (Shemoth), Exodus. Genesis depicts a world of anarchy, in which generations destroyed themselves because they lived a life without Torah and without any moral restraints whatsoever. Exodus relates how the Jewish people, with God's help, were able to abandon a life of slavery, and received the laws of the Torah as an aid to their future existence and moral and physical survival.

Leviticus, the third book of the Torah, deals not only with society at large but also with the individual. It concentrates on depicting man with all his problems and his sins, both against God and his neighbor, and it instructs him how he can refrain from sinning—and if he has sinned, how he can atone. The Book of Leviticus also tells him how to bring a sacrifice to obtain God's forgiveness.

This last point raises an important question that is generally little understood. Does slaughtering an animal forgive our own sins; does it make the sins disappear? And why, at all, did God, who from the beginning of Jewish history talked to His people and allowed Himself to be addressed in return, need a physical sacrifice? People who are unfamiliar with the laws of the Torah ask why a nation that gave the world the Ten Commandments and the Torah should believe that sins can be forgiven by paying ransom in the form of sacrifices. Here we are reminded again of the saying in Koheleth, according to which there would appear to be no difference between animals and people. Both live and die, so how can an animal atone for the sins of a human being?

Indeed, it appears difficult to understand what God says to the Jews in the opening words of Va-Yikra, in the weekly portion of the same name. The first few sentences of the *parashah* contain the words, אדם כי־יקריב מכם קרבן ליהוה (*adam ki-yakriv michem karban le-hashem*): "When any of you brings an offering to God."

The Midrash explains the meaning in a very simple manner, by pointing out that a sacrifice as such does not expunge the sin. The sacrifice is merely intended as a way of teaching people how to rid themselves of their bad deeds. Rabbi Yohanan says, "A man who sacrifices an animal for his sins has to be present when the sacrifice is made, and he should say: 'I have sinned, and I did wrong. I pray that God may help me, so that the sacrifice that I am bringing will make me understand how my sins have changed my personality, and how much evil I have created around me—so much so that I should be punished on my body, as the priest does to the animal on the altar. However, God is not interested in punishing me physically. He only wants to teach me, in order that I shall undertake this minute never to repeat what I have done.'" The sinner said this publicly, in the presence of the priests and the people, which means that the sacrifice represented an important step toward his rehabilitation.

However, the Torah says, "*adam ki-yakriv michem karban.*" The Torah wants to say that a human being is special. Following the Midrash, our rabbis conclude that any differences between humans and animals are derived from this verse. Indeed, the most striking difference indicated above is that only man has the capability of bringing sacrifices in the broadest sense of the word—not only animals or first fruits from his crop, but even things that are essential for his own spiritual or material well-being. Human beings are even prepared to sacrifice their own physical existence—sometimes for the sake of complete strangers. Soldiers get killed shielding comrades with their own bodies, in the same way that we regularly hear about people sacrificing their lives while protecting others during a catastrophe. Throughout the centuries hundreds of thousands of people have sacrificed themselves for their ideals, without ever demanding or expecting to receive in their lifetime any personal reward, except hoping that future generations would benefit from their efforts. We also have examples of physicians testing new and unproven medicines on themselves—and so we could go on and on.

Animals, on the other hand, are incapable of sacrificing. An animal basically lives only according to its instincts, and it will not give anything of itself—not food or anything else material. An animal certainly is incapable of contributing ideas, and least of all will it sacrifice its life for moral or any other considerations. We do of course know that dogs are devoted to their masters, and there are countless stories of dogs having entered a burning house to save their owners—but only their owners, and not another person they did not know. For a dog's instinct tells him that he needs his master, in order to continue receiving food and protection. No animal will sacrifice itself for someone it has never seen before, and from whom it does not expect food or physical care.

The question therefore presents itself, what it is in the nature of a human being that enables him to make physical sacrifices? The answer is that the only thing more powerful than his physical life is his spiritual existence. When we ask what benefit he expects to receive from his sacrifice, there is only one answer: the survival of his soul. The soul of man—and only man has a soul—causes him to sacrifice his physical life for something far higher: eternity.

Now we understand why the Torah says that human beings are different from animals, because they are capable of sacrificing themselves. Connected with the above are, of course, many other differences between human beings and animals, for humans possess intelligence, the power of rational thought, the ability to communicate in writing and speech, and so forth. Here, too, we see the connection with the earlier-mentioned verse from Koheleth, where it says, "Man's fate is like that of the animals; the same fate awaits them both: As one dies, so dies the other. All have the same breath.... All come from dust, and to dust all return." But then Koheleth adds, "Who knows why the spirit of man rises upward and why the spirit of the animal goes down into the earth?" So it looks as if the author, even in his most pessimistic mood, recognized the essential difference, namely the eternity of the human spirit.

Our sages comment that there are still other ways to recognize the spirituality of man. The body, the physical element of all creation, deteriorates as it gets older. Yet elderly people, when they are scholars and remain mentally active, gain spiritually in old age; they become more learned and more understanding as they grow older, whereas those who reject spiritual nourishment and values will find their minds degenerating together with their bodies.

There is a famous and moving story about Chaim Weizmann, Israel's first president. Toward the end of his life he became partly paralyzed, and his physical activities were severely impaired. His scientific interest, however, continued unabated, and when one night he was sitting at his home with two fellow scientists, he told them that he had solved a chemical problem, the answer to which had escaped him for years. Weizmann noticed the two looking at each other, and he said, "I know what you are thinking. He is partly paralyzed, and he has one foot in the grave, so what does he think he can do? I'll tell you: my body may be almost dead, but my mind is very much alive, and it will stay alive even after my body is gone. This explains why I am even now able to solve an intellectual problem."

This is what the Torah tells. When one sins, he has to bring a sacrifice to God and confess that he did wrong. This must be interpreted in the sense that everyone of us is obliged to surrender the animal part in himself. Only when we see to it that we can be called אדם (adam)—a "human being"—shall we have the right to sacrifice.

Parashath Tzav

וידבר יהוה אל־משה לאמר: קח את־אהרן ואת־בניו אתו ואת
הבגדים ואת שמן המשחה ואת פר החטאת . . . ואת כל העדה
הקהל אל־פתח אהל מועד.

"God said to Moses, 'Bring Aaron and his sons, their garments, the anointing oil, the bull for the sin offering...and
gather the entire assembly at the entrance to the Tent of
Meeting.'"

The scene described in the above lines and in the succeeding
paragraph of the Book of Leviticus deals with Moses' consecration of Aaron and his sons, at the express command of God.
Aaron was honored in front of all the people, not for his own
greater glory, but in recognition of the burden that was to be
placed upon his shoulders and those of his descendants, namely
the responsibility for the spiritual future of the Jewish people.
The Midrash adds that God said to Moses, "Aaron loves justice
and hates evil, and because of this he and his sons deserve
everything I have told you to give them." In this context we are
told to understand the words קח את אהרן (kach eth aharon) as not
merely meaning "take (or bring) Aaron," but in the sense of
"draw him close to you"—give him your sympathy.

Was it because Aaron was so perfect that Moses had to go
out of his way to honor him? But how does this square, for
instance, with the occasion when Moses failed to return in time
from Mount Sinai, and the Children of Israel panicked, and in
their fear decided to make themselves a Golden Calf. According
to the Midrash, instead of putting an end to this abomination,
Aaron said to himself, "I know that the people are doing wrong,

162

but I cannot possibly leave them to their fate. Therefore I have no choice but to join them, and in this way, when they are accused, I shall be blamed together with them."

In other words, Aaron knew the gravity of the sin of defying God and Moses by failing to stop the Children of Israel from making the Golden Calf. However, he loved his people so much that he was simply unable to abandon them; rather than look on how they destroyed themselves, he decided that he would accept Divine punishment, if at least he succeeded in keeping them together. This explains the Midrash, according to which God told Moses, "I know Aaron, and I even understand his failures. This is why I want you to draw him close to you, and thus show him your sympathy."

The above example illustrates how difficult it often is to understand God's reasoning by merely observing a situation from the outside. In this case, in order to save the Children of Israel, God was prepared to forgive even the negligence and the bad example of one of their most exalted leaders.

There is a related midrash about this same portion, according to which the nations of the world asked God, "What is the matter with the Jewish people? Why is it that they always have to suffer and sacrifice?" And God answered, "This is the way the Jewish people live and survive."

Here, again, we are faced with an aspect of God's plan with the Jewish people that at first glance seems inscrutable. History shows that there is indeed no nation in the world whose survival has demanded so many sacrifices. It looks like a vicious circle, for the longer the Jewish people survive, the longer they continue to suffer, and the more sacrifices are demanded of them. Some of these sufferings are so dreadful that it is not surprising other nations should ask themselves whether the Jews are indeed God's chosen people—and if they are, how this election must be understood.

Neither is this question asked by Gentiles only. Throughout history the Jews—both as a people and as individuals—have had to struggle for recognition and survival, so that we can understand that some Jews wonder whether there isn't something essentially wrong with them.

We are dealing here with more than an existential problem. There almost seems to be a mystery here. Among the several hundred nations in the world we will find scarcely one that is not automatically accorded the recognition that is traditionally denied to the Jewish nation. And yet, whereas many nations that never suffered persecution have in the course of time disappeared, the Jewish people—with or without recognition—continues to exist. No less surprising is the way in which the Jews emerge from their troubles and suffering. Despite the fact that we live in a world that does not seem to learn from its mistakes, a world that continues to discriminate, maltreat, and destroy its minorities, the Jewish people manage to bounce back after every disaster. The painful memories remain, and the suffering is not forgotten, but even in our own generation we have witnessed how refugees from the pogroms in Eastern Europe reclaimed the soil of their ancient homeland, and how people who barely survived the death camps built a Jewish state that can in many respects vie with the most advanced and progressive nations in the world. The majority of these people had never held a spade or a gun in their lives!

Thus it has been throughout Jewish history—ever since a ragged band of tribal Hebrews left Egypt, to conquer their Promised Land after a forty-year sojourn in the wilderness of Sinai. The more primitive and harsh the conditions, the stronger the Jewish people emerged. Here, therefore, lies the answer to what God meant when, in answer to the question why the Jews always had to suffer, He answered, "This is how they survive."

Even so, we might ask from where the Jews draw the strength to face up to so many difficulties. It would seem that they owe a great deal to the examples of their leaders. Starting with Abraham, the Jewish people have always had very special leaders, who, rather than aggrandize themselves, placed the interests of their followers before their own. Abraham, far from considering himself important, said to God: ואנכי אפר ועפר (ve-anochi efer va-efer), meaning: "I am but dust and ashes." Moses, of whom the Torah says that he was "the most modest of men," similarly was a totally self-effacing leader, who said of himself: ואנחנו מה (ve-anachnu mah), "What are we?"

In the course of his own life, Abraham, our first patriarch, gave the Children of Israel countless examples of disinterested service that they would remember throughout their generations. One such example was when he argued with God not to destroy Sodom and Gomorrah, even if the inhabitants were so bad that they deserved any punishment coming to them. Our narratives state that God did not decide to destroy Sodom and Gomorrah only in order to punish the inhabitants for their sins, but also in order to assist Abraham, so that it would be easier for him to disseminate his own moral ideas, which stood in stark contrast to those of Sodom and Gomorrah.

The people of Sodom must have seen Abraham as their greatest threat. We know how Abraham always welcomed visitors. His tent was open on all sides, and he invited all passersby for food and drink. In Sodom, on the other hand, it was forbidden to invite strangers. The best way to counter Abraham's influence was therefore to discourage all contacts with the outside world. Our narratives contain an interesting story on how this was done: Visitors to Sodom were made to sleep on a special bed, on which they had to fit. If the guest was too short, he was stretched until he had reached the right length, but guests who were too long had a piece chopped off their legs. This parable shows how hostile societies force people to conform to their own ideas. Like all parables, it contains a lesson about human behavior, and modern examples of countries such as Russia, China, and Vietnam, where people are make to "fit"— in other words conform to the prevailing ideology—by violent means, prove that it has lost none of its relevancy.

The best way for Abraham to protect his way of life would certainly have been to see Sodom and Gomorrah destroyed. Yet the Torah tells that Abraham was not happy. He bargained with God for their survival, even depreciating himself by saying that thousands of people should not lose their lives for his sake. He believed that his ideas were right, so that they would prevail anyway.

The Jewish people have had other leaders such as Abraham, leaders who were open to the world, positive and constructive, and who realized that hatred and destruction on one hand, or withdrawal and isolation on the other, were no solution; leaders whose moral impulse drove them to inspire and unite their followers. Their example, from generation to generation, is what has molded the Jewish way of life.

A no less remarkable aspect of the Jewish mentality is the absence of hatred for people who abuse us, as measured by a desire for taking revenge when for a change the circumstances are to our advantage. The Jewish people originated in a part of the world where blood feuds were—and still are—a time-honored custom, and yet it has never been a Jewish practice. In our generation, even Holocaust survivors who would prefer to avoid contacts with Germans, Poles, or Russians would not think of inflicting harm upon their former tormentors. Similarly, despite almost sixty years of Arab hostility, and a history of almost traditional animosity and terrorism, the Jewish people do not hate the Arabs; the thought of going out to boycott, kill, or destroy in turn would not give them any satisfaction.

Despite their many sad experiences, the Jewish people do not segregate themselves, on the one hand, or disintegrate, on the other,—because of one overriding reason: they believe in life. Hatred kills, hatred is destructive, and it destroys the hater as thoroughly as his enemy. A person who hates is incapable of living. Despite this, Jews have traditionally been accused of almost every kind of crime or calamity that has happened in the world, from kidnapping and warmongering to poverty and epidemics. One of the most dreaded sicknesses during the Middle Ages was the "Black Death," and many times, when a plague epidemic broke out in rat-infested areas, the Jews were accused of having maliciously caused it. There even was proof, for it so happened that far fewer Jews died of the sickness than Christians! The Jewish explanation, that they lived separate from the general population, and that their strict adherence to ritual laws regarding physical purity and hygiene also helped to prevent infection, was in vain. To mention only one example: Jews have traditionally buried their dead away from residential areas, but even today it is not uncommon in certain European countries for people to be interred in church cemeteries inside villages and towns. Another well-known superstition, that Jews used the blood of Christian children for making *matzoth*, frequently made the populace look for Jewish culprits when a child had suddenly died or disappeared.

Most of the world may be too educated to believe some of the cruder stories, but even in the twentieth century, superstitions remain. These days they may concern the control of the mass media by Jewish press lords, or Jewish financiers who impoverish the world and finance wars between peace-loving nations. All this, as always, poses the question why we insist on fighting windmills, and whether Jews would not be much better off if they stopped presenting themselves as the guardians of a moral doctrine.

The answer to this question is negative, if only because—regardless of the reaction of individual Jews—as a nation we are incapable of resigning our trust. We are incapable of going down to the level of our adversaries, but continue to be driven by an inner compulsion to try to raise it. This is the message—and the mission—of the Torah.

A look at Jewish history also tells us why. As soon as the Children of Israel had crossed the Red Sea, and realized that they were free from their oppressors, they raised their voices in song. The Torah says: אז ישיר משה ובני ישראל (*az yashir moshe u-venei yisrael*). The translation reads, "Then Moses and the Children of Israel *sang*," but the Hebrew says *"will sing,"* and our sages ask, "Why does the Torah talk in the future tense?"

One answer is that the Jewish people have taken it upon themselves to continue to sing, now as well as in the future. Singing means not giving up hope, or being cast down by adversity. The Jewish exiles in Babylon resisted their tormentors' demand to "sing us one of the songs of Zion"—but they only hung up their harps on the poplars; they did not break them, or throw them away. The Jewish faith is a faith of hope: hope of freedom and redemption. One of the central messages of the Jewish prophets is that one day there will be freedom and justice for all people. We hope for the realization of the prophecy of Isaiah, according to which there will come a time when the lion will lie down with the lamb, a time when the weak will live together with the strong, without the fear of being devoured or abused. A just and righteous society means righteous people, and this is why so many of our prayers express the firm belief in a change of human nature.

On the question of how this situation will come about, opinions differ. Some think that this spiritual change will be achieved in the evolutionary way, whereas others believe that the ultimate redemption of the world will be preceded by a profound crisis, which will sweep away the old world and its ideas. Our sages of the Babylonian and Jerusalem Talmud believed in the evolutionary process. According to them, redemption does not merely mean physical freedom, the release from material or social dependency, for the Torah talks about a new outlook and a new way of life.

The Talmud reports a dialogue between Rabbi Eliezer ben Azaryahu and his colleagues on the question of whether a Jew must remember the Exodus from Egypt "by day and by night," or only during the daytime. Some of them were of the opinion that we are obliged to remember the Exodus from Egypt day and night, whereas others believed that this duty refers only to the daytime. We could ask whether there is a difference—and if so, why it is so important. I believe the answer is connected with the question of how the redemption of the world will come about: through a gradual process, which slowly and persistently continues day and night, or as the result of a violent and destructive crisis, a sudden revolution during the day (or night). The Exodus, the first recorded large-scale national liberation in history, was not a message for Jews only, but for the entire world. This means that it must be viewed within the larger framework of human evolution, which is why our sages concluded that the ultimate redemption would come slowly and gradually, in other words "by day and by night."

The things that affect our world also happen to individuals. Changes in our external condition may occur suddenly or slowly, but changes in our thinking or way of life take time. They do not happen from one moment to the next, but have to be patiently worked at—with many ups and downs on the way. However, our Torah has taught us never to despair, and it has implanted in us not only a will to survive, but also the means to achieve this: a tradition of devotion and sacrifice. The Midrash tells that Moses said to Aaron and the elders of the people: לא שררה אני נותן לכם אלא עבדות אני נותן לכם (lo serara ani noten lachem ele aveduth ani noten lachem), "I did not intend you merely to dominate [the Jewish people], but to serve them." Aaron showed that he was ready to accept the ultimate consequence of this view during the incident with the Golden Calf. God said: עמו אנכי בצרה (imo anochi betzarah), "I, too, am with you in your troubles." Aaron reasoned that if God was with the Jewish people when they were in trouble, he, too, could not stay away; he wanted to be with them—even if they were wrong. This is the meaning of God's command to Moses, to "bring Aaron," or—as the Midrash puts it—"to draw Aaron close to him," for it was the love of Aaron, and of all those in Jewish history who supported and continue to support the Jewish people in their suffering that enables the Jewish people to survive.

Parashath Shemini

ויקחו בני־אהרון נדב ואביהוא איש מחתתו ויתנו בהן אש
וישימו עליהן קטרת ויקריבו לפני יהוה אש זרה אשר לא צוה
אתם : ותצא אש מלפני יהוה ותאכל אותם וימותו לפני יהוה :
ויאמר משה אל־אהרן הוא אשר־דבר יהוה לאמר בקרבי אקדש
ועל־פני כל־העם אכבד.

"Aaron's sons Nadab and Abihu took their censers, put fire
in them and added incense; and they offered unauthorized
fire before God, contrary to his command. So the fire came
out from the presence of God and consumed them, and
they died before God. Moses then said to Aaron, 'This is
what God spoke of when he said: "Among those who
approach me I will show myself holy; in the sight of all the
people I will be honored."'"

The story that is related here happened only a little while
after the חנוכת המשכן (chanukkath ha mishkan), the inauguration of
the Tabernacle. The course of events, and its moral, seem very
simple: God punished Aaron's sons Nadab and Abihu in order to
teach the Israelites that nobody was above the law, however
important he might be in his own right—even if he was a son of
the high priest, or one of his assistants. Nadab and Abihu
committed a sin, for, as the Torah says, "they offered unauthorized fire before God." For this they were punished and killed.

The question is nevertheless why their sin was so grievous,
and why they had to die.

A little further on in the same portion of the week, we find

God instructing Moses and the Israelites about "clean" animals, the kind they were permitted to eat, and "unclean" animals, the ones they were not permitted to eat. The Midrash explains that God intended to make a clear distinction between the things that were good for them and those that were not good for them. As to the question why certain things were considered bad for Jews, and not for others, the Midrash gives the example of a physician who went to visit two seriously sick people. One patient he permitted to eat everything, whereas the second was told to abstain from certain kinds of foods. When asked why he gave the one such complete freedom, and restricted the other, the physician answered, "The man whom I permitted to eat everything is in such a bad state that nothing I can say or do will change his condition. So let him eat and drink. The other person has a good chance of getting well and living a useful life. Because of this, I have permitted him to eat only those things that will not impair his condition." In exactly the same way God has forbidden the Jewish people to eat food that will harm their spiritual and physical well-being.

But what is the connection between the inauguration of the sacrificial office in the Tabernacle and the dietary laws? More specifically, what is the connection between what happened to Aaron's children and *kashruth*, and the final introductory words to this *parashah*, in which God declares, "Among those who approach me I will show myself holy; in the sight of all the people I will be honored."

To understand all this, we must go back to the question of what the sons of Aaron did to deserve death. In the Talmud we find two seemingly contradictory explanations. In tractate *Eruvin* it is written that the children of Aaron committed a grave sin. There it is told that Nadab and Abihu questioned the leadership of Moses and Aaron. In fact they said as much as, "till when will these two old people lead this nation? It is about time that they should die, so that we can lead the Jewish people." To this God answered, "We shall see who will die earlier, Moses and

Aaron or you." This explains what they did, and what made them sinners.

In contrast to this, we read in tractate *Zevachim* that Nadab and Abihu died for קדוש השם (*kiddush ha-shem*), the Sanctification of God's name. This suggests that they did not die because of their sins, but in order to glorify God. In the *Midrash Rabba* dealing with the weekly portion of *Shemini* we read that, following Nadab and Abihu's death, Moses said to his brother Aaron, "On Mount Sinai God told me that He will sanctify His name through the one who is nearest to Him. I believed that I would be the one, or that He would take you, but when I saw Nadab and Abihu killed, I realized that your children were closer to God than you or me." The Midrash continues that when Aaron heard these words from Moses, he stopped mourning.

I quote the Midrash to show that our sages believe Nadab and Abihu—although sinners—were among the greatest and most righteous men of their time. To understand this, we should also look at what the Talmud Yerushalmi writes about the two. There Rabbi Uzi is quoted as saying, "Nadab and Abihu were no less devoted to the Jewish people than Moses and Aaron, and everything they said or did was out of concern for them."

We should recognize that Nadab and Abihu faced a serious problem. They had come to realize that the Israelites had become totally dependent upon their uncle Moses and their father Aaron. Recent history had shown that they could not imagine life without them.

For example, Nadab and Abihu could not forget what had happened in the recent past at Mount Sinai, when Moses had ascended the mountain and returned six hours late. The people had completely lost their heads and become so frightened that they built themselves an idol, so that they would have something to look after them. They believed that Moses was dead, and wondered who would take care of them in this barren desert. In fact, there was no recognized leader other than

Moses; there was as yet no one who had shown that he was capable of taking Moses' place. So they decided to collect all their silver and gold and fashion a "leader." Maybe the Golden Calf would help them and save them!

Nadab and Abihu had seen all this, and they understood that if the Jewish people were to survive, there would have to be a future leader in whom they could believe, and whom they would trust and listen to. This is why the Talmud, in tractate *Eruvin*, comments that they said to each other, "Look how they follow Moses and Aaron. What will happen to this people when these two shall have gone. Everyone has to die one day, and the new generation of potential new leaders should at least manifest itself while Moses and Aaron are still here, to make the people realize that they will have capable leaders even after the old generation shall have died."

Having said this, they acted—and immediately erred, in several ways. According to the Torah, God warned Aaron after the calamity by saying, "You and your sons are not to drink wine or other fermented drink whenever you go into the Tent of Meeting, or you will die.... You must distinguish between the holy and the common, between the unclean and the clean...." Nadab and Abihu had not distinguished between the holy and the common, by bringing in "unauthorized" fire. Second, the warning against drinking wine or beer (שכר = *shecher*) strongly suggests that they must have been drunk. Third, they wanted to show the people that they could act independently and decide for themselves what was forbidden and permitted. In effect, they started to teach the Jewish people in the presence of Moses and Aaron, their elders—something that is completely against Jewish law—with the purpose of establishing their authority in the eyes of the Israelites.

Even if we assume that everything they did was intended to reduce the Jewish people's dependence upon Moses and Aaron, God did by no means agree with their methods. The Torah teaches that not only the goal is important, but also the way in which it is achieved. To use a well-known expression, the end does *not* justify the means. The Torah demands that the way we follow toward achieving a purpose shall be the right one. If not, the purpose, even if it is achieved, is invalid.

For example, the Torah asks us to honor our father and mother—unconditionally. Nadab and Abihu did not honor their elders, but rationalized that there were situations where disobedience was not only permitted, but a necessity. The Talmud is very insistent on this point, and it gives a number of examples from the lives of our sages to demonstrate how parents, even if sometimes they were unreasonable or wrong, were deferred to. The Jesuits, on the other hand, in their time taught the Roman Catholic believers that it was permissible to shed the blood of those who did not see things their way. The followers of Mohammed have for many centuries taught that it is a "holy duty" to fight unbelievers.

The Jewish view can be exemplified by the dream Jacob dreamed after he had run away from his brother Esau. He saw angels going up and down a ladder to the heavens—in other words gradually, step by step. We, too, are expected to pursue our most elevated goals step by step, to avoid causing injustice on the way, and to prevent us from falling down in the process.

The above enables us to understand the three questions we asked earlier. Nadab and Abihu had a good purpose, but they, and through them the Jewish people, had to be taught once and for all that even good intentions may not be pursued at all cost. They did not distinguish between "clean" and "unclean," between what was permitted and not permitted, between what was "good" for them and the Jewish people and what was "not good." Neither did they understand that they had no right to change what their seniors—let alone God Himself—had decided.

The death of Nadab and Abihu teaches us three things: If we want to live, we have to accept the Torah, even if we do not understand all its commandments. For example, the rules of *kashruth* should not be changed, even if we do not always understand their meaning. Aaron's children believed, wrongly, that they could make changes. Second, we may not bring "unauthorized fire" into the Sanctuary. Our Sages say that a Jew can be a sinner, in other words deviate from the commandments, and still be a full and valid Jew. However, he may never claim that the Torah permitted him to deviate, by unilaterally interpreting its meaning. And third, if we want to achieve a good purpose, we have to follow the correct way.

There was a reason why God so strongly and forcefully upheld Aaron's authority, for teaching the Jewish people these principles could be done only by the *cohen ha-gadol*, the high priest, and as long as he was in office, no one—not even his deputy—could act in his name.

What was the work of the *cohanim* in general—why were they so important? One reason was that they were the mentors of the Jewish people, charged with their spiritual care on the most diverse occasions. There are some wonderful narratives about the way pilgrims who came to Jerusalem in biblical times to sacrifice or to pray were looked after by the members of the priestly family. Upon his arrival, the pilgrim—regardless whether he was rich or poor, important or unimportant, whether he came from the Sharon, Galilee, or Beth She'an—applied to the *Shaar ha-Ezra* ("Gate of Help"), an institution that today would be called the "visitors desk". There one of the *cohanim* would take charge of him, from the day he arrived until the day he left Jerusalem. He would see to it that the visitor received lodging and food, he would be his friend and act as his counsellor and social worker. This kind of treatment and care was essential for the unity of the Jewish people. The *cohanim* and the Levites were expected to give the example of how people should care for each other. Let us see what the Torah says: כי יהיה בבני ישראל נגע ונגש אל הכהן (*ki yihyeh be-venei yisrael nega ve-nigash el ha cohen*), "If any of the Children of Israel is afflicted, he should go to the cohen." Nadab and Abihu did not behave as was expected of persons of their status; neither did they honor their teacher Moses and their father Aaron. Regardless of their intentions, there was a serious danger that the people would learn from their negative example, a danger that the people would say, If the priests act like this, then why not us? So, even though—or because—God loved and appreciated Nadab and Abihu, He sanctified His commandments through His devoted friends, so that everybody would understand "that even for good and loyal people I will not change My Law."

Parashath Tazri'a-Metzora

זאת תהיה תורת המצרע ביום טהרתו והובא אל־הכהן: ויצא הכהן אל־מחוץ למחנה וראה הכהן והנה נרפא נגע־הצרעת מן־הצרוע

"God said to Moses: 'These are the regulations for the diseased person at the time of his ceremonial cleansing, when he is brought to the priest: The priest is to go outside the camp and examine him. If the person has been healed of his infectious skin disease....'"

Both *Parashath Metzora* and the preceding portion, *Parashath Tazri'a*, which are often read together, deal with the purification for various illnesses and other forms of uncleanliness. Prominent among these was leprosy, an infectious disease that could seriously disfigure the sufferer.

The above-quoted opening verse of the portion of *Metzora* again contains a seeming contradiction. First it says that the sufferer is to be "brought to the priest," following which we read that the priest "is to go outside the camp and examine him."

For a better understanding of this, we should first understand the connection that our sages made between leprosy and another—not physical, but equally infectious—sin, namely gossip. The Midrash explains how Moses warned the Israelites not to gossip, so that they would not undergo the same fate as Moses' sister Miriam, who became leprous as a result of having slandered her brother. Because of its infectious nature, sufferers of leprosy were traditionally placed in isolation, as continues to be the case in certain countries where the illness still exists. Slander, too, is intended to place somebody outside the community, and the moral of Moses' warning was therefore that slander would be punished by an infectious disease that would cause the slanderer in turn to be shunned by his fellowmen. As the Talmud puts it: מידה כנגד מידה (midah ke-neged midah), "Measure for measure."

The Talmud tells the following story about a certain Rabbi Alexander, who, when passing through the town of Zippori in Galilee, was attracted by a voice calling, "Who would like to have long life and good fortune?" Looking around him, he saw an old peddler waving a piece of paper.

"Who would like long life and good fortune," the peddler called again, "come near, and I will tell you the answer."

A crowd started forming around the old man. Rabbi Alexander also joined and, addressing the peddler, said, "Show me what you have."

The peddler held out his piece of paper, and on it were written the words from Psalm 34, מי־האיש החפץ חיים אהב ימים לראות טוב נצר לשונך מרע ושפתיך מדבר מרמה (me ha-ish he-chafetz chaim ohev yamim lir'oth tov netzor leshoncha mera u-sefateicha medaber mirmah), "Whoever of you loves life and desires to see many good days, keep your tongue from evil, and your lips from speaking deceit."

"Remember," the old man whispered to the bystanders, "to control your tongue and to refrain from spreading evil language about your fellowmen, and you will live long and happy lives."

Rabbi Alexander was very much surprised to hear such wisdom from the mouth of an ignorant peddler. But what impressed him even more was the fact that, although he had known the words of this psalm all his life, their true meaning had up till this moment escaped him.

We could go on quoting parables and sayings about the dangers of gossip and slander. It will suffice, however, to tell a story about a certain rabbi who took his pupils on an excursion. By midday they all had a hearty appetite, and they decided to look for a place where they could find a kosher meal. They went from one inn to another, but none of them appeared to be good enough. Finally, they found a small place that seemed to fit their requirements, and soon all of them were enjoying their meal. The rabbi, slightly amused at the thought of how extremely particular they had been in searching for a really kosher place, said to them, "Boys, I sincerely hope that you will always be as careful about what comes out of your mouth as you have been about what is going in."

The Torah wants to warns us against idle talk, but the question is how we can avoid it. Let's face it: a bit of gossip is the spice of life, and very few people can resist it. What is gossip? In its most innocent form it is curiosity, which causes us to speculate aloud to a stranger about the reasons why something has happened, or why someone has behaved in a certain way. Even if our intentions are kind, our talk nevertheless often is careless. For it is very tempting to add a little bit of drama, and to ascribe less than entirely unselfish or honorable motives to another person's behavior; if this wasn't the case, there would be no gossip.

In its worst form, however, gossip is slander, and at this point we already have transgressed far beyond the point of honesty or propriety. This is what Miriam did, when she criticized Moses' marriage to a Cushite woman. As a punishment, she was smitten with leprosy, and she was healed only after Moses interceded on her behalf.

The Torah tells us, therefore, to stay away from gossip and slander. However, the real story of this *parashah* concerns the two kinds of *cohanim* mentioned in the opening words: the *cohen* who has sufferers brought to him, and the *cohen* who goes out of the camp to examine them. In exactly the same way there have always existed two kinds of leaders. We are not—at least not here—referring to politicians, but to socially responsible people with ears and eyes open for real problems, and a desire to solve them. The first kind want to help, but are afraid to stick out their necks, or to interfere in other people's situations without having been asked. They are generous and willing, but they prefer to wait until a problem is brought to their attention. The second kind of leader, on the other hand, actively confronts problems; they are what we would call the "pastoral type." To the second category belonged, for example, the Lithuanian Rabbi Israel Salanter, the founder of the *Musar* movement, and Rabbi Israel Baal Shem Tov, the founder of Chassidism in Eastern Europe, both of whom were tireless fighters for social causes without being in the slightest influenced by what people said, either about them, or about the efficacy of their assistance.

In one of the countless stories about Rabbi Salanter, one of his pupils asked him, "Don't you ever get tired trying to improve people? Don't you realize that you are not getting anywhere? Why do you keep beating your head against the wall?" Rabbi Israel smiled, and said, "There was a moment once that I thought I had reached the same conclusion. Then, on a cold winter day, I noticed a woman peddling matches and all kinds of knickknacks. She was calling, "Needles! Matches! Buy my needles, matches!" and from time to time she would stop a passerby and repeat her question. But nobody seemed willing to buy, so I made it a point to follow her and see how she managed to make a living.

I did this for several days, and every time again I was surprised to see how little she sold. Finally I went up to her and asked her, "Why don't you stop punishing yourself by walking around in this freezing weather? You don't seem to be selling anything. Come on, go home, and warm yourself."

The old peddler woman gave me a puzzled look, and answered, "Young man, I know my business better than you. I have been peddling for many years, and it is true that I don't have so many buyers. But you would be surprised to know that every evening when I count my takings, there always is enough money to buy food for myself and my children."

"From this," Rabbi Salanter concluded, "I learned that you

have to continue saying and doing what you think is best, even if it looks as if nobody is listening."

It looks, therefore, as if there were two kinds of *cohanim*: the first kind waited for the patient to be "brought to the priest," whereas the second kind went "outside the camp... to examine him," and heal him—in other words, went out of his way to search for those who needed his assistance.

In the previous discussion on *Parashath Bo* we referred to the six occasions that the Torah tells us "to remember," because they contain a pivotal lesson for Jewish survival. They were the Exodus from Egypt, the Shabbath, the receiving of the Torah at Mount Sinai, the way the Children of Israel provoked God in the desert, the curse of Amalek, and Miriam's punishment for slander. Why was this latter incident so important? The answer is that any stable society depends upon the relationship between its members. The same, but on a larger scale, applies to the relations between different societies. Slander is the ax at the root of mutual trust and the interdependence between man and his fellow. On the individual level, we have only to look around us to see how often people stoop to insinuations and purposeful lies to undermine an opponent. The same thing applies to governments, except that in international politics we use techniques like propaganda and disinformation. This is why the Torah tells us: זאת תהיה תורת המצורע (*zoth tehiyeh torath ha-metzora*), meaning that this principle of avoiding contagion is an important commandment in its own right, and that neglecting it risks our existence.

Philosophers have through the ages asked themselves what were the fundamental principles that determined the existence of our world. Right at the beginning of the Torah, in the narrative of the Creation, the completion of the successive days is denoted with the words, "And it was evening, and it was morning, one day,... a second day,... a third day,.. a fourth day,... a fifth day—until the sixth day, when suddenly we read, "And it was evening, and it was morning, *the* sixth day." The Talmud, in *masecheth Shabbath*, tells us that the extra ה (the numerical value of which is five) of יום הששי (*yom ha-shishi*) was added at the point when the work of Creation was finished, to imply God's condition to Israel that the world would continue to exist only if the Jewish people accepted the Torah and their interpretation; if not, it would sooner or later revert to chaos.

How can we ensure that our world will continue? By realizing that our individual deeds help to improve or destroy life. This idea, too, can be illustrated by a parable. Rabbi Yehoshua ben Chananyah once asked one of his colleagues, "Can you tell me where is the middle of the world?"

The other rabbi answered, "Exactly where you are standing."

Rabbi Yehoshua said, "Very nice, but how do I know that you are right?"

"Simple," said the other. "We'll take a rope, and each of us will pull at one end. No matter where we stand, you'll see that we'll stay exactly where we are. So that spot must be the middle." Precisely the same principle applies to our efforts to improve the world, when every individual acts as if, as far as he or she is concerned, the center of the world is right underneath his or her own feet. The individual is the most important. Ultimately, peace and war are not decided by governments alone, but by individuals. We may not be able to move the world, but all that may—and should—be asked of us is that we accept responsibility for the quality and seriousness of our efforts.

There once was a Jewish tailor in a village in Eastern Europe, who was renowned far and wide for the high quality of his work. One day he was summoned by the local landlord, who wanted to order a new pair of pants. The tailor went to take his measurements, following which he returned home to buy cloth and make his preparations. After barely a week the landlord sent a servant to ask whether his pants were ready. They weren't—and neither were they after two weeks, or after four weeks, or after six weeks. The eighth week the landlord was so enraged that he decided to go and see for himself why it took so much time for his pants to be finished.

"What do you think you are?" he shouted at the tailor. "When will my pants finally be ready?"

Proudly the tailor held up the pants, from which he had just that moment removed the last stitches.

"Here they are, sir," he said. "First try them on, and then we'll talk."

Quickly the landlord put on the new pants, and a delighted look spread over his face.

"Wonderful, really perfect, but I still do not understand why you should need eight weeks to finish a single pair of pants, when the entire world was created in six days."

"But, sir," the tailor retorted, "how can you compare? Look at your new pants, how perfect they are, and then look at the sorry state of the world!"

People will have to recognize that they are not free to do what they want, but that they have to listen to the Torah. If everybody did what he thought right, the world would soon become unmanageable. Our sages tell a story, according to which God took the first man on an excursion through Paradise, showing him every beautiful tree He had created. "Look," God said, " how beautiful the world is that I have made. From now on it will be your responsibility to see to it that it will not be destroyed." Man has the ability to choose between good and evil. A great responsibility rests on every individual, particularly in the present century, when we are learning to develop artificial intelligences, and more and more activities can be performed by a simple press on a button. Most of these buttons serve worthwhile purposes, but there are a few that can destroy— wholesale!

The portion of *Tazri'a* begins with the words אשה כי תזריע וילדה זכר (*ishah ki-tazria ve-yaldah zechar*), "if a woman has conceived and she has born a male...." The Midrash comments that these words are intended to remind the Jewish people of the words of the prophet, "How we are missing the days of old," meaning that the children born in those days were unable to do as much harm as the modern generation. The old world certainly had its share of injustice and cruelty, but never on such a potentially massive scale as today. This thought alone should be enough to cause us to remain alert and to be constantly aware of our responsibility to avoid "contagion"—of any kind.

Parashath Acharei Moth

(6) והקריב אהרן את־פר החטאת אשר־לו וכפר בעדו ובעד ביתו.

(11) והקריב אהרן את־פר החטאת אשר־לו וכפר בעדו ובעד ביתו.

(17) וכל־אדם לא־יהיה באהל מועד בבאו לכפר בקדש עד־צאתו וכפר בעדו ובעד ביתו ובעד כל־קהל ישראל.

(6/11) "Aaron is to offer the bull for his own sin offering to make atonement for himself and his household."

(17) "No one is to be in the Tent of Meeting from the time Aaron goes in to make atonement in the Most Holy Place until he comes out, having made atonement for himself, his household, and the whole community of Israel."

The above quotations from *Parashath Acharei Moth* in the Book of Leviticus form part of a discussion on the priestly rites for the Day of Atonement, the one day during the year when the high priest entered the Holy of Holies inside the Sanctuary. No fewer than three times the text repeats that Aaron has to ask forgiveness for himself. The obvious reason, as our sages explain, is that nobody should be allowed to ask forgiveness for others until he has atoned for his own sins, and he knows that they are forgiven. Only when he himself has been absolved can he pray on behalf of others.

Even so, we could ask why the Torah insists on this triple

absolution. First of all, why three times, and not four or six times. Three is, of course, a significant number in many cultures. Three is the minimum number needed for something to be stable or lasting. A chair, for instance, can stand perfectly well on three legs; it does not need four legs, but it cannot possibly stand on two. Also in the Jewish tradition the number three conveys the idea of stability and completeness. In the Book of Ecclesiastes we read, for instance, החוט המשולש לא במהרה ינתק (ha-chut ha-meshulash lo be-meherah yinatek), meaning "A triple thread does not easily come apart." This saying is often applied to learning Torah, in the sense that once a grandfather, a father, and a son have applied themselves to the study of Torah, there is an excellent chance that the tradition will be carried over to the grandchildren as well.

The triple atonement of the high priest therefore emphasizes the seriousness of the act. There was, however, another—even more important—aspect to his atonement. A person who sins does not only harm others, but even more so himself. He injures himself, and he becomes a worse person. Cruelty and injustice to others invariably damage the perpetrator; they coarsen and desensitize him, causing him to lose the ability to distinguish between good and bad. This is why G-d tells people to atone for themselves, because of the harm they have inflicted upon their own person, and not only because they have harmed others.

The reverse also holds true, for the more unselfish and caring a person is to others, the more his character will be enriched and ennobled. Giving charity is a good example. Our sages comment that giving charity obviously helps the receiver, but that it benefits the donor even more. Rabbi Chananiya ben Akassia says that God wanted to privilege the Jewish people, and that this is why He gave them the Torah ve-mitzvoth. For the performance of the mitzvoth helps to improve our character; it ennobles our nature, and even makes us feel better. All this is summarized in our Scriptures by the saying שכר מצוה מצוה שכר עברה

עברה (*sechar mitzvah mitzvah, sechar averah averah*), which means as much as "Good makes you do good, and evil makes you do evil."

All this explains why the high priest had to examine himself so carefully. First he had to ask himself whether he had possibly harmed anybody, either directly or indirectly, and whether his transgressions were of a kind capable of atonement. Following this, he had to ask himself whether he really understood the seriousness of what he had done, and whether he was certain that he would be able to prevent a recurrence. For without an awareness of sin, and without a desire to make good, the high priest's atonement was neither possible nor valid. This highly personal aspect of the high priest's atonement also explains why on *Yom Ha-Kippurim* he entered the Holy of Holies all alone. None of his colleagues, not even his deputy, was allowed to accompany him inside.

We might ask what happened if the high priest came to the conclusion that his sins did not allow him to atone for himself, and therefore not for his family nor the rest of the nation either. That such a situation was not entirely hypothetical is proven by the fact that on two occasions the high priest found it necessary to resign, and on the spot handed over his responsibilities to his deputy. For, according to the Torah, there are sins for which no atonement or reparation is possible. Thus the Torah warns, לא תקחו כפר לנפש (*lo tikchu kofer le-nefesh*), "Do not accept blood money." According to Jewish tradition, human beings are not merely material assets that can be added up, bought, or sold, let alone destroyed. People represent values, to which no price tags can be attached. This is why God condemns a murderer not only because of the physical life he has taken, but in particular because he has destroyed a nonphysical value: a parent, a spouse, a breadwinner, a friend.

The Rambam, in the chapter *Hilchath Rotzeach* of his *Yad Chazakah*, emphatically warned the Beth Din not to permit a murderer to pay restitution for his victim. Even if a family were prepared to accept compensation, in return for forgiveness, they were forbidden to do so, since the victim's life was the property of God, so it was not up to the family to settle the material problem by accepting compensation in place of the victim's life. According to the Rambam, every assault on another human being is an affront to God Himself, in whose image we are all created.

We now understand why the Torah emphasizes the importance of atonement, particularly for the high priest, who had been appointed as the spiritual leader of the Israelites. If the high priest wanted them to embrace the right values, he himself had to be pure and clean in all aspects of his behavior. For how could he atone for others, if he could not properly atone for himself? And how could he be expected to control others, if he was unable to control himself?

It should be clear to us that the Torah, in the *pasuk* we are discussing here, does not talk only about the high priest, but, by extension, about all those who aspire to lead others, since the fate of their followers, be they relatives, a congregation, or an entire society, depends first of all upon their example. It is very typical of Judaism that it has always emphasized every person's responsibility for *himself*. How often do we hear comments like, "Let's face it. Society is bad, so what does it help to try and give a good example. I might as well join the rest." Our sages long ago came up with a powerful counterargument when they said that all of us must always look at the world as if exactly half of it was good, and exactly half bad. This means that each one of us is able to tip the scale toward a better society!

In other words, let's stop complaining about the sins and deficiencies of others. What counts for us is our *own* conduct. If *we* behave in the right way, we might in the process affect the behavior of others. Talking about other people's shortcomings can never be an excuse, or a remedy, for our own inadequacies. God warns us, by the example of our highest leaders, that we are at all times accountable for our own deeds, and for the effect they have on others.

The Torah itself places all this in even starker relief when it shows us how soon after the dedication of the Sanctuary the above principle would be put to the test. The name of this *parashah* is *Acharei Moth*, "After the death...," referring to the death of Aaron's two sons Nadab and Abihu, as a punishment for having entered the Sanctuary and offering "strange fire before God." On the eighth day following the inauguration of the Sanctuary, Aaron took up his duties as high priest. According to our sages, there was even more happiness on this occasion than when God had created heaven and earth, and the *Zohar* comments that the Israelites sang, "Who loved Israel more than Aaron, and who loved Aaron more than Israel."

Then, suddenly, came the tragic deaths of Nadab and Abihu, as if to remind the Israelites—and in particular Aaron and his children—of the frailty of human nature. What were Nadab and Abihu's sins, and what made them so serious that they had to die? Our narratives conclude that they had committed three sins, namely offering strange (in other words, "unauthorized") fire in the Sanctuary, approaching God inside the Holy of Holies, and acting on their own, without having either asked or received permission from Aaron. Even so, many of our sages declare that Nadab and Abihu were righteous men. The Midrash comments that the Torah, by specifically mentioning these transgressions, suggests that they had no other sins.

The deaths of his two sons was a bitter blow to Aaron in particular. The Talmud relates how Moses consoled Aaron by telling him something God had confided to him at Sinai. Apparently God had said that, following the dedication of the Sanctuary, He would sacrifice someone close to Him. "All the time," Moses told Aaron, "I believed that God was referring to you or me, but now I realize that your sons must have been closer to God than either one of us." Among other things, this commentary also demonstrates the high esteem in which Nadab and Abihu have traditionally been held by our sages.

Why then were they punished so severely? The answer is

that, even if their sins were not capital sins, the Jewish principle is that the higher the position, the greater the responsibility, and therefore the greater the sin and the resulting punishment.

The Rambam reminds us that certain deeds committed by unauthorized persons are considered a desecration of God's name, and as such a capital sin, punishable by death. This does not apply only to indifferent or wicked people, but also—and in particular—to people who because of the exalted positions they occupy are expected to give an example. God will not exonerate them because they are so important; the opposite is the case, and this is what the Torah means when it says בקרובי אקדש (be-kerovai ekadesh), "I will be sanctified through the lives of those who are close to Me."

The high priest had to examine himself and atone according to a far stricter yardstick than any of the other Israelites. The moral of this portion is, therefore, that Jewish morality does not place the leader above the law. If ordinary people can influence each other's behavior—both for good and for bad—how much more does this apply to those who are supposed to guide them. Because of this, the criteria by which the leader has to be judged, as well as the sanctions for his failure, should be stricter than those applied to ordinary people.

Parashath Kedoshim

וידבר יהוה אל־משה לאמר: דבר אל־כל־עדת בני־ישראל
ואמרת אלהם קדשים תהיו כי קדוש אני יהוה אלהיכם.

"God said to Moses: 'Speak to the entire assembly of Israel
and say to them: "Be holy because I, your God, am holy."'"

This is another one of the very rare occasions on which God
told Moses to call the entire congregation together. According
to the Midrash, Rabbi Hiyya bar Abba taught his students that
this section was proclaimed in the presence of the whole congregation because most of the fundamental teachings of the Torah
depend upon what is said here.

Holiness is the cornerstone of the Jewish faith. Holiness
relates to the moral conduct God requires from us, particularly
in our relations with our fellowmen. Holiness in Judaism is not
an abstract quality associated, as in most other religions, with
some deity or object, such as a stone, or even a place, but an
attribute of God, and the symbol of human moral perfection.
Neither is holiness something mysterious that can be understood only by a select few, but a characteristic of everyday
life—a human property God wants to be disseminated to and
shared by all people.

The Torah tells us: ואתם תהיו־לי ממלכת כהנים וגוי קדוש (ve-atem tiheyu
li mamlecheth cohanim ve-goy kadosh), "You will be for Me a Kingdom
of Priests and a Holy Nation." This refrain is repeated over and
over again in different versions, most explicitly so in the following verse from *Parashath Kedoshim*: והייתם לי קדושים כי קדוש אני יהוה ואבדל

אתכם מן־העמים להיות לי לעם (ve-he'item li kedoshim ki kadosh ani ha-shem va-avdel ethchem min-ha-amim lehioth li le-am), "You are to be holy to Me, because I, God, am holy and I have set you apart from the nations to be My own nation."

Three aspects are particularly apparent. First, God wants the Jewish people to be holy *to Him*, in other words to be accountable to Him. Second, God wants the Jewish people to be holy *"because I am holy"*; God wants us to emulate Him in our conduct. The third aspect, finally, the separateness of the Jewish people, is also connected with holiness because—following early rabbinic sources—our interpreters have traditionally understood the verb קדש (kadesh) to mean "distinguished" or "set apart." In other words, God set the Jewish people apart in order to bear witness to Him among the countless idolatries of the world.

The idea of holiness runs like a red thread through our entire life. It as it were forms a garland surrounding all our life's experiences, from birth till death. The father's prayer during the redemption ceremony of his firstborn son contains the words ונאמר קדש־לי כל־בכור (kadesh li kol bechor), "Sanctify to Me all the firstborn." Besides this we have Kiddush, from the word kadesh, the prayer recited over a cup of wine to consecrate the Shabbath; the Kedushah, the third blessing of the Shemoneh Esrei (or Amidah) prayer; Kiddushin, the consecration of the marriage; and finally Kaddish, the sanctification of G-d in the prayer for our departed.

Holiness, therefore, is something human beings are expected to aspire to, but we all realize that achieving this ideal state is a rather forbidding task. This explains why people or groups in certain societies who are particularly preoccupied with the idea of holiness often tend to isolate themselves and to withdraw from human society, believing that this is the only way in which they can avoid the dangers of moral or spiritual infection or contamination. From a Jewish point of view, however, they are very much mistaken.

As we mentioned before, Moses related this portion in front

of the assembled community to establish that this *mitzvah* lays the foundation of all other rules about the relationship between man and his fellow, as well as to emphasize that holiness cannot not be pursued in isolation but has to be practiced in public. Those who succeed become holy to God. One of our contemporary religious philosophers described the Jewish faith as "not a question of what man does with his solitude, but what man does with the *presence of God*: how to think, feel, act; how to live in a way that is compatible with our being a likeness of God; how to so conduct ourselves that our lives can be an answer to all that God wants of us." This is the Jewish concept of holiness. As we said before, this is by no means an easy task to fulfill, but at the same time the one and only entirely realistic approach.

Parashath Emor contains the verse: ונקדשתי בתוך בני ישראל (*venikdashti be-toch benei yisrael*), which we may interpret almost literally as meaning that God wants to be sanctified with and among His own people. Our narratives contain a parable that might help us understand this Jewish concept of קדושה (*kedushah*), or "holiness."

An artist had painted many beautiful pictures, but he wasn't satisfied. His ideal was to paint the most beautiful thing in the world.

One day he met a old man, and he asked him what, in light of his long experience, he considered to be the most beautiful thing in the world.

"That is not difficult to answer," said the old man. "Faith is the most beautiful thing."

Next the artist asked a young girl who was soon to be married.

"Love," she answered, "is the most beautiful thing in the world. It sweetens all sorrows, it makes you feel rich, and without it there can be no beauty."

Next, the artist decided to ask a soldier.

"What do you mean," the soldier answered, "peace is the most beautiful thing in the world! How can it be otherwise? War is ugly, it brings sorrow and darkness. Peace, on the other hand, is all happiness and light. Where there is peace, there will also be beauty."

Now the artist had three subjects: faith, love, and peace, but he still was at a loss how to paint them.

It was time to return home, and having arrived near his house, he saw his wife and children standing outside their front door. Suddenly he realized that he had found the most beautiful place in the world: here were his children, in whose eyes he saw reflected faith; his wife, whose smile revealed her love; and finally his home, where he would always find peace—all the things the old man, the young bride, and the soldier had told him about. He knew what his painting was going to be!

Jewish tradition, too, takes this picture and frames it within an aura of sanctity. Judaism transforms the home into a sanctuary. And everything that applies to the small, intimate society of our home also applies to society at large—in the same way as all our obligations as individuals apply to the Jewish nation at large. The holiness that God demands of us must express itself in behavior that our fellow Jews will recognize as holy.

The foregoing will make it clear that the holiness that the Torah demands of the Jew is not the same kind of holiness as understood by other people, in the same way that the justice of the Torah is of a different category than the justice commonly practiced in the world. Others may try to practice holiness by living apart, by withdrawing into their own private world, out of fear or contempt for what others enjoy. Judaism, however, sanctifies life. Judaism wants us to participate fully in all the activities of this world, despite the evil, the apathy, and the absurdities with which we are continually confronted, because of its firm conviction that man has the power to do God's will—and triumph. This also explains why Jewish justice cannot be class justice or group justice—and this rules out justice that inflicts suffering or practices inequality. Torah justice, if properly practiced, must be applicable to every place and every age.

This rules out justice as meted out in Communist courts, or by self-styled judges such as the Red Brigades or the Mafia.

The practice of true justice, too, is possible only if קדשים תהיו (kedoshim tiheyu), if we are holy. Holiness is to do all things in a holy way: to become—or try to become—another kind of person. According to the Torah, a holy man does not affront or insult, he does not push, he will not benefit himself at the expense of his fellowmen. This kind of attitude even determines our behavior toward our enemies. In the book of Proverbs we read: בנפול אויבך אל־תשמח ובכשלו אל־יגל לבך (be-nefol oyevcha al-tismach u-bi-cashelo al-yagel libcha), meaning: "Rejoice not when your enemy falls, and let not your heart be glad when he stumbles."

I am often reminded of a story in the Talmud about Rabbi Avihu ben Avima. Rabbi Avihu's father was so old that he spent his days alternately waking and dozing on a couch adjacent to the hall where his son was teaching Torah to his students. One day the old man briefly woke up to ask for a drink of water, but by the time Rabbi Avihu came to him with the water, he had already fallen asleep. Instead of returning to his students, Rabbi Avihu stayed next to the couch until his father woke up again. In taking his old father a cup of water, Rabbi Avihu no more than fulfilled the commandment to honor his parents. However, this same commandment did not oblige him to stay and wait for his father to wake up again. He simply regarded it as his human duty to do what he did, and from this point of view his conduct may be considered holy.

The Torah says ולמדתם אתם לעשות אתם (ve-limadetem otam la'asoth otam), "You shall learn them and practice them." A boy returned from school in an excited mood, and his father asked him, "What are you so happy about?"

"I learned a lot of Torah," the boy answered.

"That is not a sufficient reason," the father replied, "your happiness should not only result from how much Torah you were taught, but how much the Torah taught you."

This is what kedushah refers to: all our large and small daily acts of consideration and respect for our fellowmen that are not a part of the *mitzvoth*, but logically follow from them as an acquired way of life. *Parashath Kedoshim* does not talk about the performance of the *mitzvoth* but about the daily practice of all that they have taught us.

Parashath Emor

ויאמר יהוה אל־משה אמר אל־הכהנים בני אהרון ואמרת אלהם
לנפש לא־יטמא בעמיו: כי אם־לשארו הקרב אליו לאמו
ולאביו ולבנו ולבתו ולאחיו: ולאחתו הבתולה הקרובה
אליו אשר לא־היתה לאיש.

"God said to Moses, 'Speak to the priests, the sons of
Aaron, and say to them: "A priest must not make himself
ritually unclean for any of his people who die, except for a
close relative, such as his mother or father, his son or
daughter, his brother, or an unmarried sister who is
dependent on him because she has no husband."'"

This passage at the beginning of *Parashath Emor* tells us that
the priests of the Jewish nation were allowed to mourn only for
their most immediate relatives. The verse deals only with the
ordinary priests; with regard to the *cohen ha-gadol*, the high priest,
even stricter rules applied, for a little further on the Torah
informs us that the high priest was not even allowed to mourn
for his father and mother.

Our interpreters explain that the paramount duty of the
cohanim was to be close to their people, with whose spiritual care
they were entrusted, and this would have been impossible if
they cared more for certain persons—even close relatives—than
for others. This also explains why the *cohanim* were not allowed
to go to a cemetery, because a priest could not be involved with
death, or suffering in general, in situations where he was unable
to be of practical assistance. His task was to look after the living

and to support them in their troubles. At the same time—once the funeral was over, and the body was no longer present—the *cohen*, as a spiritual leader of the Jewish people, was obliged to go and console the mourners.

In this portion we read that God said to Moses, *"Speak* to the priests, the sons of Aaron, *and say to them. . . ."* What is the purpose of this repetition of "speak" and "say"? Rashi explains that God wanted Moses to caution the adults among the *cohanim*, and at the same time instruct them to caution their children that they, too, should avoid the sin of defilement.

This brings us to the age-old discussion of how we can educate a child so that it will follow the right way in life. Some claim that it is sufficient when a child receives the correct example from his father and mother, in other words, if his immediate environment is good, the child will automatically follow in his parents' footsteps. Others maintain that society—the environment, school, and friends—is the most important influence. We all know examples of children from wonderful homes who, for a variety of reasons, failed in life. As against this, there are examples of children who have become outstanding citizens, their indifferent or even negative home influences notwithstanding. How are we to understand this? How can we ensure that a child will turn out to be good? What are the crucial, formative influences on his or her development?

The Talmud and Midrash contain a number of opinions according to which inherited traits are of crucial importance. Rabbi Jonathan said, "If someone is a scholar, and if his son is a scholar, and his grandson is a scholar, the Torah will not be forgotten in his house, because—as the prophet said—'My spirit that is upon you, and my words which I have put in your mouth, shall not depart from your mouth, nor from the mouths of your children, or from the mouths of your childrens' children.'" What Rabbi Jonathan meant was that future generations remain mindful of the example of their forefathers. The "genetic inheritance" is important, and as long as the parents give the proper example, there is every chance that the children will follow in their way. Our sages say, מעשי אבות סימן לבנים (ma'asei avoth siman lebanim), "The deeds of the parents are a good omen for the children." This is also why, in the K'riath Shema, we are commanded: ‏...וקשרתם אתם לאות על־ידכם והיו לטוטפת בין עיניכם. ולמדתם אתם את־בניכם לדבר בם בשבתך בביתך ובלכתך בדרך ובשכבך ובקומך (u-keshartem otam le-oth al-yedeichem ve-hayu le-totafoth beyn eyneichem. Ve limadetem otam eth beneichem ledaber bam be-shivtecha be-veteycha uve-lechtecha ba-derech uve-shachbecha uve-kumeicha), "...tie them as symbols on your hands and bind them on your foreheads. Teach them to your children, talking of them when you sit at home and when you walk along the road, when you lie down and when you get up."

It is not enough to teach our children theoretically how to live; we have to "bind" the younger generation through what we are doing with our hands and with our heads. There can be no doubt, therefore, that both heritage and the home are extremely important, and that they can have a powerful influence on the younger generation.

Elsewhere in the Talmud and Midrash we find comments pointing in a different direction. In effect they say that it is not only his background that decides whether a person will be good or bad. The most important thing is said to be his environment and his opportunities: the chances that he is offered—or that he missed, often through no fault of his own.

Combining these two views, we may conclude that there is no single cause; all the above-mentioned factors, the home, the school, the street, a person's companions, as well as chance conditions, may pull in different directions. Even so the home remains the central, formative environment, and the young child cannot help being profoundly influenced by the way he sees his parents behave. Modern psychologists even claim that this influence begins immediately after birth, and that a baby who is no more than a few months old is affected when its parents quarrel. This is why Moses said אמר ואמרת (emor ve-amarta), "Speak [to the priests] and say to them." In other words, the *cohanim* were expected to pass on their message—and their example—to those below them through their practical deeds.

Summarizing, we may conclude that God asked the *cohanim* not merely to behave like any other person, but to be a living example—and to pass on this example "down the line." From this it follows that a priest, in his capacity as a spiritual leader, had to be so profoundly aware of his obligations that he could not permit himself to be depressed or to mourn. This is why he was not allowed to expose himself to any kind of situation where he was powerless to offer practical assistance.

In this context, we should relate what the Talmud, in *masecheth Baba Metzia*, tells about Rabba bar Avuha, who once found the prophet Elijah seated in a cemetery of idol worshipers. "What are you doing here," he asked, "are you not a *cohen*? Surely you know that a *cohen* should not enter a cemetery?"

Elijah replied, "Don't you know the laws of *taharah* (purity)? Tell me what is written there?" And he continued, "Rabbi Shimon Bar Yochai said that the cemeteries of idol worshipers are not called cemeteries, since the prophet said ואתן צאן מרעיתו אדם אתם (*ve-aten tson marito adam atem*), which can be translated as, You are the shepherd's flock, because you are called people.

What did Rabbi Shimon Bar Yochai mean? Did he want to say that idol worshipers are not people? The very idea runs counter to accepted Jewish tradition. Judaism recognizes all of G-d's creatures as human beings. This is also how our sages interpret it, when they remind us that "God accepts both the good and the bad of people," commenting that the text does not specify "*cohanim*, Levites, and Israelites," but simply states "people." A Gentile, if he behaves correctly, should be accorded the same reception as even the high priest. The Talmud states that "we honor every man because he is created in the image of God." Rabbi Akiva commented that the Torah says חביב אדם (*chaviv adam*), and not חביב האדם (*chaviv ha-adam*), "Beloved is man, because he was created in the image of God." Not: beloved is *the*—special or specific—man, but simply *man*. Not merely learned people, or

beautiful people, or rich or influential people, but every creature
that was made in God's image. Our patriarchs did not insist on
honors, titles, or degrees, and neither did our prophets or sages.
On the contrary, all our historical leaders, prophets, and sages
are known by their first names! Abraham, Moses, David, Akiva!
What counted were their deeds, and through them, their names
became as it were their titles. Every man can aspire to become as
illustrious as Moses. The Gaon of Vilna (the *Vilner Gaon*) said
with a play on words in Yiddish: "*Will nor* ("if only you want"),
you too can be a *gaon*—a genius."

So why did Rabbi Shimon Bar Yochai suggest that idol worshipers are not people? And what was Elijah doing in the cemetery, which was a ritually forbidden place, where he would only
be troubled, without being able to help anybody? Rabbi Shimon
Bar Yochai looked at the way of life of the idol worshipers, and
he concluded that, since they did not regard people as human
beings in the image of God, the saying "You are the shepherd's
flock, because you are called people" did not apply to them.
Because of this, the prophet Elijah decided that the idol worshipers' cemeteries were not cemeteries in the Jewish sense, and
that visiting them would not cause any particular emotions,
either happy or sad.

The above dealt with the power of a practical example, not
only that of the *cohanim* and their offspring and successors, but
with respect to all Israelites, including the modern generation.
This is why the Torah repeats אמר ואמרת (*emor ve-amarta*), "Speak
[to the priests] and say to them." Tell the leaders that if they do
the right thing, their successors will learn from their practical
example—not as a result of what they hear, but because of what
they see with their eyes.

The Midrash contains a story showing how a child who has
received a proper education will almost instinctively know how
to make the right decisions. There was a man whose father was
very old, so that he depended upon his son for his every need.
One day the man said to his oldest son, "I am going to visit your

grandfather. Why don't you come with me?" The boy readily agreed, and his father continued, "I am suddenly reminded that your grandfather's suit is getting very shabby. Go and get my old suit from the cupboard, and we shall take it to him."

The father waited and waited, but the son did not return. When he went into the house, the father saw that his son had cut both the trousers and the jacket right down the middle. Angrily, he called out, "What have you done? You have ruined the suit that I wanted to give to your grandfather."

The son looked at him, and said, "I am sorry father, but I had no choice. I was suddenly reminded that one day you too will be old, and when your suit gets shabby, I will want to bring you an old one from the house. So I decided that we should take grandfather half, and that the other half would be left for you."

The father immediately realized how thoughtless he had been. "You were absolutely right," he said to the boy. "Right now we shall first go and buy a new suit for your grandfather, and when I am old, and my suit is worn, you will also bring me a new suit."

The reaction of the son in this story reflects the kind of behavior that can be learned only through practical example. What the Torah wants to teach us in *Parashath Emor* is that it is the example that counts, and that it is their overall experiences, first and foremost within the family circle, but also at school and in the street, that determine the future of our children.

Parashath Be-Har

וכי־ימוך אחיך ומטה ידו עמך והחזקת בו גר ותושב וחי עמך.

"If one of your countrymen becomes poor and is unable to support himself among you, help him as you would an alien or a temporary resident, so that he can continue to live among you."

This next to last portion of the Book of Leviticus deals largely with the subject of redemption—redemption of land, of property, as well as of people who have lost their freedom because they had become poor and had to sell all or part of their property. What the introductory verse of this *parashah* intends to say is that a Jew should never allow the situation of one of his fellowmen to decline so seriously that he falls, and it becomes difficult to put him back upon his feet. In fact, we should start supporting him the moment his position begins to show signs of being shaky, to prevent the decline from getting out of hand.

In fact, this biblical verse provides the foundation for what is generally regarded as the most fundamental and comprehensive of all Jewish virtues, namely גמילות חסדים (*gemiluth chasadim*), to be translated as "bestowal of lovingkindness." In this we include all expressions of care and kindness toward one's fellowman in the broadest sense of the word. *Gemiluth chasadim* is a far broader concept than charity, since charity mainly involves money given to the needy, whereas *gemiluth chasadim* also includes all kinds of services, which may be rendered to poor and rich alike. *Gemilath chesed*, in fact, helps to prevent charity, by removing the underlying cause.

Maimonides, in his *Hilchoth Tzdakah*, writes that there are eight levels of charity, each one more elevated than the next. The highest degree of charity is that which is rendered with the purpose of helping somebody to become independent of charity. For example, a long-term, free loan might enable a family who have had a rough patch as a result of sickness or unemployment to rehabilitate themselves. The same applies to the businessman who helps a struggling young colleague to establish himself by supplying him with contacts. This is what the Torah means when it says והחזקת בו (*ve-hichzakta bo*), help him—help him to stay on his feet, so that he will not fall, and thus become a burden upon himself and society.

It is really surprising to realize that the above commandment dates back thousands of years. It is difficult to say whether the society in those days was inherently riskier than that of today. On one hand there would have been few traffic accidents, while the prevailing religious and social conformity must have prevented many violent crimes. On the other hand, people were unprotected against the vagaries of nature, such as droughts, locust plagues, and crop failures, and the lack of proper medical services resulted in many untimely deaths.

We, who live in the twentieth century, have learned to avoid risks by shifting the accent to prevention. We wear safety belts in our cars, we guard our homes with alarms, we avoid eating certain foods, we submit to periodic medical and dental examinations, and we have savings and pension plans to prepare ourselves for our retirement and the uncertainties of old age.

One of the main modern methods to prevent at least the consequences of an accident or illness is of course insurance. However, insurance policies are intended to avoid our own troubles, whereas the Torah commandment was given to help us prevent the troubles of our fellowman. It is very well that we insure our cars against accidental damage, but does this teach us to respect the rights of fellow road users and pedestrians? Careful driving and road sense, thus preventing accidents, are a far better example of fulfilling the Torah commandment about preventing tragedies to others.

Unfortunately not every tragedy, whether accident, war, poverty, or sickness, can be prevented or insured against. Life will continue to hold surprises, both pleasant and unpleasant. This is as it should be, if only to ensure that we do not lose our awareness of our neighbor. Thank God our society has not lost its sensitivity for those in need. In fact, it would seem that our capacity for sacrifices increases as the situation gets worse. By contrast, the most glaring examples of indifference and neglect can often be encountered during times of prosperity, when people's thoughts are far removed from economic crisis or war, and all they have to do is think of themselves.

Of course, such acts of personal heroism in times of emergency are wonderful and virtuous, but it would be far more beneficial if we could eliminate the need for sacrifices of this kind from the outset. This is the thought expressed in the above-quoted words from *Parashath Be-Har*: "If one of your countrymen... is unable to support himself, help him..., so that he can continue to live among you." Support him while he is still able to stand upon his own feet. In other words—to use a well-known expression—"An ounce of prevention is better than a pound of cure!"

This idea applies of course to all areas of life. How often doesn't it happen that parents are suddenly confronted with a crisis by the delinquency of their children. Whatever the reasons, whether bad company or neglect, such things do not usually happen out of a clear sky. More often than not they could have been prevented by parental care and supervision, and by a more flexible or more authoritarian attitude. Prevention must be timely; it is no use being wise after the event.

Similarly we are aware that both world wars, with all their indescribable horrors, resulted from negligence and a lack of serious effort to stop the rot before things got out of hand. The nations allowed peaceful relations to erode until they were beyond rescue. If all the heroic deeds of soldiers and resistance fighters, as well as all the countless other people who daily risked their lives to print underground papers, or who braved suffering and torture to rescue hostages or act as couriers, could have been marshalled to rescue peace when it could still be saved, our present world would be a far better and more hopeful place.

Does this mean that prevention can avoid all problems? Or that we can—or should—help our fellowmen under all circumstances? What about a situation in which more than one person lays a claim to our support? How, for example, do we solve the shortage of dialysis equipment, and to whom do we allocate the available hospital beds and personnel? Do we give young people preference over the old? But don't old people have families, children, hopes—and memories? The same problem arises with regard to heart transplants and similar costly operations, where the number of patients that can be saved is limited by the technical and financial resources that society can place at our disposal. How do we decide who shall live and who shall die?

And what do we do in a case when we, too, are in serious danger? When we are not only unable to help, but we are confronted with a choice between our life and that of somebody else?

Obviously we are faced here with a serious moral dilemma, for which the Torah commandment to support our neighbor does not seem to provide an answer. Our sages recognized this problem, and the Talmud, in tractate *Baba Metzia*, discusses a hypothetical situation that is directly related to our subject. It describes a situation in which two people are walking in the desert. They are exhausted and thirsty, and one of them has preserved just enough water to ensure his arrival at their destination. However, if he shares this water with his traveling companion, it is almost certain that both of them will die. What must he do—share the water, and temporarily stave off both their deaths, or keep whatever little he has for himself, and have it forever on his conscience that he has caused his companion to perish?

Rabbi Bar Petora is of the opinion that both should drink and take their chances, rather than one of them having to see the other die. Rabbi Akiva disagrees, invoking the Torah verse וחי אחיך עמך (ve-chai achicha imcha), "Your fellow shall live *with* you." He interprets this as meaning that only when you are *both* able to live are you expected to come to your fellow's rescue; if not, "your life comes before that of your fellowman."

How do we understand these two diametrically opposed conclusions of Rabbi Bar Petora and Rabbi Akiva? In order to answer this question, we should realize that in the case under discussion there are three possibilities:

1. to give the water to our companion;
2. to share the water;
3. to drink it all ourself, and thus save our own life.

What these three solutions have in common, however, is that in all cases at least one person will have to die. The only question is who. It would seem that Rabbi Ben Petora had the more emotional approach. We may assume that, given the unavoidable outcome of whatever decision was taken, he would not have gone so far as to accuse the survivor of transgressing the Sixth Commandment, "You shall not murder." However, he was deeply conscious of the psychological consequences for the person who would have drunk all the water, and as a result would have had to witness the death of his friend. Rabbi Ben Petora believed that he would never have been able to forgive himself! This is why he decided that they should both drink.

Rabbi Akiva, however, reasoned that for the owner of the jar to surrender his water to his companion—or even share it— would be tantamount to suicide, which is forbidden under Jewish law. And since sharing the water would be useless, since neither person would survive, the only remaining course was to drink it himself and thus ensure his own life.

Rabbi Akiva's decision was governed by a moral impulse. We

must note that Rabbi Akiva did not mean to say that an individual should not sacrifice his life under any circumstance, as is proven by his own martyrdom at the hand of the Romans, which he welcomed as a unique opportunity to fulfill the precept ואהבת את יהוה אלהיך בכל־לבבך ובכל־נפשך ובכל־מאדך (ve-ahavta eth ha-shem eloheicha be-kol levavecha u-ve-kol nafshecha u-ve-kol me'odecha), "You shall love God with all your heart and with all your soul and with all your strength"—even when he had to pay for this with his life.

Why did Rabbi Akiva use a different yardstick when, rather than the survival of a hypothetical person, his own life was at stake? The answer is simple. It is written ואהבת לרעך כמוך (ve-ahavta eth re'echa kemocha), We shall love our neighbor like ourselves—but not at the price of killing ourselves. This is not selfishness, but basic morality, and—although God may spare us from ever being faced with such an awful choice—it is a morally and emotionally balanced decision.

In all other cases, we must apply what the Torah says in this portion: "If one of your countrymen becomes poor and is unable to support himself, help him... so that he can continue to live among you." Here there is no room for selfishness—not in the Torah, and not in our modern society. We are fortunate that we have been able to eliminate many of the risks that threatened people in biblical times. Even so, there are still more than enough uncertainties left, so that the biblical precept about preventive support for our fellow in need has not lost any of its urgency or topicality.

Parashath Be-Chukotai

אם־בחקתי תלכו ואת־מצותי תשמרו ועשיתם אתם: ונתתי
גשמיכם בעתם ונתנה הארץ יבולה ועץ השדה יתן פריו.

"If you follow my decrees and are careful to keep my
commandments, and do them, I will send you rain in its
season, and the ground will yield its crops, and the trees of
the field their fruit."

The Midrash comments that it is strange that the Torah,
after exhorting us to follow God's decrees, and to keep His
commandments, should then add: "and *do* them." Doesn't one
include the other? Aren't "following" and "keeping" the same as
"doing"?

The answer is that we are arequired not only to accept the
commandments but to perform them in an active and practical
way. It is possible, theoretically, to keep the commandments of
the Torah in the spirit, by agreeing with them, and by thinking
and theorizing about them. However, the words "and *do* them,"
stress that for a Jew, intentions are not good enough, and that
what is required are מצות מעשיות (*mitzvoth ma'asioth*), in other words
the practice of the commandments. Rather than being a specula-
tive faith, Judaism requires positive action—and this applies not
only to the religious commandments, but to all other aspects of
our lives.

To illustrate the idea that is expressed in the above Midrash,
we may indeed take a look at our everyday existence. Suppose
we ask someone who has worked hard most of his life, and who
seems physically and mentally exhausted, what he would most

like to do during his remaining years. The odds are that his answer will be something like: "So far my life has been one continuous grind; getting up early, rushing off to work, going here and there, with only an occasional brief holiday and hardly a moment to think of myself. If I could drop my work tomorrow, there is nothing I would like better than to relax—to sleep late, to take my time to eat, to go where I want and when I want, without anybody telling me what to do, and without having to plan my day."

There must be many people who think like this, and yet I am convinced that they are making a big mistake. The fact is that work and responsibility are an integral—and essential—part of our life. Not, however, in the sense of a punishment, because it says in the Torah that "by the sweat of our brow we will eat our food," but because we cannot exist unless we have a purpose in life. Work gives us not only a purpose, but also self-esteem. The moment someone feels he is no longer important and of some use to other people, he risks losing his motivation—not only the motivation to help others, but the will and desire to look after himself. In Psalm 128 we read: יגיע כפיך כי תאכל אשריך וטוב לך (yagia kapeicha ki tochel ashreicha ve-tov lecha), "You will eat the fruit of your labor, and you will be happy, and all shall be well with you." Our sages asked themselves about the meaning of this duplication of "happiness," and "well-being," and they answered, "When you enjoy the fruit of your labor, you will be happy in this world, and well in the next."

This applies to people of all ages, but also—and in particular—to people who have retired from a busy working life. It is a well-known fact that a disproportionate number of people die very shortly after their retirement. It seems that the sudden termination of a life-long routine, and the lack of an alternative occupation—be it part-time work, a hobby, or some voluntary communal activity—can be a traumatic shock for the human system. Another well-known and proven observation is that elderly patients, even those who suffer from a so-called "incurable" disease, have a much better chance of prolonging their life as long as they feel that they have a purpose, and there is something they can look forward to.

After the above explanation, it should be clear what is meant by the verse with which we opened this *parashah*: "...be careful to keep my commandments, and do them." To understand the commandments, and in order to have the strength to perform them—or any other useful activity—we must have a purpose. If we understand and enjoy the commandments, and observe them with determination and conviction, we can surmount every difficulty, but if we regard them as only a philosophical ideal, let alone as senseless or burdensome, we weaken ourselves and thereby increase our chances of breakdown and failure.

There is a story about a man who had worked very hard all his life to build his small workshop into a thriving factory. He became wealthy, and at a given moment decided that it was useless to continue working in order to earn even more money. So he retired and, not having any other hobbies or preferences, decided to devote his remaining days to leisure and enjoyment. He divided his property among his children, leaving enough for himself to fulfill his every whim or fancy.

Two years later he had become a changed person; he had fallen into a depression, he hardly talked, and he had completely lost his appetite. His family was seriously worried about his health. The eldest son consulted a physician, but after a thorough physical examination had yielded negative results, the father eventually agreed to submit himself to psychotherapy. Soon afterwards he confided to his therapist that his sleep was disturbed by wild dreams about being forcibly fed a diet of dry, tasteless, and undigestible food, without any salt or sugar. So realistic was the sensation, that the taste—or rather the lack of it—stayed in his mouth the whole day, completely spoiling his appetite for any normal food. Following this, the psychologist concluded that the man felt superfluous, and that the thought of being useless was ruining his life. He contacted the man's children and told them that if they wanted their father to get well, they should once more let him take an active part in running his business. They followed his advice, and after a short time the man was cured, and ate and slept as soundly as before.

Job said אדם לעמל יולד (adam le-amal yevaled), "Man is born to work." Without purposeful activity, life merely means existence. There is a saying in the Talmud, in tractate Shabbath, according to which זקני עם הארץ כל זמן שמזקינים דעתם מתטרפת עליהם; זקני תלמידי חכמים כל זמן שמזקינים דעתם מתישבת עליהם (ziknei am-ha-aretz kol zeman she-mazkinim da'atam metarefeth aleihem; ziknei talmidei ha-chachamim kol zeman she-mazkinim da'atam mityasheveth aleihem), "The older untutored old men become, the sillier they are; the older scholarly old men become, the steadier their mind." Here, again, we see that the word "retirement" should by no means be taken literally, and that it would be very unwise to regard the end of gainful employment as the signal for mental or physical idleness.

In light of the above, we understand why the noted first-century tanna (a sage from the time of the Mishnah) Rabbi Nehunyah Ben ha-Kanah used to pray every time he left the Beth ha-Midrash: "I thank You, God, that You have set my portion with those who sit in the houses of study and in synagogues, and not with those who sit in theaters and circuses." Rabbi Nehunyah strengthened and enriched himself from day to day, whereas those who were merely chasing pleasures became weaker and poorer because they were aimless.

This concept of study is taken so far that people who exercise their minds should never worry about the purpose, or the value, of their efforts. The Torah says: אלה הדברים אשר אנכי מצוך לעשות היום (eleh ha-devarim asher anochi metzavecha la'asoth ha-yom), "These are the things I want you to do today." Once again the emphasis is on doing, and our interpreters explain that this means we should not worry about the results of our efforts. The activity contains its own reward, in that it prevents the mind from becoming sluggish and deteriorating. Whether there is a visible result or not, or if much of what is learned is soon forgotten, is irrelevant to the purpose. Our obligation is to do; as regards the outcome, God assures us that we may leave that to Him.

This is the meaning of the verse from *Parashath Be-Chukotai*: אם־בחקותי תלכו ... ועשיתם אתם (*im be-chukotai telechu... va-asitem otam*). Following God's decrees by doing them is the best way to assure ourselves both longevity and happiness.

Parashath Be-Midbar

וידבר יהוה אל־משה במדבר סיני באהל מועד באחד לחודש
השני בשנה השנית לצאתם מארץ מצרים לאמר: שאו את־ראש
כל־עדת בני־ישראל למשפחתם לבית אבתם . . .

"And God spoke to Moses in the Tent of Meeting in the
Desert of Sinai on the first day of the second month of the
second year after the Israelites came out of Egypt. He said:
'Take a census of the whole Israelite community by their
clans and families....'"

According to the Midrash, God counted the Children of
Israel every now and then because they were dear to Him. For
instance, He counted them when they left Egypt (the Torah
states that there were "about six hundred thousand men on
foot, besides women and children"), and He counted them after
thousands had been killed because of the sin of the Golden Calf,
to see how many of them were left.

In the present case, at the beginning of the second year after
the Exodus, God told Moses to take a census of the Israelites to
raise their morale and to remind them of the promise He had
made to Abraham, to make his descendants "as numerous... as
the sand on the seashore." As a matter of fact, in the Talmud, in
tractate *Yoma*, our sages refer to a verse in the Book of Hosea, in
which God says by the mouth of the prophet: "Yet the number
of the Israelites will be like the sand on the seashore, which
cannot be measured or counted." It is pointed out that this verse
contains an inner contradiction: "the number of the Israelites"
suggests something finite, which—at least theoretically—can

be counted. Yet the prophet continues with the words, "which cannot be measured or counted." Our sages answer that the two parts of the quotation refer to two different situations. Whenever the Jewish people do God's will, they become so numerous that they cannot be counted, but when they disobey, their numbers automatically decrease to a point where they can be counted.

There is another interpretation, but for this we first have to enter in somewhat more detail into the concept and the meaning of counting as such. For what reason, or purpose, did God ask Moses to count the Jewish people? Surely G-d knew how many Jews there were? Apart from this, we usually count the things of which we like to have a lot, such as money, in the hope that we shall find more than we expected. In the case of the Jewish people, however, God was not so much interested in their numbers as in their quality. After all, the Torah states specifically that God chose the Jews because they were a small nation. There must have been a very important reason why God time and again wanted to count the Jewish people, and the answer is that it was the *act of counting*, rather than the numerical outcome, that was important. The counting was to be a guide for the Jewish people on how to behave among themselves. There are two ways of counting: according to value, or according to number. Human society is "departmentalized," in the same way as, to mention just some examples, there are differences between animals, plants, or money. Just as there are wild and tame animals, or large and small animals, and in the same way as there are flowers, grasses, shrubs, and trees, or coins and bills in all kinds of different denominations, we can subdivide people by, for example, professions, intellect, or wealth. People who handle money are interested only in absolute values, and thus the bank teller or supermarket cashier carefully sorts coins and bills according to denomination. There simply is no other way — where money is concerned.

The Jewish people, on the other hand, were counted

together, as equal individuals. Even with money, certain denominations are counted together because they have the same value. So it was with the Jews, except that there was only one "denomination." God wanted the Jewish people to be counted collectively, as equals, instead of as groups divided by status, rank, or intelligence. The counting symbolized their equality, and therefore also their responsibility for each other. This has been the Jewish tradition from time immemorial, and in this respect the Jews might well be the most democratic nation on earth. When we look at the *tallith*-shrouded figures on the *bimah* during the Torah reading in the synagogue, we cannot know that one person might be a rabbi or a millionaire, and the other a shoemaker or a bookkeeper. This only goes to show that God does not distinguish between scholars and *amei ha-aretzim* (simple, or uneducated people) or between the rich and the poor.

There is a story about a simple man who asked his rabbi whether he could be considered as valuable from a human and Jewish point of view as the learned and influential people in the community. The rabbi, rather a snob, indicated that actually he was not quite his equal. At which the simpleton asked, "Does this mean, Rabbi, that nine people as learned as you would be sufficient to make a *minyan?*"

"Of course not," the rabbi replied, "under any and all circumstances ten is the minimum."

"I see, Rabbi," came the reaction, "then ten people like me can make a minyan."

The rabbi took the point!

From a Jewish point of view not only a simpleton but even a sinner is a Jew, and therefore continues to be counted with everybody else; today his behavior may deserve censure, or even punishment, but tomorrow he may have changed. Here we have the other way of explaining the talmudic commentary on the earlier quoted words of the prophet Hosea: "Yet the number of the Israelites will be like the sand on the seashore, which cannot be measured or counted." God is not interested in counting quantity, but in quality, and when the Jewish people go in His ways, their collective value rises to a point where it can no longer be measured. But even if they do not, enough value remains to enable it to be counted.

King David said in Psalm 104: יתמו חטאים מן־הארץ ורשעים עוד אינם (yitamu chata'im min ha-aretz u-resha'im od einam), "But may sinners vanish from the earth and the wicked be no more." The Talmud states that the way to virtue is paved by the removal of sin, rather than the sinner, from the world. The Jewish ethic does not require the sinner to be cast out, since he retains his innate capacity to choose between good and evil, and any time he decides to change his way of life, he is redeemed and his sins no longer exist. For this reason we pray that God will take away the sins, and not the sinners. This is what God intended to impart to the Jewish people when He instructed Moses to count them. Because He loved the Jewish people, he wanted to raise their morale, to let them know that they were all equally valuable to Him, regardless of status or position, or whether they were guilty or innocent, and that they could always be proud to form a part of the Jewish people.

Our sages add that the Torah was given in the desert, to the accompaniment of thunder and lightning and a violent trembling of the earth. These phenomena signified that no ordinary occurence was taking place. According to the Midrash, the nations of the world came to Balaam and said, "Why should the Jews receive a faith? What do we need another religion for, when it will only cause more upheaval, more coercion, and more bloodshed?" But Balaam answered, "Don't worry, this will be a faith without אש ומים (esh va-mayim), without fire and water." The Torah was given amid fire and water to signify that it would never be imposed by violent means.

The second notable aspect is that the Torah was given in the desert. The desert does not belong to anybody, and the same applies to the Torah. Although the Torah was placed in the charge of the Jews, God wanted it to be clear that the Torah was

for everyone—regardless of race or nationality—who was prepared to accept it, and that nobody should claim it as his exclu-
sive property. As regards this, it is interesting to read King
Solomon's prayer at the dedication of the Temple in Jerusalem,
when he said:

> As for the foreigner who does not belong to Your
> people Israel, but has come from a distant land because of
> Your name—for men will hear of Your great name and
> Your mighty hand and Your outstretched arm—when he
> comes and prays toward this Temple, then hear from
> heaven, Your dwelling place, and do whatever the for-
> eigner asks of You, so that all the peoples of the earth may
> know Your name and fear You, as do Your own people
> Israel, and may know that this House I have built bears
> Your name.

The Torah laid the foundation for freedom, justice, and
equality among Jews and Gentiles alike—including sinners and
criminals.

This latter point can be illustrated by one particular *halachic*
rule—only one of many similar rules—dealing with civil trial
procedure. When the Sanhedrin tried a suspect, and found him
to be guilty, but there was one person in the court—even an
ordinary person, not necessarily a law student or a rabbi—who
believed that the sentence was a miscarriage of justice, it was his
duty to rise and argue in the defense of the accused. Not to do so
was considered a sin. All this follows from the Torah principle
that every person is a part of God, because he was born in His
image. We therefore have to distinguish between two things:
the right of society to remove a criminal from its midst, to
prevent him from doing further harm, and the right of the
condemned person to protection as a human being created in
God's image.

The Book of Numbers is the fourth of the Five Books of
Moses. The first, Genesis, relates the story of the creation. The
second, Exodus, records how the Jews became a nation and

received the Torah, to show the world the way to justice and freedom. The third book, Leviticus, focuses on the priests and the sacrificial laws and teaches us the distinction between "the holy and the profane, and the pure and the impure." Without these laws no orderly society would be possible. The fourth book, Numbers, of which the present *parashah* is the first portion, relates the wanderings of the Israelites in the desert. Its commandments, contrary to the cultic and sacrificial commandments in Leviticus, deal to a large extent with the relations between man and his fellow. The Torah's "bill of rights," according to which all people are counted together, signifying their equality, therefore typically belongs in this volume. Deuteronomy, the fifth and last book of the Torah, is essentially Moses' repetition of all the foregoing, and as such its message is that if indeed we listen to the Torah and heed its commandments, also in the human and personal sphere, every person will feel his value enhanced. If someone knows that he is important, his morale will be boosted, and he will give his best, to the benefit of society and himself.

Parashath Naso

וידבר יהוה אל־משה לאמר: דבר אל־אהרן ואל־בניו לאמר כה
תברכו את־בני ישראל אמור להם: יברכך יהוה וישמרך: יאר
יהוה פניו אליך ויחנך: ישא יהוה פניו אליך וישם לך שלום.

"And God said to Moses, 'Tell Aaron and his sons, "This is
how you are to bless the Israelites. Say to them, 'The Lord
bless you and keep you; the Lord make His face to shine
upon you and be gracious to you; the Lord turn His face
toward you and give you peace.'"'"

The Midrash records a discussion between Rabbi Yehudah
and his colleagues on the commandment of the priestly blessing,
in which they ask themselves what made the Jewish people
deserve this important privilege of being blessed by the *cohanim*.
Rabbi Yehudah maintains that the blessing is a consequence of
the greatness of Abraham, since it was Abraham who received
God's promise that his children would become a great nation,
through whom all the nations on earth would be blessed.

The other rabbis, however, are of the opinion that the Jewish
people owe the privilege to the patriarch Jacob, and they refer to
the Torah, where God commands Moses: כה תברכו את בני ישראל (*koh
tevarechu eth benei yisrael*), "So shall you bless the children of Jacob."

Actually, the most interesting aspect of the above midrash is
why this discussion between the rabbis took place at all, for
nowhere else in the Talmud or Midrash do we find our sages
discussing what entitled the Jewish people to some *mitzvah* or
other, such as the Shabbath, the *sukkah*, or any of the other
commandments.

The answer is that Rabbi Yehudah and his fellow rabbis were

220

not discussing the entitlement of the Jewish people to the blessing as such, but the question what they had done to deserve a priestly class like the *cohanim*, who expressed their devotion to their people by blessing them every day. The discussion was, therefore, not about the *mitzvah* of the blessing, but about the privilege of having this kind of *cohanim*.

Here, indeed, was an unusual aspect, in which the Jewish people differed from many other societies. Most priests and ministers of the dominant world religions have traditionally occupied positions of great prestige and power within—and even outside—their respective religious communities. In Western civilization, the cultural environment with which we are most familiar, the Church has for over fifteen hundred years exercised considerable social and political influence. Kings used to be the nominal heads and protectors of the national Church—in Great Britain this is still the case today—and thanks to this cooperation between the worldly and ecclesiastical authorities, the Church was able not only to amass great wealth but to control the lives of individuals in both worldly and religious affairs. In passing we might mention that in particular the Jews and other "heretics" for many centuries suffered from the autocratic behavior of priests, bishops, and popes.

By and large this situation persisted until well into the twentieth century. Only after World War II did the traditional Church in many countries lose some of its power, although in many other countries new forms of religion have sprung up that in many cases approach, and sometimes even exceed, the bounds of exploitation of the believers. We only have to mention the "television ministries," and all kinds of Western and Oriental cults, whose operations resemble giant commercial enterprises, and whose leaders own extensive properties and fly in private airplanes, paid for by the "voluntary" contributions of their members. Simultaneously their sheer mass and lobbying power enable them to exercise considerable political influence.

Only against this background do we begin to realize how

different was the situation of the Jewish priesthood. On one hand, the *cohanim* were a hereditary class, but this status, instead of forming the basis for a powerful vested interest, circumscribed their power and ability to amass property and wealth. According to our sages, Moses told Aaron and the elders of the people in the name of God, לא שררה אני נותן לכם אלא עבדות אני נותן לכם (*lo serara ani noten lachem ele aveduth ani noten lachem*), "I did not intend you to dominate [the Jewish people], but to serve them." Another example of this difference between the Jewish priesthood and that of other religions is that God purposely excluded the tribe of the Levites from owning land. When Eretz Israel was divided among the twelve tribes, only the Levites were not allotted any territory. They did, of course, have to reside somewhere, so a number of "levitical cities" were designated, scattered throughout the territories of the other tribes, to serve as residential and administrative centers for the Levites. For the rest they owned no worldly property, their subsistence being derived entirely from the תרומות ומעשרות (*terumoth u-ma'aseroth*), to be translated as "contributions and tithes," mainly in the form of agricultural staples such as grain, wine, and oil, but also cattle, which the people brought to the priests and Levites.

Whereas the *cohanim*—the direct descendants of Aaron— were responsible for the service in the Sanctuary, the Levites— the progeny of the remaining members of the tribe of Levi—fulfilled a large variety of secondary tasks, both in the Sanctuary and outside it. The Levites were the main contacts between the priesthood and the general population. According to numerous descriptions in our rabbinical literature, Eretz Israel was divided into districts, and each district had a number of Levites whose specific responsibility was to make the rounds of the villages and towns, not only to collect the *terumoth*, but also to maintain contact with the general population and to attend to its social and spiritual needs. Conversely, when a resident of, for example, Galilee or the Sharon district went to Jerusalem, he would find the Levites there as helpers and hosts.

This leads us to another characteristic difference between the Jewish priesthood and that of other faiths: whereas in most cultures the priest traditionally represented the establishment, and therefore sided with the ruling powers, the Jewish priesthood was always on the side of the people, with whom it maintained close daily contact.

This is also evident from the way the *cohanim* blessed. Every priest was expected to bless the Israelites every morning before the start of his daily activities in the Sanctuary. The blessing was pronounced from a special raised platform, called the דוכן (*duchan*), which explains the term "duchenen," as the pronunciation of the priestly blessing in the synagogue is often called. Before pronouncing the blessing the *cohen* made a special *berachah*, which ended with the words, ...אשר קדשנו במצוותיו לברך את עמו ישראל באהבה (...*asher kideshanu be mitzvotav levarech eth amo yisrael be-ahavah*), "...to bless his people Israel *with love*." According to *halachah*, the priest had to love the people in order to be able to bless them; blessing without love was regarded as a ברכה לבטלה (*berachah le-batalah*), literally a "blessing in vain," but in effect a profanation of God's name. Rabbi Kook, the former chief rabbi of Eretz Israel, himself a *cohen*, whose life and thoughts were a shining example of love for his people, was of the opinion that this obligation to love rested on every Jewish leader, and not merely on the *cohanim*; according to him, anyone who felt himself unequal to this responsibility should not attempt to undertake leadership.

Yet another interesting aspect is the fact that the priestly blessing, consisting of six strophes, forms a short paragraph right in the middle of *Parashath Naso*. Not only is this *parashah* one of the longest portions of the Torah, but the priestly blessing appears almost suddenly among all kinds of other verses of a far more technical and prosaic nature, such as the ones dealing with the arrangement and purity of the camp, the numbering of the Levite clans, and details about the sacrifices at the dedication of the Sanctuary. A commandment as important as the priestly blessing could almost get lost in such a long *parashah*, and it certainly creates the risk of detracting from its importance.

In addition, *Parashath Shemini*, one of the portions before *Naso*, already contains the sentence וישא אהרן את־ידיו אל־העם ויברכם (*va-yisa aharon eth yadav el-ha-am va-yevarchem*): "....then Aaron lifted his hands toward the people and blessed them." However, the kind of blessing that Aaron pronounced is not mentioned at this point, and one of our interpreters, the thirteenth-century Rabbi Gershom, explains that in *Parashath Shemini* Aaron did not bless the Israelites because he was commanded to, but as a more or less spontaneous act, because he loved them.

Here, in *Parashath Naso*, however, we are talking about an obligation on the part of the *cohanim* to bless. It is by no means unusual for priests to bless their flock, but at the same time it is very often not their first task that comes to mind. Often priests are much sooner associated with issuing instructions and enforcing religious discipline than with service and subservience. The priests who served in the Sanctuary pronounced their blessing before they embarked upon their serious duties for the day, in other words before they became preoccupied by their other tasks. This was to ensure that they could focus their complete attention upon the people who were assembled before them. Often when people do the same thing day after day, the task becomes routine and boring, and here was one responsibility God did not want to be performed automatically. Looking at the *berachah* the *cohanim* pronounced prior to their blessing, we see that the words "who has commanded us" are in the plural, whereas the words "*his* people Israel" are in the singular. This shows that the blessing had to be an individual blessing rather than some formal and collective ritual act. Surveying the people from his raised platform enabled the priest to see them as individuals and to realize that he was not dealing with a crowd. This helped the priest to feel that every Jew was an individual who had to be taken care of, and whose problems were also the *cohen*'s concern. After giving his blessing in this way, the rest of the *cohen*'s daily work could not be automatic, and he would remain conscious of his duties to the people during the day.

The above helps us to understand why the Torah emphasizes that אהרון ובניו עשו כאשר צוה יהוה (*aharon ve-banav asu ka-asher tsiva ha-shem*), "Aaron and his sons *did* as God asked him." Why does the Torah stress this? Is there any reason to doubt that Aaron or his sons would not act in accordance with God's instructions? The answer is that the *cohanim* did not act routinely, but in the way God expected of them, namely by serving the Jews as individuals, and *be-ahavah*, with love. Their blessing came from the heart. This also means that they did not restrict themselves to a blessing with words only, but that they followed up what they promised in their daily work, which is, of course, a necessity for a blessing to be turned into reality.

There is a story about the great nineteenth-century Rabbi Israel Salanter, the founder of the *Musar* ("morality") movement in Eastern Europe, according to which a very troubled woman came to him to pour out her heart. As was his custom, Rabbi Salanter listened patiently, and when she was finished, he blessed her, saying that he would pray to God to help her. Following this, he expected the woman to leave, but she refused to budge. Rabbi Salanter asked her whether there was anything else she wanted.

"Yes," she said. "Tell me, Rabbi, when one of your family has a problem, do you bless them?"

"Of course," Rabbi Salanter answered.

"And what else do you do?" the woman continued.

"Well," Rabbi Salanter said, "of course I try to do everything that I can to help practically, too."

To which the woman replied, "That is what I am waiting for, Rabbi, please *do* something."

From this, Rabbi Salanter said, he learned that it is not sufficient to leave it at words. The Torah says: וישא אהרן את־ידיו

אל־העם (ve-yisa aharon eth yadav el-ha-am), "Aaron raised his hands to the people." He used his hands to help, not just his mouth to bless.

This is the answer to the discussion between the rabbis to which we referred at the beginning. They were asking, to what the Jews owed this important privilege of having cohanim who, rather than boss their flock around, looked after their people; priests who, rather than look after their own interests or those of their patrons, cared for their people and blessed them with love. In other nations priests were elected or appointed by the ruler; they were seldom independent, and this could not fail to be reflected in their behavior. Also the striving for power and influence all too easily resulted in corruption and personal enrichment. The Jewish priestly function, by contrast, was hereditary, and the cohanim were by definition excluded from possessing property or wealth. Which other nation had priests who did not own material goods, and who for this reason alone could not raise themselves above the ordinary people—except when standing on the duchan, from which they blessed them?

During the blessing the cohanim stretched out their hands to the people. There is an interesting symbolism in this gesture, in the sense that when we stretch out our hands toward someone, people can see whether our hands are clean, or whether we have anything to hide. This teaches us that a prior condition to all prayer and spiritual meditation is to have "clean hands" and demonstrate correct moral behavior. One without the other would be a mockery and invalidate the act. The Talmud, in tractate Megillah, states that a cohen who has a defect on his hands is not fit to pronounce the benediction. This, too, has to be understood in both a literal and a symbolic sense. The cohen had to be physically perfect in order to participate in the service, but in the symbolic sense it meant that if his hands were not "clean"—in other words, if his record or his reputation was blemished—he was considered unfit to lead others. The cohanim had to be spotless, both in their private and public lives, in order

to be able to lead a nation that was intended by God to be an
עם סגולה (am segulah), an "exceptional nation."

Finally, apart from the importance of their personal behavior, the *cohanim* were intended to be an example. In a sense they
acted as role models for all other leaders. In the final analysis
people cannot be better than those who stand above them.
When these leaders are selfish and corrupt, how can we expect
the nation as a whole to be any better? Now we understand why
the mission with which God charged the *cohanim*, to bless their
people with love, was so important for our Jewish survival, both
as a *mitzvah* and as an example for instilling ethics and morale in
the Jewish people.

Parashath Be-Ha'alotcha

וידבר יהוה אל־משה לאמר: דבר אל־אהרון ואמרת אליו
בהעלתך את־הנרות אל־מול פני המנורה יאירו שבעת הנרות.

"God said to Moses, 'Speak to Aaron and say to him,
"When you set up the seven lamps, they are to light the
front of the lampstand."'"

The candelabrum in the Sanctuary consisted of a central
shaft bearing three branches on each side, giving seven lamps in
all. "Setting up" the lamps meant that the lights had to be
kindled until the flames ascended of themselves, and in such a
way that the flames on the six branches lit up the central shaft.
Our sages say that the central shaft had to be lit up in order that
people should not say that "God was in want of its light."

According to the Midrash the Jewish people asked God,
"Why do you want us to light the candelabrum to provide a light
for You—when You Yourself and Your entire creation are
light? What can the light of this tiny candelabrum do for You?"
To which God answered, "Indeed, I do not need your light for
Myself. The flames of the candles are meant for you, to enable
you to demonstrate to the entire world that you are ready to
light the way to a better and brighter way of life." So far the
Midrash.

To enable us to understand this verse from the Torah, and
the connected midrash, we must take the idea of spreading light
in the wider sense of the dissemination of not only light but
"enlightenment," i.e. knowledge. In the same way as the flames
of the *menorah* in the Sanctuary had to be directed toward God,

both "enlightenment" and knowledge can bear fruit only if they are directed toward a purpose.

Some might say that we are suffering from an overdose of enlightenment, and that the world was a happier place when mankind was more ignorant. However, knowledge as such is not the culprit, and neither are the teachings of Moses against the study and dissemination of any kind of knowledge about whatever science or worldly experience. This also means, of course, that Judaism welcomes all kinds of inventions that enable man to make his life easier and more comfortable.

Nor are our Jewish beliefs opposed to research into the nature of our world or the universe. The proposition of the sixteenth-century astronomer Copernicus that the earth revolved around the sun, and the moon around the earth, shattered the age-old belief that our world was the center of the universe, which in turn caused a profound scientific and philosophical revolution. In particular the Church was unable to come to terms with this idea, and in Italy the hapless Galileo Galilei, who supported the Copernican theory, was forced to recant his views in a degrading public ceremony. Judaism, on the other hand, did not have—and will never have—any problem with the Copernican theory or similar astronomical issues. From a traditional Jewish religious and philosophical point of view it simply is not important whether the sun revolves around the earth, or the reverse.

Another example of this problem is the popular discussion about the date of the Creation. According to our Jewish tradition the world was created 5748 years ago at the date of writing, the year 1988. Scientists will tell us, however, that they have discovered fossil remains of plants and animals that are millions of years old. We also have skeletal parts of human beings who must have walked the earth 100,000 years ago. Doesn't this contradict the Jewish orthodox view of the Creation? Not in the least—for the simple reason that *Torath Yisrael* does not necessarily talk in the language of our secular calendar. When in

Be-Reshith we read ויהי־ערב ויהי־בקר יום אחד (*va-yehi erev va-yehi boker yom echad*), "And there was evening, and there was morning—one day," we are not talking about our day on earth, but about God's day. To illustrate this, we may refer to the unforgettable experience of the first astronauts, when they observed our earth from the depth of space. In the midst of this vast emptiness, in which the light of the universe was evenly diffused without throwing shadows anywhere, they suddenly realized that they were dealing with an entirely new dimension, in which light and dark, and day and night, as they had always known it, had absolutely no meaning. We, earthlings, experience what we call day and night as a result of a purely physical phenomenon, the earth's rotation relative to the sun. The moment we leave the earth, concepts such as day and night take on an entirely different meaning. There, out in space, it suddenly becomes impossible to talk about a conventional day or a conventional night. This is why, when we read, "And there was evening, and there was morning—one day," we are talking about days and nights as defined by God.

In other words, as far as Judaism is concerned, no scientific discovery is capable of bringing us into conflict with our faith. But, we could ask, if everything is acceptable and explainable, then what do we need our faith for? Isn't Judaism intended to provide solutions to the mysteries of our existence and all those other questions for which there are no normal answers? This week's portion, *Parashath Be-Ha'alotcha*, helps us to receive an answer.

It is an undeniable fact that man has achieved a lot in the course of the relatively short period of civilized existence. Looking around us, we are amazed at the almost unbelievable things we are able to do, and the incredible comforts we have created, even when compared with the generation of our grandparents.

Yet, taking all these blessings into account, it is surprising that our present generation is not much happier and more carefree than that of our grandparents—not to speak of people who lived several centuries ago. How primitive and perilous were their circumstances. Only a hundred years ago the majority of people performed hard, physical labor; many of them never ate a square meal; women and children died in childbirth, and infectious diseases carried off a large percentage of the survivors at a premature age. Transportation was slow, and communications almost nonexistent; leaving one's country was tantamount to saying farewell to one's relatives for life. The industrial civilization, which after many centuries followed the agricultural era, has almost run its course; we have entered the postindustrial era, dominated by services and clean, technology-intensive occupations. People live much longer, the work week is being cut, and an ever-smaller percentage of workers will be able to provide for a steadily expanding class of senior citizens and other nonproductive groups. Who could have dreamed—not a thousand, but a hundred years ago—that it would be possible to heat or cool a house at the press of a button, launder and dry clothes without even looking at them, or meet relatives across the ocean less than a day after leaving our home? What would our grandparents have said if, instead of time and again seeing their precious food spoiled, they had learned that it can be stored away, for a year in necessary.

In short, with so many opportunities for luxury, comfort, and enjoyment, why is it that we are not happy, not grateful? Why do we feel oppressed and depressed, and why do we have that hunger inside, as if there is someone sitting inside us, who prevents us from enjoying life?

God told Moses to instruct the cohanim: "When you light the seven lamps, see to it that the wicks of the six branches are turned toward the central shaft." This means that all the flames had to be focused on one important, central point. Not the lighting was important, but where the light shone. In the same way, any human knowledge and any human inventions can bring happiness only if they are "directed toward" something, and if they are used for the purpose for which God created them. This is the meaning of the midrash about the sages who asked God why He wanted the lights we kindle to shine toward Him, when He Himself was the source and center of all light God answered that indeed He did not either want or need the light for Himself, but that if we did not direct our light our energy and our knowledge—toward something, we would surely waste it. "The light has to be before Me," God said, "to remind you—and through you all the world—of the way I have shown you, and that everything you do has to have a purpose. Only then will you be able to enjoy it."

The above also enables us to understand the meaning of what the Torah says later on in the same portion: ויהי בנסע הארן משניאיך מפניך (va-yehi be-nesoa ha-aron va-yomer moshe kumah ha-shem ve-yafutsu oivecha va-yanusu mesaneycha mi-peneycha), "Whenever the Ark set out, Moses said, 'Rise up, O Lord! May your enemies be scattered; may your foes flee before you.'" This is followed by the verse: ובנחה יאמר שובה יהוה רבבות אלפי ישראל (u-venuchoh yomer shuva ha-shem rivavoth alfei yisrael), "Whenever it [the Ark] came to rest, he said, 'Return, O Lord, to the countless thousands of Israel.'"

Two situations are pictured: one where the Jewish people, with the Ark at their head, were on the move, and another where the Ark rested, a situation of seeming tranquility. The explanation is connected with the differences between the Jewish people and other nations in terms of their history and existential experience. Most people like to look ahead and plan their decisions, in order to eliminate uncertainties wherever possible. In reality, however, this proves to be a difficult if not hopeless task. There are a myriad of external circumstances that we cannot control, and even if we know what we want, the implementation of our intentions depends upon other people, and we do not know how they will react. The same applies to our children. Every parent wants to plan his children's future, but ability, environment, and a thousand other chance circumstances can make this future take a different direction. In the same way as individuals plan, so do nations and societies, and much of a nation's morale depends upon the outcome. The more successful it is, the higher its morale: economic, technological, and military successes result in buoyancy; backwardness, unemployment, and defeat produce depression and malaise.

The history of the Jewish people has traditionally shown the same, except that their reaction has been different. During periods of national flourishing and political and economic power and prosperity, the nation sooner or later became spoiled and its resolve softened. On the other hand, some of the most shining examples of character, creativity, and morale date from periods of depression and oppression. Economic deprivation and persecution have proved to bring out traits of spiritual creativity, generosity, and unselfishness that often were absent in times of affluence. The lesson is that the potential greatness of the Jewish people does not lie in its material culture but in its spiritual and ethical development. This is what Moses indicated with his juxtaposition of the Ark when it "set out" (in other words traveled ahead of the people and had to be defended against potential enemies) and when it "rested" (because there were no enemies about and the people felt safe). When the Ark was forced to move from place to place, because the Jewish people were on the move, and their lives were insecure, Moses was not worried, and he confidently declared that "God will scatter our enemies." But the moment the Ark rested, the Israelites became complacent, and Moses asked God to "bring back the countless thousands of Israel" who threatened to get lost.

The same lesson applies in our modern age: the moment Jews are under pressure, they shows their true grit. They band together, and their mutual solidarity and devotion helps to pull them through. However contradictory this sounds, it is during times of oppression and persecution that the risk of disintegration of the Jewish people is slightest. As long as our people retain their identity and purpose, individuals may become tired of the

practice of Judaism, but at the first sign of trouble their conscience is reawakened and they rejoin the fold. At this point
people know where to find God, who is never far away, and He
helps to "scatter their enemies."

But when the Ark "rests"—when the Jewish people are
settled and secure—then the people begin to draw away, and
this creates a danger to our survival. This is the situation to
which Moses' call applies: "Return, O Lord, to the countless
thousands of Israel," to save all those who are threatened to be
lost because of assimilation and indifference.

Now we understand what God meant in this portion: as long
as everybody lights his own flame, and we allow the lights to be
scattered in all directions, we will remain unfulfilled and vulnerable. But when we light the candelabrum toward Him, in other
words, if we remain mindful of the purpose for which God gave
us His light—in the broadest sense of the word—and keep our
flames turned toward Him, we will not only survive, but experience happiness and contentment in the process.

Parashath Shelach Lecha

שלח לך אנשים ויתרו את־הארץ כנען אשר־אני נתן לבני
ישראל איש אחד איש אחד למטה אבתיו תשלחו כל נשיא בהם.

"Send people to spy out the land of Canaan. Of every tribe
of their fathers shall you send a man, every one a prince
among them."

It was about a year after their departure from Egypt. The
Jewish people had crossed the Sinai desert, and they were now
standing at the gates of the Promised Land. At this point God
told Moses to take one representative of each of the twelve
tribes to spy out the land.

Before we go into details about what happened to these
spies, we should compare this verse with a similar verse in
another part of the Torah, the first chapter of the Book of
Devarim, and try to explain what looks like a difference between
the two. In Devarim, Moses says to the Jewish people, "You
came to me, every one of you, and said, 'Let us send men before
us, that they search the land for us.'" This means that the people
asked for the spies to be sent, whereas in this portion of the
week, *Parashath Shelach*, it is told that God told Moses to send the
spies.

A second question comes to mind: what was the purpose of
sending out twelve people on a spying mission? Especially in
olden times, people were not accustomed to seeing foreigners in
their cities, so that any strange face—and certainly twelve new
faces—were immediately noticed. Twelve people were a crowd,

and as such they could not avoid arousing suspicion. The Book of Joshua describes a similar spying mission, but there Joshua sends only two people. Why are there twelve in this case?

We could ask a third question: Moses wanted the spies to investigate whether the people that lived in the countries of Canaan were strong or weak. What did Moses mean, when he himself told the Jews, "Listen, people of Israel, you are today going to cross the Jordan, to overcome nations greater and mightier than yourself, cities great and fortified up to the heaven, a people great and tall, the sons of the Anakim...." So apparently Moses—and presumably the other Israelites—knew what to expect. Why did Moses have to send spies to confirm what he already knew?

From this follows a fourth question: why were the people so upset when the spies came back and reported to Moses how fierce the people of Canaan were, and how strong their cities. They knew it already—and still the Torah tells us that the people were scared and "cried all night." Why?

The Torah continues to tell us how God and Moses were very angry about the report of the spies, particularly about the way they related the details in a manner that frightened the Jews. But why did this make them sinners? After all, they had been asked to look and report what they saw, and this is exactly what they did.

We can find some of the answers in the Talmud, in volume *Sotah*, where it is stated that God told Moses that he was permitted to send spies if he wanted to do so. "As for Me," God said, "I promised you that the land was good, and that it will be delivered into your hands. But if you have doubts, and if you would like your people to see the land, I will not prevent you from doing so."

This explains how the Jews were permitted to go and see for themselves what the situation in Canaan was like, but it does not answer all the questions we asked before. It does show, however, how far the Jewish people, by insisting on sending the

spies, were removed from the unquestioning faith they had
shown at the time they stood at Mount Sinai. At Mount Sinai
they had not asked what was written in the commandments.
There they had shown complete confidence that if God gave
them a Law, they would be able to observe it.

If they had shown a similar faith when they stood at the
gates of the Promised Land, they could have entered the land
thirty-nine years earlier, and all their suffering in the desert
would not have happened. Even more so, the entire generation
that had left Egypt could have entered Eretz Israel, and would
not have had to live their lives in the desert and eventually die
there, without achieving their goal.

This did not happen, however. The Jews did not possess the
same unshakeable faith in God as they did when they received
the Torah at Mount Sinai. They asked that their representatives
be allowed to check what kind of land they were going to enter.
According to the Torah, the people were even divided among
themselves, and this explains why Moses had to send twelve
people, one from each tribe. When these twelve people came
back, all they could do was confirm what Moses had in fact told
them before—but they did this with words that struck fear into
the heart of every one of them.

Indeed, they did not tell any lies, and even brought back some
of the wonderful fruits from the land, to show how good they
were. But they added a conclusion, namely: Do you really
believe that people who possess such a wonderful land will let us
take it away from them? "After all," they said, "if it were a bad
land, people would not mind very much giving it up, and moving
somewhere else. But it is a good land, and thus they will fight to
the death to keep us out. Even if, in the end, we would succeed in
conquering one of the kingdoms, we could not hope to stay
there. The Negev is settled by the Amalekites. The Jebusites live
in the hills. Along the sea coast are the Canaanites. Besides this,
all of them have already developed strong traditions. The Jewish
people, on the other hand, received the Torah only a year ago, so

that they have hardly had an opportunity to develop a characteristic way of life."

This is why the spies advised against entering the land, for if the Jews were to do so, they would—so the spies concluded—adopt the customs and habits of the local inhabitants, and before they knew it the Torah would be forgotten. All this very likely was the truth, but in their reporting the spies exceeded their authority. For they had been sent to observe and bring factual reports rather than to draw conclusions.

Doesn't their complaint somehow have a familiar ring even today? Jews in the State of Israel and abroad say: Eretz Israel is a wonderful land. But the people who live there do not behave in the right way. They are not polite, they are not helpful, they are very selfish. They are opinionated and stubborn. This is nothing new, however, for already in the Book of Exodus God warned the Children of Israel that they were "a stiff-necked people." That was the problem then, and that is what it is today. In fact, however, it is both a curse and a blessing. For however stubborn they are, it has helped the Jewish people to survive for thousands of years and to realize God's promise that no enemy would ever destroy them completely. God also assured the Jewish people that there would never come a day that they would abandon the Torah. Moses said: God shall be blessed for separating us from the confused, for giving us the Law of Truth and planting everlasting life in our midst. And the prophet promises: נצח ישראל לא ישקר (netzach Yisrael lo-yeshaker), the Glory of Israel will not fail.

Now, maybe, we can understand why the spies were blamed, to the point that they were considered sinners. They had every right to tell what they had seen. But they did not have the right to draw conclusions and to tell the Jewish people that they would endanger both their physical existence and their spiritual survival.

Our narratives present a somewhat more detailed picture of how the spies reported their conclusions to their brothers.

Some of them said, "Let's go into Canaan, not like a nation that wants to live by itself, in isolation from the rest of the people, but like individuals, with the baggage we are carrying (in other words, the Torah). This way we shall be able to convert our environment to our own way of life." Several others among the spies advised, "Let's go back to Egypt, for the Egyptian army has drowned. The land is in a state of chaos. We can build a new Egypt that will suit us—but let's not go into this strange and unknown land that might destroy us totally."

It is clear that such divisions and lack of unanimity sowed doubts and fears into the hearts of the Jewish people. In short, they became scared to be independent and to fight for their existence. Our narratives tell that Pharaoh, before he finally freed the Children of Israel, also was of the opinion that as soon as the Jews left, and as soon as they found themselves all alone in the desert, they would want to return to Egypt. "It is in the Jewish nature to hate restrictions," he said. "Once they will be on their own, and are living in their own little country, they will once more long for wider horizons and greater opportunities." It is clear, therefore, why the words of the spies sowed doubt and confusion and made the people feel insecure.

There is no greater sin in a time of crisis than to frighten people into believing that they will lack the strength to stand up to their ordeal. We have seen this once again in the Second World War. Hitler started conquering the European nations psychologically even before he attacked them physically. Germany's rearmament was widely publicized, and the German propaganda machine and fifth column planted the suggestion that nobody would have a chance to fight this strong Germany. This is a similar kind of demoralization that the spies were guilty of in the time of Moses. The moment the people no longer believe in their strength, they are defeated even before the war has started; without the proper morale, people might be killed, even though they are in effect stronger than their enemy.

One of our great religious leaders, Rabbi Meir Isserles, commented that God did not punish the people of Israel by the fact that He caused an entire generation to die in the desert. For if they had entered the Land of Israel without belief, they would surely have been killed in the course of the fighting, and then they—and all the generations following them—would have been wiped out.

Parashath Shelach of the Torah teaches that one has to believe in what he does; otherwise he will fail, and might even be destroyed.

A second lesson of this *parashah* is that the Land of Israel is not merely intended as a land for absorbing people who have nowhere else to go, because they were thrown out from somewhere else. God has linked the Land of Israel with the values of Sinai. החי בישראל כאלו קיים את כל התורה (*ha-chai be-eretz yisrael, ke'ilu kieem eth kol ha-torah*), "To live in the land is like fulfilling the entire Torah." If Eretz Israel had been a land just like any other, the Jews would have forgotten it long ago. Instead of this, Eretz Israel is bound up not only with the eternity of the Jewish people but also with the eternity of the Torah. Together, Eretz Israel and the Torah are essential for the survival of the Jewish people.

Parashath Korach

ויקח קרח בן־יצהר בן־קהת בן־לוי ודתן ואבירם בני אליאב ואון
בן־פלת בני ראובן: ויקמו לפני משה ואנשים מבני־ישראל
חמישים ומאתים נשיאי עדה קראי מועד אנשי־שם: ויקהלו
על־משה ועל־אהרון ויאמרו אליהם רב־לכם כי כל־העדה כלם
קדשים ובתוכם יהוה ומדוע תתנשאו על־קהל יהוה.

"Now Korach, the son of Izhar... and certain Reubenites—
Dathan and Abiram—took men; and they became insolent
and rose up against Moses with 250 Israelite men, well-
known community leaders who had been appointed
members of the council. They came as a group to oppose
Moses and Aaron and said to them: 'You have gone too far!
The whole community is holy, every one of them, and the
Lord is with them. Why then do you set yourselves above
the Lord's assembly?'"

Rashi, the interpreter *par excellence* of the Torah, comments:
What exactly did Korach take? He took men, but with the
purpose to put himself on one side, in order to separate himself
from the community, and to protest about the priesthood to
which Moses had appointed his brother Aaron.

The entire episode—Korach's rebellion, Moses' reaction to
it, and the fatal punishment to which Korach and his followers
were subjected (for they were swallowed by the earth)—is not
at all clear, and we shall need to explain it.

As for the substance of Korach's accusations, it looks as
though he was partly right. For Korach was a Levite, like Aaron,

and he and his fellow conspirators believed that "the whole community was holy, every one of them." Wasn't the whole of Israel an עס סגולה (am segulah), a "chosen nation"? So why could only members of Aaron's family be appointed to the priesthood, and not other Levites—let alone people belonging to any of the other eleven Jewish tribes?

What was the sin of Korach and his followers? Already at this point I should add that Korach was not so seriously discriminated against as he believed. Indeed, Moses told him, "Isn't it enough for you that the God of Israel has separated you from the rest of the Israelite community and brought you near himself to do the work at God's tabernacle? He has brought you and all your fellow Levites near Himself, but now you are trying to get the priesthood too?"

In a sense it is very hard to understand Moses' reaction to this revolt. Let us not forget that it was not the first time that the people rebelled against him. First there had been the incident with the Golden Calf, a terrible sin—for even while Moses was away to receive the Torah, the Israelites were busy fashioning an idol. God was angry, Moses was angry—and yet Moses asked God to forgive them.

In the portions immediately before *Parashath Korach* we find two other examples. There it is told that the Jewish people wanted meat instead of manna. First they had complained that they were going to die of hunger in the desert. So God gave them manna. Now the complaint was, "We have lost our appetite; we never see anything but this manna!" Again God became extremely angry, and Moses was at his wits' end, and hardly knew how to handle such a stubborn and ungrateful lot. Yet Moses, being a good shepherd, asked God to forgive them. Even God gave in to the Jews, and told them that they would receive the meat they had asked for—"until it comes out of your nostrils, and you will loathe it."

Again, in the portion before *Parashath Korach*, we read how the Jewish people did not want to enter Canaan, because the stories of the scouts who had just returned from their spying mission had struck fear into their hearts. In this case, too, Moses asked God to be lenient with them, and God forgave them.

Looking back at the way Moses handled these various rebellions, we see that in every case Moses was extremely dissatisfied with his people's behavior. Yet in all cases he had seen to it that nobody had suffered any physical harm. But in the case of Korach he proved unwilling to forgive.

This is strange, for not only did the rebellion concern only 250 persons, rather than the entire community, but by destroying them, Moses deprived the tribe of Levi, and to some extent that of Reuben, of all their leaders, generals, and so forth. So why did he do it?

Moses summoned Dathan and Abiram, but they refused to come. In fact, they were quite abusive to Moses, saying, "Isn't it enough that you have brought us out of a land flowing with milk and honey to kill us in the desert? And now you also want to lord it over us?" Therefore, this time, after one more effort at intervening on behalf of the guilty men, Moses accepted G-d's verdict that the rebels would have to die.

The question is, therefore, what caused Moses to change his attitude so severely? Our narratives tell us of Korach: פקח גדול הדור היה (pikeach gadol ha dor hayah), in other words, that he was one of the outstanding men of his generation. He possessed brilliant gifts, but apparently Korach, too, saw himself as a unique individual, rather than an ordinary person. A wise man once said: Each individual is like three persons. The first person is the one he sees himself. The second person is the one that is seen by the world around him. The third person is the real one. Without a balanced evaluation of these three elements—one's own opinion, that of the sur- rounding world, and one's real personality—a person cannot be a leader. Korach saw himself as a great and talented man, but he obviously refused to consider the opinions of others.

Even this is insufficient to grasp what happened with Moses

and Korach in this case. Therefore it is important to know that Moses really understood Korach and his people, and at the outset even accepted their complaints. He even invited them for a discussion, and when they refused to come, Moses and the elders went to them, and said: Look, we do not mind that you have different ideas—I am not a dictator. You should not think that I want you to accept my opinion because I am the leader. There may be differences of opinion, as long as they do not lead to hatred, so that we can no longer talk to each other and are no longer prepared to listen to an explanation.

Jewish tradition allows differences of opinion, but it has to be with the purpose of achieving the right goal. Since Korach, Dathan, and Abiram refused to listen to Moses, and since he realized the destructive consequences of their behavior, he told the community, "Move back from the tents of these wicked men!" And the ground under them split apart, and they, with their families and all their possessions, were swallowed alive by the earth, and the earth closed over them, and they vanished forever.

There is a well-known saying in the *Ethics of the Fathers*, according to which כל מחלקת שהיא לשם שמים סופה להתקיים (*kol machaloketh she-he le-shem shamaim, sofah lehitkayem*), "Every controversy that is for God's sake will be of lasting worth in the end." But, at the same time, מחלקת שאינה לשם שמים אין סופה להתקיים (*machaloketh she-eyn le-shem shamaim, eyn sofah lehitkayem*), "The controversy that is not for God's sake will have no lasting worth."

According to the Midrash, Moses said to Korach and his people, "Look, it is not that I wanted to favor my own family. If I had selfish motives, I would give the priesthood to my own immediate family." The reason the priesthood had gone to Aaron and his sons, as Moses told Korach and his people in no uncertain terms, was that God did not want the selection to the priesthood to be subject to the same criteria as those applied by other nations. Jewish leaders needed special qualities. A Jewish priest had to be ready to be a slave to his people, and to listen to every complaint, whether it was justified or not. When God gave the priesthood to Aaron and his children, He told them, "I am not giving you dominion over the Jewish people, I am giving you slavery." The priest or the leader had to be an example through his actions and behavior. The Talmud says: If there is a stain on the garment of a leader, he shall be convicted to death. This of course does not literally refer to a stain on his clothes, but to actual misbehavior or a crime. Leaders—let alone priests—cannot be judged like ordinary persons, because they have to set an example to others. For this reason their behavior has to be far more careful, so that people cannot suspect them of misbehavior.

God appointed Aaron and his children to the priesthood not just because they were more capable and talented than other people. He chose them because for the priesthood more is needed than capability and talent; it requires compassion, understanding, devotion, and a lot of patience. To the sorrow of Moses, Korach and his community refused to accept this argument, and they replied, "Your attitude and understanding of what is needed to be a leader is completely mistaken. Leaders should not be involved with the people, for as soon as they are, the people will lose their respect for them. Leaders should keep themselves apart, to make sure that they will be feared and respected, and that their orders are obeyed."

This is what opened Moses' eyes to the question that was involved here. The issue was not which person would be the high priest, but which type of person. It was a question of principle, namely how a leader should lead his nation—as a dictator, or as a brother who cares for his people. There were no two ways; it was one way or the other. Therefore it was impossible to forgive the revolt, as he had done previously. The welfare, if not the existence, of the Jewish nation was at stake.

Let us look at some of the things that are happening in our lifetime. Many nations that received their freedom after the Second World War are now ruled by dictators. Their populations are suffering, and many more people are being destroyed under these newly independent regimes than during their worst years of suffering under imperialist colonial rule. Moses understood this point, and he concluded that the evil had to be destroyed at the roots. Failing this, the problem would spread. It was a thoroughly bad idea, and therefore dangerous.

Now we can understand Moses' radical change of attitude compared with the previous revolts. In fact, even after Korach and his people had been destroyed, and all the other rebels had died of the plague, their influence still remained. This is why God decided to give a sign that proved Aaron's suitability as high priest to the rebellious Israelites. God told Moses to get twelve staffs, one for each of the ancestral tribes. On each staff was to be written the name of the leader of the particular tribe, after which the twelve staffs were to be placed in the Tabernacle. God said to Moses, "The staff belonging to the man I choose will sprout, and I will rid myself of this constant grumbling against you by the Israelites."

So it was done, and the next day the staff with the name of Aaron on it had not only sprouted, but had budded, blossomed, and even produced almonds!

The symbolism of the tribal staff is a deep one. The staff is a leadership symbol, used throughout the ages. The leader could use it to point the way, to signal to his followers, or to rouse and inspire them, by holding it aloft. And of course the staff could be used to punish unruly subjects.

There are two kinds of rulers. The first kind rules with a stick, to punish any subjects who refuse to obey. This kind of ruler forms the majority. The second kind tries not to punish, but to reform and rehabilitate the sinner. This is the longer and more difficult way, but if the leader has the right feeling and patience, he has a good chance of succeeding. By telling the tribal leaders to place their staffs in the Tabernacle, Moses said as much as, "Try for once to rule without a stick. If you are more successful than Aaron, you can be the leaders."

Aaron and his children were leaders of the second kind. They talked to everyone quietly and tried to explain calmly to the sinners that the way they were going was not the right way. I am sure that all of us have experienced more than once in our everyday lives that we get further when we talk to someone in a pleasant way than when we shout and rant. Therefore we should put aside our big sticks, we should stop bullying and putting fear into people, but instead try to educate and rehabilitate.

Aaron's staff in the Tabernacle sprouted and blossomed. This proved what Moses had said, and it convinced the Jewish people that Aaron and his family were indeed the fittest persons for the priestly leadership. But it proved more than that: it proved what this type of leadership is capable of. The staff, which Korach and his people would have liked to use as their symbol of power, to rule and to punish, became instead a symbol of gentleness and beauty, for it blossomed and produced almonds.

The story of Korach tells us that everyone of the B'nai Israel has the right to explain his way of thinking, but on two conditions: that his purpose is to promote unity, and that the second person is given the same right.

Parashath Chukkat

וידבר העם באלהים ובמשה למה העליתנו ממצרים למות במדבר כי אין לחם ואין מים ונפשנו קצה בלחם הקלקל. וישלח יהוה בעם את הנחשים השרפים וינשכו את־העם וימת עם־רב מישראל.

"But the people grew impatient on the way; they spoke against God and against Moses, and said, 'Why have you brought us up out of Egypt to die in the desert? There is no bread! There is no water! And we detest this miserable food.' Then God sent venomous snakes among them; they bit the people and many Israelites died."

The "miserable food" of which the Children of Israel complained was the manna, with which God had sustained them ever since their departure from Egypt. As a punishment, God sent fiery serpents among them, and many of them died. The Torah continues to tell that the people regretted the things they had said against God and Moses, and realized that they had sinned. Moses prayed for the people and asked God to take away the serpents. God answered, "Make a snake, and put it on a pole, and anyone who is bitten, can look at it, and he will survive."

Our sages ask why God, of all things, sent serpents to punish the Children of Israel, and they answer: What better way was there to punish them for their calumny than by means of the very animal that was punished for its slanderous statements in the Garden of Eden. And what better punishment was there for the denigration of the heavenly manna—which, according to our tradition, tasted like whatever one wanted—than the serpent, for whom all foods had only one taste, that of dust.

The reference is, of course, to the crafty serpent that seduced Eve, and made her transgress God's instructions, for which it was cursed and condemned to crawl on its belly and eat dust all the days of its life.

The Torah tells us that the serpent was craftier than any of the animals God had created. Although God had warned Eve that she must not eat from the tree in the middle of the garden—or even touch it—for fear she would die, the serpent convinced her that there was absolutely no reason to be afraid. "You will not die," the snake said, " but God knows that when you eat of it, your eyes will be opened, and you will be like God, knowing good and evil."

Our sages even give a description of the serpent, saying that he walked upright, that he talked a "holy" language (to the meaning of which we will refer later), and that his first words had been against God, claiming that God had only been able to create because He Himself had eaten from the Tree of Knowledge. So far the Midrash.

A long time ago our sages concluded that the sin of Adam and Eve in eating of the Tree of Knowledge was not an individual or incidental transgression, but a fundamental and perpetual sin, that would leave its mark upon all human generations to come.

It is this emphasis on knowledge, rather than on proper behavior, that has been the cause of much of the world's misery. The full name of the tree from which the serpent said Adam and Eve could not eat is "Tree of Knowledge of Good and Evil." There has always been much speculation about the correct interpretation of this name, some saying that it refers to knowledge of good and evil, whereas others maintain that the reference is to universal knowledge. Whatever the case may be, God had provided an environment for Adam and Eve that would have enabled them to thrive with or without knowledge. To protect them, God specifically forbade them to eat from the Tree of Knowledge, but Adam and Eve believed that they could build their world with knowledge, instead of through their natural gifts and the moral innocence that God had instilled in them at the moment of their creation. They thought the Tree of Knowledge would help them and further their purpose.

Throughout history people have commited all kinds of sins under the guise of furthering knowledge, or introducing ideas and ideals that would improve the world—even justifying the destruction of human lives or societies with the argument, "you have to destroy in order to build something better." Apart from the untold misery this argument has caused, the underlying principle, like all principles that are carried to extremes, is wrong. For sometimes nothing is built to replace the existing order, and when it is, more often than not we see that the underlying idea is, in turn, short-lived and in no way justifies the sacrifices that have been made to achieve its implementation.

The Jewish traditional view is that one does not destroy until proper preparations for something new have been made. A simple *halachic* example is the rule applying to the replacement of an old and derelict synagogue, which prescribes that a new structure should be built around the old one before it may be torn down.

If this rule applies to inanimate nature, how much weightier it is when we talk about human creation. Our worst executioners invariably claim to have a "sacred mission," and they typically dress up all kinds of vice in the garb of concepts like liberalism, progress, culture, or civilization, meanwhile inflicting physical and mental torture upon countless millions of human beings.

According to our sages, the serpent *also* talked a "holy language," which in this case we could interpret as the use of sweet and seductive words, which the snake knew would appeal to its human victim. One of our human characteristics is our belief that we deserve more than we have. Of course, ambition is a healthy desire, but the snake abused it in order to deceive Eve and convince her that by eating from the Tree of Knowledge she could be like a god, and would be able to create worlds. In the process, the snake turned Adam and Eve's innocence into a perpetual human weakness and liability.

Complaints against God are a recurrent phenomenon in our world. We know that life can be hard and uncertain, and that few people always receive everything they want or deserve. This leaves the field wide open for agitators such as the serpent, who say, "Why should you be satisfied with what you have? Don't you see that you are being shortchanged, and that with a little bit of effort you can achieve all your desires? All you need is to be free, and not to be tied down by all kinds of restrictions." Another type of agitator will say, "The problem with the world is that it is unjust. As soon as all property and opportunities are equally divided, there will no longer be any problems."

All these arguments are what we might call "the Big Lie." One does not have to be a great philosopher to realize that unbridled freedom does not create happiness. Freedom does not mean that everybody can take what he wants or live the way he wants. This is not freedom, but license, and it makes all our lives more difficult rather than easier. We only have to look at the world around us to realize how quickly people tire of all kinds of newfangled ideas. The French Revolution got completely out of hand before a new order could be introduced in France. Mao Tse-tung's Cultural Revolution set China back two decades socially and economically, and Soviet Russia's most persistent problem, seventy years after the Communist Revolution, is to achieve self-sufficiency in food production in what still is a largely agricultural society.

But neither have escapist movements such as "Flower Power," or cults and drugs proved to be a solution. They are merely the last resort of those who, after rejecting what they call "the Establishment," have nowhere else to go. They represent the ultimate unfreedom: a flight, under the guise of idealism or romanticism, into the dead-end street of nihilism. Apparently, materialism and rationalism aren't everything, and their blessings and general consequences have time and again proved to be of a very mixed kind.

The human character does not really change. The external circum- stances change, but people's basic needs and problems remain the same. What is needed is a reflection on our enduring values. The Jewish ethic and morality, and an unselfish interest in our fellowman, are yardsticks that are able to give our lives purpose and direction. For one thing, we should not always look at what other people have, but learn to live our lives according to our own capabilities and needs, while seeing to it that others receive the same opportunity.

Every person has his own individual needs, pleasures, and priorities, and even the relative absence of material wealth does not rule out enjoyment and satisfaction—provided we have other people to share it with. Our rabbis said: It is not so important how many people love me, or how much they love me. What is important is how many others I love, and how much. There is an interpretation by one of our rabbis of the verse ואהבת את יהוה אלהיך (ve-ahavta ha-shem eloheicha), "You shall love your God," and he asks: How can God *demand* that we love Him, when love is an emotional state? We can understand that God asks us to honor our parents, to celebrate the Shabbath, or to build a *sukkah*. But how can we force our feelings? The answer is that if we follow God's commandments—in other words, behave in this world the way God told us to—we will automatically come to love Him, because our emotions will become involved. What begins as a commandment, a duty, ends up as a natural and logical behavioral impulse. This is, for instance, how we discover that it is better to love than to be loved, or that it is more enjoyable to give than to receive. These are only some of the secrets of our human existence!

The symbolism behind this entire problem is represented by

the snake. The snake has a habit of biting people, and we could well ask, why? As far as we know the serpent does not enjoy blood any more than dust. So why does he kill? The answer is simple. A snake does not kill merely to eat, but also out of hate and to inflict damage. There is an old story about a discussion between a snake and a gossipmonger. The gossip asked the snake, "Why do you kill and destroy?" To which the snake answered: "You should be the last one to ask me such a question. You are much worse than I, for you also kill and destroy. But whereas the effect of my bites is restricted to my victim only, the damage you do spreads far and wide."

At this point let us return to what happened to the Children of Israel in the desert. They were punished for complaining—not only about Moses, but about God as well. What was it that caused their dissatisfaction? They had come to loathe the manna, which they considered too "light," meaning that it was absorbed by their bodies even without chewing. God punished them by sending venomous snakes, but upon Moses' intercession, God promised to remove the snakes and heal those that had been bitten and were as yet alive. In order to achieve the latter, Moses was told to fix a brass snake upon a high pole and tell the victims of the snake bites to gaze at it.

Why did God choose a snake as a remedy, since the snake was not only a known idol among heathen nations in antiquity but also a symbol of materialism and easy achievement? The answer is that God wanted to confront the sufferers with their materialist attitude and teach them that without spiritual content life is impossible. In the same way that the serpent destroyed the lives of Adam and Eve by agitation and slander, the Children of Israel would have been unable to continue, and they would have died in the desert if God had allowed their ungrateful complaints.

At the same time, looking at the brass snake on the pole forced them to look up and gaze toward the heavens, enabling them to focus their thoughts upon God.

The story teaches us that we should not provoke individuals or groups against each other, nor should we allow ourselves uncritical acceptance of all kinds of new ideas that are promoted in the name of scientific, social, or cultural progress, for in many cases they will fail to bring the satisfaction we expect

The snake is a symbol of the "brassy," materialist, and superficial aspects of life, and its function is to remind us in both our private and public lives to look beyond the food we eat, in other words the material side of our life, but also to attend to the nonmaterial, spiritual aspects. For, as the Torah tells us: כי לא על הלחם לבדו יחיה האדם (lo al ha-lechem levado yichiyeh ha-adam), "Man does not live by bread alone." To live, we need not only food but spiritual nourishment as well.

Parashath Balak

ועתה לכה־נה ארה־לי את־העם הזה כי־עצום הוא ממני אולי
אוכל נכה־בו ואגרשנו מן־הארץ כי ידעתי את אשר־תברך מברך
ואשר תאר יואר.

"Now come and put a curse on these people, because they
are too powerful for me. Perhaps then I will be able to
defeat them and drive them out of the country. For I know
that those you bless are blessed, and those you curse are
cursed."

In this portion of the Torah we are told how Balak, the king
of Moab, summoned his prophet Balaam and begged him to
curse the Israelites, as they were too mighty for him to defeat in
battle. He had good reason to be worried. The Israelites had just
defeated the Amorites and occupied the kingdom of Bashan, and
they were now encamped along the Jordan, close to the Moabite
territory. But how could Balak expect a curse to achieve what he
could not achieve in battle?

Parashath Balak tells us about the various opinions among
enemies of Israel about the best way to destroy her. The Torah
relates a number of debates between Israelites and their antago-
nists and enemies about the justification and safeguarding of
the Jewish way of life. Some examples are the midrashic narrative about Abraham and Nimrod, and the contentions between
Isaac and Ishmael, and Jacob and Esau, about their conflicting
worldviews. The Torah also records a debate within a nation,
namely when the Egyptians discussed how they could prevent

255

the Children of Israel from becoming too numerous, for fear that they would join Egypt's enemies and subvert the country.

The present case is rather different, however. The Torah tells in considerable detail how King Balak went out of his way to have Balaam brought to him and have him curse the Israelites, and the question is why—and what he hoped to gain from this.

The interpreters of the Torah explain that all these examples teach us that the Jewish people were hated from the early years of their existence—a situation that in various forms and with different arguments has persisted throughout our history. One of our Hebrew poets once expressed it as שנאת עולם לעם עולם (sin'at olam le-am olam), "Eternal hatred for the eternal people." According to the prophet Isaiah, we must expect this hatred to continue until almost the End of Time, when the "age of understanding" will arrive.

Analyzing the reasons why anti-Semites hope to achieve this purpose of destroying the Jewish people, we can distinguish two motives. The first is because they are afraid of people who are not like themselves, regardless whether the reasons are economic, ethnic, religious or something else. For this reason they want to "keep them in their place"—in other words, try to keep them out of their country or, if they are already in the country, prevent them from competing by the imposition of all kinds of restrictions. If this is not effective, there is persecution and, as a final resort, physical destruction. This has throughout the centuries been the customary method in most societies—and not merely the uncivilized ones. In our time the dictator Hitler openly confessed that the Jews posed a danger to the existence of Germany, and he and his henchmen acted out the above scenario to its bitter end. The so-called *Protocols of the Elders of Zion*, copies of which are still being printed and distributed in more countries than we like to remember, are proof that there is still a fertile soil for this form of paranoia about the influence of the Jews.

The second reason is not so much connected with fear of economic competition, but with a refusal to accept the Jewish-inspired morality and way of life. The Jewish presence, and the resulting confrontation with the demands of the Torah—or the Old Testament, as it is usually referred to in Western societies—can be unsettling. Who do these Jews think they are anyway? What kind of presumption is this claim to be a "chosen people," this segregation from the rest of society, this cultivation of alien customs, and eating of special kinds of food? The best way to put a stop to all this is to forbid these rituals and force these Jews to mix and assimilate.

There are numerous historical examples of this attitude, from Greek and Hellenist times until our own era. The reason why people believed that this strategy of suppressing the spiritual side of Judaism would be successful is that the Jews always were a small people, during much of their history even without their own country. Since, as a result, they lived as a minority among far more populous nations, many of which were under the sway of powerful state religions, it was believed that as soon as their spirit was broken, the Jews would automatically assimilate and disappear.

Not many years ago a book was published, written by the late President Sadat of Egypt subsequent to his decision to go to Jerusalem and make peace with Israel. In it he gave his views of the future developments in the Middle East, including the future of the Jewish state. Sadat did not have a great love for the State of Israel, but he had come to the conclusion that it would be too costly to defeat Israel by force of arms, and that this would demand an intolerable sacrifice in human and economic terms. He realized that, given the fierce Jewish determination, the existing political and economic support for the Jewish people, and the military strength of the State of Israel, even the sacrifice of several million Arab lives would be unable to force a decision in favor of the Arabs. Thus he concluded that the easiest way to conquer Israel was by making peace. This would neutralize her military might, and sooner or later assimilate this small country within the vast "Arab sea." In this way, eventually, the Jewish state would dissolve itself.

The above example goes a long way toward explaining the meaning of the dialogue between Balak and Balaam. Balak was the traditional, overt enemy who would have liked to destroy Israel by military means, whereas Balaam was an anti-Semite of the other school, who attached more importance to Israel's spiritual destruction, without the need for a military showdown. His strategy was assimilation, by far the more dangerous, because the Israelites would not have the strength to resist. His method was advising the Midianites to send their daughters in order to mix and cohabit with the Israelites, and so disrupt their family unity and destroy the nation from within.

Understanding these ways of thinking also helps us to understand Balaam and Balak. Why did Balak spend so much money and effort to enlist Balaam's services? To curse the Jews. What did he think cursing would do? It would have been more logical and practical to marshal as many soldiers as he could from among his own people and their allies, and attempt to defeat the Israelites in battle. True, the Jews had a reputation for being hardy and stubborn, but given a sufficient military superiority, he might have had a good chance of destroying his enemy. Instead he chose to call upon Balaam, who was famous and influential in this part of the world. Balaam would tell the world how bad the Jews were, and this condemnation would be sufficient to isolate them and put them effectively "beyond the pale."

This, too, can be illustrated with the help of a contemporary example. Forty years ago, with God's help, the State of Israel was reestablished. As of today, this state is slandered, besmirched, blackmailed, and boycotted by a large part of the world. Israel was established by a decision of the United Nations, whose duty is to prevent conflict, discipline warmongers, and condemn those who disturb the peace. Yet, pro-

portionately most of the sanctions and embargoes this same
United Nations has recommended, through the votes of its
Security Council, have been directed against the State of Israel.
Studying the protocols of the Security Council, we will find that
every kind of slander has been leveled against the State of Israel,
including accusations of the very crimes of which the Jewish
people have been the principal victims. Claims of military
aggression, racism, and desecration of holy places by Israel have
traditionally found a majority among the members of this
august body. One of Israel's representatives to the United
Nations once said in an address to the General Assembly: If
somebody would introduce a motion to this organization con-
demning the Jews for manufacturing Passover bread with the
blood of Christian children, I am certain that a majority could be
found.

Isn't it ironic that the highest international political authority, the General Assembly of the United Nations, has become
the tool of the Balaams of today, to instill hatred and contempt
of the Jews? Even after thousands of years they are unable to
accept that God will not allow His people to be annihilated. And,
physical force having failed time and again, the only remaining
method is to try to create a common front against the Jews, by
convincing the world that the Jews are bad, and that it is the
duty of all nations to get rid of them.

This is what the curse of Balaam means. He was a visionary,
famous for his prophecies in the entire region. People believed
him, and the very fact that he said something was sufficient to
convince people that it would come true—except, of course, that
in this particular case God put a spoke into the wheel, and
prevented Balaam from cursing Israel.

One of the remarkable aspects of this hatred of the Jewish
people is that even nations who hate each other will unite to
attack us. There is a midrash about the verse in the weekly
portion of *Balak*, according to which, ויאמר מאב אל־זקני מדין (*va-yomar
moav el ziknei midian*), "The Moabites said to the elders of

Midian...." Our sages ask: How could they talk to each other, when it is well known that they were each other's enemies? For an answer, the midrash compares the behavior of two dogs, who will fight furiously for the possession of a bone but will band together as soon as they see a wolf. In the same way Moab banded together with Midian... although the Israelites did not have a quarrel with either! This hatred is the cement that unites enemies. Hitler openly wrote in *Mein Kampf* that he hoped that the nations' aversion of the Jews would override their own best interests, and thus enable him to destroy them.

There is a passage in the memoirs of the late Eleanor Roosevelt, according to which she expressed her concern about the Nazis' treatment of the Jews to her husband, and asked him why the United States was incapable of intervening. President Roosevelt answered her by saying in so many words that a confrontation with Nazi Germany within the United States at this particular time would be perceived as a defense of the Jews, rather than a defense of the United States. Similarly, it is a well-documented fact that—even after 1942, when information about the massacres in the German concentration camps had begun to leak out—the wartime British government repeatedly dismissed calls for the rescue of endangered Jews for fear of being accused of conducting a "Jewish war." British ministers claimed that increased immigration of Jewish refugees, or Jewish residents from areas as yet unoccupied by the Germans, would arouse anti-Semitic feelings in Great Britain and detract from the war effort. "The first priority is to win the war," the argument went, "after that the Jews will automatically be saved." The Jews were *not* saved, and—however hard this sounds—a large part of the responsibility for this must be placed on the Allied governments.

God did not permit Balaam to condemn Israel, so he tried a new way — he blessed them, and he said: מה־טבו אהליך יעקב משכנתיך ישראל (*mah tovu ohaleicha ya'acov mishkenoteicha yisrael*), "How goodly are your tents, O Jacob, your dwellings, O Israel." We could understand these words as praise, and as a blessing by a heathen visionary who had come to understand that the Jewish God would not allow him to curse the Israelites. But we might also see Balaam's oracle as simply another curse—a way of showing the world how, to paraphrase a well-known expression, you can "kill the Jews by kindness."

Apparently, Balaam had recognized two aspects of Jewish solidarity and realized that unless he succeeded in neutralizing them, there was no hope of defeating the Israelites. The first aspect was the cohesion of the Jewish tribes and families: מה־טבו אלהיך יעקב, "How goodly are your tents, O Jacob"; and the second the central place occupied by the Sanctuary, the Ark of the Covenant: משכנתיך ישראל, "Your dwellings, O Israel." In the course of time the Ark of the Covenant was superseded by the Temple, and still later by the בית המקדש הקטן (beit ha-mikdash ha-katan), the "small sanctuary," in other words the synagogue.

Balaam said to Balak: You cannot destroy the Jewish people as long as they have this cohesion; as long as they show this devotion to their families; neither can you destroy them as long as they have in every place a sanctuary where they worship their God, remember their past, and celebrate their good and bad events. As long as these two continue to exist, the Jews will survive.

The Ramban (Rabbi Moses ben Nachman), the famous thirteenth-century rabbi and scholar, wrote: The Torah introduced a special portion about Balak and Balaam to impress upon our younger generation the importance of the profound hatred and discrimination with which the Jew is confronted. There indeed exists a serious danger that, where such hostile opinions become sufficiently widespread, young Jews might eventually begin to believe some of the slander about their own people. Many of today's young Jews are not very well versed in Jewish history. They have hardly any idea how much their small nation has given to the world in such varied fields as religion, philosophy, science, technology, and the arts. This is why the Ramban said that it was important for Jewish youngsters to know what even our enemies had to admit.

Balaam realized that however many soldiers King Balak would hire, he would not succeed in defeating the Jews in war. The Midrash gives a picture of what Balaam said to Balak: If you hired a multitude of soldiers, would you have more soldiers than the Egyptians, or more chariots? Eventually Balaam, too, came to realize that he could not conquer the Israelites by curses either, because of the "goodliness of their tents and their sanctuary"—their internal cohesion and unity.

Thus our enemies hope that they can destroy us by isolating us, and thus cause others to curse and persecute us. Failing which, there is one method left, namely to erode Jewish strength from within. In Balaam's time it was the daughters of the Midianites who seduced the Israelites and brought them to the worship of Baal. In our days too we are destroying our internal cohesion, but this time by assimilation, with the result that we lose our identity by not adhering to traditions that have kept us together for thousands of years.

We Jews have conquered all kinds of Balaams, but there is one problem we have not overcome until today: our worst enemy is not condemnation by others, or the enemies from outside, but internal disunity and lack of common purpose. If this is understood, it will be stopped, but if not, it can destroy us.

Parashath Pinchas

ויאמר יהוה אל משה עלה על הר העברים הזה וראה את הארץ
אשר נתתי לבני ישראל : וראיתה אתה ונאספת אל עמיך גם אתה
כאשר נאסף אהרון אחיך.

"Then the Lord said to Moses: 'Go up this mountain in the
Abarim range, and see the land that I have given the
Israelites. After you have seen it, you too will be gathered
to your people, as your brother Aaron was.'"

In effect, God told Moses to climb a mountain close to the
borders of Eretz Israel, and to look at the land from this high
point, after which he would die just like his brother, without
having entered the Promised Land. The Torah tells of two
occasions on which God showed the land to his dear ones. The
first time was when He told Abraham to leave his country, his
people, and his father's house, and to "go to the land I will show
you." Abraham went, and after he had arrived in Eretz Israel,
God promised him the land as an eternal possession for his
children. The second time was when God showed the land to
Moses — but what an enormous difference there is between
these two situations!

When God showed the land to Abraham, it was a happy
occasion, a promise for the future. The second occasion, when
He showed it to Moses, was really a big tragedy. Abraham
walked the land, and he received God's promise that his presence there would continue through his children "for all their
generations to come." When God showed the land to Moses, He
also told him that he, personally, would have no part in it. It was
like taking a thirsty man to an oasis, and telling him that he was
not allowed to drink the water. This was the tragedy. Moses'

entire life had been devoted to his people, with the one objective of guiding them to Eretz Israel and, once they had arrived there, settling them safely in the land. For this purpose he had endangered himself by returning from Midian, where he had fled following his fatal confrontation with an Egyptian overseer. He knew that his life was at risk, but he returned to fight for the liberation of the Children of Israel from Egyptian slavery, because this is what God told him to do. Moses and Aaron went to Pharaoh and told him, "This is what the God of Israel says: 'Let my people go.'" Pharaoh threw him out of his palace, but Moses did not give up until the Jews were able to leave Egypt. And let us not forget the problems Moses had with his own people until the moment that the Children of Israel were able to leave Egypt.

Once the Israelites had crossed the Red Sea, and even before they arrived at Mount Sinai where God would give them their spiritual purpose in life, the first revolt began: after having traveled in the desert for three days without finding water, they arrived at an oasis called Marah, but its water was bitter, and the people vented their disappointment on Moses. This incident was followed by a long series of conflicts and reproaches. Yet Moses, although tired of their complaints, never despaired — not even when a group of rebels under Korach attacked him, and Dathan and Abiram reproached him, saying, "Why have you brought us out of a land flowing with milk and honey [meaning Egypt] to die in the desert?" Moses accepted everything patiently, because he knew that he had a mission to fulfill, namely to bring his people safely to the Promised Land.

However, once they arrived close to their destination, the people were again not satisfied until they would receive a first-hand report about the situation in Canaan. Moses agreed to send twelve scouts to spy out the land, but following their return the Jews did not believe the word of God, but that of the spies. At this point it was God who decided that the generation that had come out of Egypt was still too much influenced by its former spiritual and physical bondage to be worthy of entering the Promised Land. For this reason the Jews would have to stay in the desert until the entire generation that had left Egypt would have died.

So they wandered for forty years. These forty years were one long litany of complaints and bad feelings between Moses and his people. Reading the Torah we realize that the Jewish people liked Aaron, but not Moses: וידברו במשה (va-yedabru be-moshe), in other words the people "gossiped" about Moses, to the point where, according to our sages, they accused him of having an affair with a married woman. But their behavior did not change Moses' devotion and compassion for his people. What better illustration of this can we find than Moses' desperate plea to God after the people had made themselves the Golden Calf: "Please forgive their sin — but if not, then blot me out of the book You have written!" Summarizing, we can say that only a man such as Moses could have had the strength of mind not to be influenced by this kind of behavior, and to be so entirely unselfish as far as his own interests and comforts were concerned.

Finally the moment arrived that would repay Moses for all his troubles and sorrows — the moment that was to be the culmination of his life's hopes and expectations. Forty years had gone by; of the generation that had left Egypt only a handful, among them Caleb and Joshua, were left, and now they were at last going to enter the Promised Land. Then, suddenly, God said to Moses, "Go up this mountain and see the land, but after this you will die." What a terrible tragedy.

Many of us will have experienced cases of people who worked and saved all their lives in the hope of being able to enjoy a happy and peaceful old age. They raised a family, they succeeded in their careers, and then they retired to enjoy their grandchildren and devote themselves to the many things for which they never had time when they were working. And then, quite unexpectedly, they died.

Such cases are tragic, no doubt about it; but they cannot be compared with the terrible thing that happened to the greatest leader the Jewish people ever had. Let us not forget how much patience Moses had needed to listen to all their complaints, how much self-control had been required to put up with their faults, and how much courage to plead time and again with God to forgive their mistakes. How did he manage to do it? Only because he loved them. What a great man Moses was! A great poet once wrote, "How small Mount Sinai looked when the great Moses stood upon it."

What did Moses feel after God had told him once and for all that he would never set foot in the Promised Land? According to the Midrash, he said to Joshua, his disciple, "Yesterday I felt capable of soaring up to heaven like an eagle. Today I am not even able to cross the Jordan, which is narrower than a lake." Our great leader and prophet asked God to let him cross the Jordan, even for a short while, but God did not permit it.

The question is, why? Our interpreters try to find the answer in the fact that — in addition to God's punishment of Moses for striking (rather than talking to) the rock when the thirsty Jews needed water in the desert — God did not think Moses would be able to lead the Jews after they had entered the land.

When we think about it, we can only conclude that this indeed would have been too much for Moses. It was not only a question of age, but of the nature of the task that lay ahead. Moses had been the leader *par excellence* to guide the Children of Israel to freedom. But meanwhile a new generation had been born, whose life would be spent occupying, dividing, and settling the new Jewish homeland. This no longer involved matters of grand strategy, but all kinds of practical aspects. Moses was made for big things; he could not deal with everyday details. Moses was a visionary, not an administrator. Moses was a ruler, not an adjudicator of petty conflicts about how the land should be divided between the tribes.

It is told about David Ben-Gurion how, during one of the first cabinet meetings shortly after the Jewish state had been founded, he commented how glad he was that Benjamin Ze'ev Herzl had not lived to see the day. For the great visionary and dreamer would not have understood the infighting and the petty compromises that seem to form an inevitable part of everyday political life. Moses was capable of fighting Pharaoh and the Egyptian nation. He was capable of leading them to Mount Sinai to receive the Torah. But he was not capable of seeing Jews fighting their brothers. In fact the Torah tells how, early in Moses' career, he became terribly upset when he saw two Hebrews hitting each other. No, the division of the country between the Jews had to be supervised by another person, able to understand and handle the pettiness of the people. This person was Joshua.

I am certain that we would be able to understand if Moses, after God had refused his entry into the Promised Land, had been so depressed that he had decided to withdraw and no longer worry about what would happen next. Not Moses, though, for the Torah tells us how he immediately asked God to "appoint a man over this community... one who will lead them out and bring them in, so that God's people will not be like sheep without a shepherd." God's answer was, "Take Joshua, the son of Nun, a man in whom is the spirit," in other words a man who is strong and does not easily despair. We therefore see that Moses, even when he realized that his role was finished, and that he himself would never witness the culmination of his mission — that even at that critical moment he did not pity himself, but that his first thoughts were for his people.

The message of this *parashah* is clear, namely that a real Jewish leader does not abandon his people. However trying the circumstances may be, as soon as he knows that his own role is finished, or that his life is coming to an end, he sees to it that another capable leader is appointed to guide the people to the chosen goal.

Parashath Mattot-Masei

אלה מסעי בני־ישראל אשר יצאו מארץ מצרים לצבאתם בידי־
משה ואהרון.

"Here are the stages in the journey of the Israelites when
they came out of Egypt by divisions under the leadership of
Moses and Aaron."

The two portions *Mattot* and *Masei* are usually read together.
The first portion deals largely with the defeat of the Midianites,
whereas *Parashath Masei*, which is also the final portion of במדבר,
the Book of Numbers, records in considerable detail the stages
in the journey of the Israelites between the Exodus and their
arrival at the border of Canaan.

We can appreciate why the Torah relates all kinds of key
events that occurred to them along the way, including the
defeat of a powerful enemy, but why should it devote an entire
page to a repetitious account, consisting mainly of the words ויסעו
ויחנו ... ויסעו ,... ויחנו ...: "They left... and they camped; they
left... and they camped." Why should it interest us to know,
thousands of years after the events took place, where the Israelites spent shorter or longer periods, particularly when some of
the names mentioned are otherwise unknown, and we may
never succeed in locating many of the other sites with whose
existence we are familiar from historical sources. Obviously,
the Torah does not intend merely to teach us Jewish history; as
usual, there is a very good reason for every single word it
contains, but before turning to an answer, I would like to digress
for a moment about the history of the Jewish people.

One way of looking at Jewish history is by dividing it into one period when the Jewish people lived in their own land and a second comprising the various exiles. Going by the historical accounts, the first period—covering the years between the conquest of Canaan and a point in time 215 years after the destruction of the Second Temple—lasted 1585 years, whereas the second period, until the reestablishment of Jewish sovereignty in the State of Israel, lasted almost 1700 years.

From the arrival of the Israelites in Canaan until the dedication of the First Temple by King Solomon, 440 years elapsed. The Temple stood for 420 years, until the year 586 B.C.E., when it was destroyed by the Babylonians, who carried off most of the inhabitants of the Kingdom of Judah to Babylon. Until the return of Ezra, and the rededication of the Second Temple, 70 years passed. The Second Temple stood for 410 years, and following its destruction, another 215 years passed until—after the final redaction of the Mishnah—Jewish life in Eretz Israel had deteriorated to a point where it was no longer possible to talk about an organized community. Excluding the 70 years spent in Babylon (and disregarding the exile of the inhabitants of the Kingdom of Israel to Assyria in the year 722 B.C.E., since they assimilated and vanished without a trace), this adds up to 1485 years.

During this period all kinds of different conditions prevailed. For example, we cannot compare the social, economic, or political situation during the time of the Judges with the situation during the kingdom of Saul. Neither can we compare the personality of Saul, and the particular stamp this first Jewish king placed on his reign, with the personalities and the reigns of David or Solomon. The latter, in particular, was a sophisticated ruler, under whose leadership the Jewish kingdom reached the peak of its fame and influence. Nor can the era of the Kings be compared with that of the Second Temple; during the First Temple period the country was independent, whereas during the second period it was in fact under Greek rule, and the

Temple was rebuilt with permission of an alien monarch. The Jewish population of Eretz Israel enjoyed a measure of autonomy, but it was by no means free and politically independent. Jewish historians, talking about the Jewish population during this time, refer to Eretz Israel as ארץ מוצאיהם (*eretz motzaeihem*), "the land of their origins." In other words, it was not the independent homeland of the Jewish inhabitants, but "the country from where they came"—their fatherland.

Following the destruction of the Second Temple, and the disintegration of Jewish community life, the Jewish people were to live outside Eretz Israel for almost 1700 years. The country passed into the hands of a succession of foreign rulers, but Diaspora Jewry continued to exist under the most varied conditions, both favorable and unfavorable. There were periods during which the Jews wandered from country to country, driven by discrimination and religious and social persecutions, but also periods of relatively harmonious coexistence and great cultural and economic flourishing. One such period was the Golden Age in Spain, which is associated with famous names such as Maimonides, Alfasi, Yehuda Halevi, Ibn-Ezra and Ibn-Gabirol, to mention only a few. However, these periods invariably created a false sense of security, and they were always followed by a reaction and even worse persecution.

Moses implanted into the Israelites a desire for freedom and an awareness of redemption. For this reason he wanted them to remain conscious of their country of origin, wherever their exile would take them. The way the Midrash puts it, Moses connected מוצאיהם למסעיהם (*motzaihem le-masa'eihem*), "their origins to their wanderings," so that they should always remain mindful from where they had come, and remember that eventually they should return to their land.

It is an old tradition that every Jew must at all times remain mindful of three things: God, his nation, and his country—Eretz Israel. The exiles in Babylon "sat at the rivers... and wept when they remembered Zion," and King David's vow,

If I forget you, O Jerusalem,
may my right hand forget its skill.
May my tongue cling to the roof of my mouth
if I do not consider Jerusalem
my highest joy,

has ever since symbolized our desire for a return to Zion.

There is a story about the Emperor Napoleon who, during one of his campaigns, passed through a village that looked as if it were deserted. Upon his enquiries he learned that the inhabitants had not fled, but that they were all in the synagogue to commemorate some day of mourning, called Tisha be-Av.

"Has there been some calamity?" Napoleon asked.

"Apparently," came the answer, "it appears that their Temple has been destroyed, and that their compatriots have been sent into exile. But the strange thing is that it all happened a very long time ago—some two thousand years, in fact—and they are still mourning!"

According to the story, Napoleon answered, "If those people have such a long memory, I do not doubt that they will one day return to their land."

The history of our own generation teaches that those who do not remember both Zion, the Land of Israel, and *emunath Yisrael*, the faith of Israel, risk losing both their land *and* their faith: in other words ultimately they will assimilate and disappear. In the course of the centuries the Jewish people never considered changing their homeland. In modern history, the very name "Zionism" is bound up with the political redemption of our people in Eretz Israel, which is why all other solutions, such as Jewish settlement in Madagascar, Guiana, or Uganda, were rejected.

The portions *Mattot-Masei* are always read during the three weeks preceding Tisha be-Av, when we mourn the destruction of the Temple. During this period we mourn things that happened thousands of years ago, and some of us might ask whether there are not many far more recent calamities to mourn and be sorrowful about? The truth is, however, that the minute a nation forgets its past, it starts to disappear. Our history is our sheet anchor, which is why the Torah tells us, אלה מסעי בני-ישראל ... ויסעו ... ויחנו ... ויסעו ... ויחנו ... (eleh masa'ei yisrael... va-yissu ... va-yachnu)—forty-one times in all.

Our narratives explain this idea by means of a parable about a king who took his seriously sick son to a distant place to cure him. It was a difficult journey, and several times the boy was so ill that the father had to stop on the way, and wondered whether he could go on. But he continued, and once they had reached their destination, the boy recovered. On the way home, the father decided to stop once more in all the places where they had been forced to rest on the way out, to tell his son all that had happened there: where they had slept, where he had caught a cold, where he had run a temperature, where he had had a headache, and so on.

For the same reason God wants us Jews always to remain mindful of the troubles during our wanderings in the desert: where the Jewish people rebelled, where they quarrelled, and where they complained about sickness or a lack of water or food. But at the same time God wants us to remember that ultimately they arrived at their destination. This is the message, both for the present and for future Jewish generations.

King David wrote, "When our fathers were in Egypt, they gave no thought to Your miracles." Our generation, too, might ask why God had to perform a miracle to take the Children of Israel out of Egypt. In fact, had He not sent them there in the first place, there would have been no need for them to undergo all these hardships, or for a miracle to extricate them from their bondage. The truth is, however, that the Israelites would never have been capable of accepting the Torah, or of taking posses-sion of Eretz Israel, if they had not been slaves first. According to our tradition, there are fifty stages of moral purity, and the Hebrews in Egypt lived at the lowest level. They simply were not prepared—physically or morally—for the task that lay ahead. At the same time, only people who had been enslaved for hundreds of years could understand what it would feel to be free, to be able to decide their own destiny, and to fight for a country of their own. And only people living in such abject conditions could have benefited so much from what the Torah had to offer. The wanderings of the Israelites in the desert were therefore a necessary part of their physical and spiritual evolution into a strong and unified people. Their sufferings were necessary, for the same reason that steel achieves its qualities of hardness and durability only after it has first been made red hot and then tempered with water. God wanted the Israelites to pass through all kinds of trials, so that they would not break down at the first crisis. The wanderings of the Israelites in the desert were as it were a quarantine period, aimed at immunizing them against any and all future shocks and disabilities, and to ensure their safe arrival at their ultimate destination.

Now we can understand the words of King David, when he commented that our forefathers in Egypt did not realize the meaning of all these miracles. They would have much preferred to be able to leave of their own free will, rather than outstay their welcome and be enslaved. This is why Moses said to them, "Look at your forefathers, Abraham, Isaac, and Jacob." Indeed, it cannot have been easy for Abraham to leave his family and the land of his birth, and to wander to a completely strange land— but he got up and left. He trusted God, and believed that it would all be for the best. Jacob, too, experienced numerous problems in his life. He was threatened by his brother Esau and exploited by his father-in-law Laban, his wives quarrelled, and there was jealousy between his children. His favorite son was sold into slavery, but he believed him killed. Yet our patriarchs persevered, and we see how toward the end of their lives all their efforts and sacrifices proved to have had a profound purpose.

The Exodus and what followed were not merely historical episodes, but a metaphor of the Jewish condition—and of our

own ultimate destination. The Torah repeats ויסעו ... ויחנו
... ויחנו ... ויסעו , ..., *va-issu va-yachnu*, to teach us that the historical events, as described in the Torah, contain a message for all
our generations, namely that our continual trials and tribula-
tions contain the seed of our survival. Looking toward the past
helps us to see the future. Taking the lesson of history to heart
helps us to maintain a long-term view ahead, and thereby surmount all difficulties.

Parashath Devarim

אלה הדברים אשר דבר משה אל־כל־ישראל בעבר הירדן
במדבר.

"These are the words Moses spoke to all Israel in the desert
east of the Jordan..."

The first words of this portion of the week, which is also the
beginning of the Book of Devarim, inform us that "these are the
words Moses spoke to all Israel in the desert east of the Jordan."
In other words, almost forty years after the Exodus, when the
Jewish people were near the end of their wanderings, and were
about to enter Eretz Israel, Moses spoke to the Jews.

Our interpreters ask why the Torah considers it necessary
to say "these are the words Moses spoke," when after all Moses
verbally transmitted the entire Torah to the Jewish people,
exactly as he had received it from God. Our interpreters have
given several answers to this question, one of which is that the
first four books of the Torah contain the literal text of everything that God spoke to Moses, whereas in Devarim Moses
repeats the same things in his own words.

A more important explanation is that the words אלה הדברים
(eleh ha-devarim), "these are the words," are words of reproof, and
that in them Moses enumerated all the places where the Jewish
people provoked God to anger. This raises three other questions: Why did Moses reprove the Jews at this point, just before
they were about to cross the Jordan? And why did he reprove
them at all—taking into account the fact that the generation

that entered the Land of Israel was not even the same generation that had given him so much trouble? Would it not have
been more correct and effective if Moses had directed his anger
at the generation of the Exodus, which had provoked God at
every turn? Third, if Moses decided that it was necessary to
remind the new generation of the mistakes of their parents, and
warn them not to repeat these mistakes, why did he wait so
long—until shortly before he died?

The answer to the third question also raises a philosophical
point, namely to what extent reprimanding people, rubbing
their noses into their mistakes, helps to change their minds.
Practical experience would seem to suggest that very often it
only makes them stubborn — *davka* as we say in Hebrew. There
is a discussion in our scriptures between two rabbis, Rabbi
Tarphon and Rabbi Eliezer ben Azarya, in which Rabbi Tarphon
says, "I wonder whether there are people today who are ready to
listen to reproof." Rabbi Eliezer adds, "I would be more surprised if I could find somebody who knows *how* to reprove." I
believe both Rabbi Tarphon and Rabbi Eliezer meant that they
doubted whether reproving people was a practical proposition,
either because the subjects of the reproof would not be ready or
able to listen, or because those who reproved did not know how
to do it in an effective way.

In other words, telling people off is not so simple, but it looks
as if Moses had come to the conclusion that this was the only
way to make the Jewish people obey. Our sages comment that
we should never reprimand someone until we know everything
about him and his circumstances, and that this explains why
Moses waited forty years, until he was sure that he really knew
the people and their circumstances.

Moses' reproaches are not the only harsh words that we read
this Shabbath. In the *haftarah* belonging to this week's portion,
the prophet Isaiah addresses the following words to the Jewish
people הוי גוי חטא עם כבד זרע מרעים בנים משחיתים (*hoy goy chote am keved avon
zera mar'im banim mashchitim*), "Ah, a sinful nation, a people loaded

with guilt, a brood of evildoers, children given to corruption." This is very tough language indeed, and remembering the discussion between Rabbi Tarphon and Rabbi Eliezer, it certainly was uttered by people who had a right to speak. And yet it seems as if neither the reproaches of Moses nor those of Isaiah contributed much to improving the Jewish people. In the end even the Temple was destroyed, Jewish independence was lost, and the Jewish people exiled.

The above dilemma of whether or not to reprove others does not only apply to the Jewish people as a nation, but on a small scale also to every individual. Shall we tell our friends the truth—or at least what we *think* is the truth—and risk getting the cold shoulder because they are embarrassed and feel that they have to justify themselves? Maybe we are not obliged to tell others the truth, and maybe we do not even have the right to do it. I do not want to be misunderstood; I am not advocating that we should tell lies, but a closer look at the situation often reveals that truth is a very relative thing.

Our sages note that Moses, as well as the prophets Isaiah and Jeremiah, use one particular word when they express their anger and pain about the behavior of the Jewish people, namely the word איכה (*eichah*). Moses said: איכה אשא לבדי טרחכם ומשאכם וריבכם (*eichah aseh levadi tarchachem u-masa'achem ve-rivchem*), "How can I bear your problems and your burdens and your disputes all by myself?" The prophet Isaiah said: איכה היתה לזונה קריה נאמנה (*eichah hayetah le-zonah kiryah ne'emanah*), "See how the faithful city has become a harlot!" and Jeremiah lamented: איכה ישבה בדד העיר (*eichah yashvah badad ha-ir*), "How lies the city deserted." Even God, when he saw that Adam had transgressed by eating from the Tree of Knowledge, used the word *eichah* when he called Adam to account: אייכה (*ayekah*), "Where are you?" God knew very well where Adam was, but what He wanted to say was, "What happened to you, to cause you to do what you did?"

In other words, Moses, Isaiah, and Jeremiah, when reproving the Jewish people, asked them, "Where were you?" in the

sense of, "Why did it happen; why did you do it?" *Eichah* therefore expresses wonder: "How could you be like that?—I am so
surprised about your behavior that I do not really know how to
handle you." To reprove in this way, one has to know the person
or the people one accuses very well; one has to be very devoted
to them and love them deeply to be able to react in this way. The
Torah says הוכח תוכיח את עמיתך (*hochiach tochiach eth amitecha*). Our
sages interpret this as meaning: "Accuse someone only if he
knows that you are his friend, and want his good." If you want
to be a moralist only, it is better not to reprove at all, because
you will not achieve your purpose.

There is a well-known story about one of the great chief
rabbis of Kovno, Rabbi Isaac Elhanan Spektor, according to
which one of his assistants was always complaining about the
behavior of the community. Every day he would come to the
rabbi with yet another story about how this one had misbehaved, or how that one had insulted his neighbor, and so forth.
One day Rabbi Elhanan became really fed up with his stories,
and he said to him, "Both of us are interested in improving
people, and preventing them from doing whatever they are
doing. But there is one difference between us, the same difference that exists between a cat and a housewife. Both of them
want to rid the kitchen of mice. But whereas the housewife
wants to catch the mice to stop them from eating her food, the
cat wants to catch the mice to eat them herself." In other words,
a housewife regrets that there are mice, whereas a cat would be
sorry if there were no mice, because she would have nothing to
eat. The same applies to reproaches: most people want to
improve others, but not all of them have the same reason.

The best illustration of the positive example is Moses himself. Moses knew all the failures of the Jewish people, yet he
loved them so much that he could not bear the idea of them
being punished; he even implored God "rather to strike him out
of His Book [the Torah], than let the Jewish people be destroyed." And the prophet Isaiah, in the earlier mentioned *haf-*

tarah, says, ואשיבה שפטיך כבראשונה ויעציך כבתחילה אחרי־כן יקרא לך עיר הצדק
קרית נאמנה: ציון במשפט תפדה ושביה בצדקה (*ve-ashivah shofetaich ke-va-
rishonah ve-yoatzaich ke-va-techilah acharei-chen yikare lach ir ha-tzedek
kiryah ne'emanah: tsion ba-mishpat tipadeh ve-shaveiha be-tzedakah*), "I
will restore your judges as in days of old, your counsellors as at
the beginning. Afterwards you will be called the City of Righteousness, the Faithful city."

These are the kind of people who have a right to reproach,
not only because their criticism is born out of love, but also
because at the same time they hold out a promise that if we
change, everything will turn out right.

We Jews are a strange people, in many ways without a
parallel in the world. Most nations celebrate their great
moments, their victories on the battlefield, and the birthdays of
their heroes. They celebrate their successes, but hardly ever
mention their failures. The Jewish people are exactly the opposite. We do not celebrate Moses' birthday, the capture of Jerusalem by David, the establishment of the Jewish commonwealth,
or the inauguration of the Temple by Solomon. Instead we
remember the Babylonian exile, we mourn the death of David,
and we mourn on the day when the Temple was destroyed and
the Jewish people were exiled. Our sages explain that we commemorate the destruction of the Temple in order to remind
ourselves that our defeat was not due to a lack of soldiers, or the
fact that we had fewer weapons than our enemies. Instead they
say, לא נחרבה ירושלים אלא על שנאת חנם (*lo nichrevah yerushalayim eleh al
sinath chinam*), "Jerusalem was destroyed only because of senseless hatred." Not only did we not like each other, we hated each
other!

In this connection the Midrash tells an interesting legend:
When Jeremiah saw that the Temple was destroyed, he was
afraid that the Jewish people would no longer be permitted to go
back to their land. He went to the graves of our patriarchs and
begged them to implore God to forgive the Jews, so that He
would allow them to return to their land. First Abraham

appeared before God, and he said, "For the most part of my life I was denied children from my wife Sarah. Only when I became a hundred years old did You grant me a son. I was so happy, because I understood that from him would issue the people to whom You promised the Land of Israel. Suddenly, one day, you called me, and told me to go to Mount Moriah to sacrifice my son. Is there a tongue in the world that could express the sorrow I felt at this moment? Yet I did not hesitate, and I took my son, and I was ready to sacrifice him. Now, because of my obedience to You, and my readiness to carry out Your commands without hesitation, don't I have the right to ask You to forgive my children?" God answered, "No."

Now Isaac went, and spoke: "God, I was only a young boy, and I had a happy childhood. My mother let me feel that for her I was the most important thing in the world. All my father's actions showed that I was the child he had hoped for and waited for all his life. But one day my father told me to go with him, and he asked me to stretch out my neck, because he was going to sacrifice me to You. Yet the thought of running away did not enter my mind. I submitted for the sake of Your name. Doesn't this give me the right to ask you to release my children from their pain, and return them to their land?" But God answered, "No!"

Now it was Jacob's turn to try to move God to mercy. "God," he implored, "my life was so confused and painful. My father Isaac did not like me. He preferred Esau. Esau wanted to kill me, so I had to run away to my uncle Laban, who swindled me. For twenty long years I worked for him, day and night. Then I could not take it any more, and I managed to return to the land of my birth. But it was not a happy situation. My wives quarrelled, my children fought each other, and at a given moment they even sold their own brother. I suffered it all, only because I wanted to weld their tribes into a Jewish nation, as You had commanded me. Don't I deserve that You take my suffering into account, and free my people?"

God did not answer, so Jeremiah appealed to Moses. He said, "Moses, please have a try; you suffered so much at the hands of this people, and more than once you were able to change God's mind." Moses went, but he did not succeed. God told him, "This is my decree, and I will not go back on My word. They [the Jewish people] will have to suffer for what they did."

Jeremiah was heartbroken and confused. What could he do now? Suddenly Rachel arose from her grave; she went up to God and said, "God, will you also forget what I did in my life? Jacob, who loved me with all his heart and soul, worked seven years to be able to marry me. When the time came, my father sent my sister Leah to him instead. I could have gone and told him, but I did not do it because I did not want to shame my sister. So I sacrificed myself."

Immediately God turned merciful, and He said, "Because of you, Rachel, I will restore the Jewish people to their land. Stop crying, and dry your tears, for there is a reward for your deeds, and your children will return to your borders."

What can we learn from this midrash? Why did God refuse to consider the sacrifices of Abraham, Isaac, Jacob, and Moses? All of them were ready to die for *kiddush ha-shem*, yet God took into account only the sacrifices of Rachel, and listened only to her pleas.

It would seem to me that there is a big difference between all the sacrifices of our patriarchs and of Moses, on one hand, and the sacrifice of Rachel, on the other. The former proved ready to sacrifice themselves by laying down their lives, but only Rachel was prepared to sacrifice by living with her fate. Her entire life she was forced to share Jacob, the husband she loved, with her sister, and because of this God accepted her sacrifice as the greatest. She was not dying for her convictions, she was not required to be a hero for one short moment only; she was *living* her martyrdom.

The deeds of Rachel teach us that it is not enough to accept Judaism only as a principle, however beautiful. We must live our

Jewish lives every day, and be prepared to accept the consequences. As our sages said: Only if we mourn and personally suffer the destruction of Jerusalem and her Temple can we hope to see the rebuilt Jerusalem and Zion.

Parashath Va-Etchanan

אעברה־נא ואראה את־הארץ הטובה אשר בעבר הירדן ההר
הטוב הזה והלבנון.

"Let me go over and see the good land beyond the Jordan—
that fine hill country and Lebanon."

Thus pleaded Moses with God, but God was angry with him,
and He answered, "Enough! Do not speak to me any more about
this matter. Go up to the top of Pisgah [literally: the highest
point of the mountain].... Look at the land with your own eyes,
since you are not going to cross this Jordan."

This stern and uncompromising message is counterbalanced
by the *haftarah* accompanying this week's portion from the
Torah, namely the famous verse from Isaiah: נחמו נחמו עמי יאמר
אלהיכם (*nachamu, nachamu ami yomar eloheichem*), "Comfort, comfort,
my people, says your God."

According to the Midrash, our sages said: If only the Jewish
people would keep two shabbatoth, they would be granted
redemption. This immediately raises two questions: Why does
the Talmud not stress that we should observe every Shabbath?
And, are these two shabbatoth indeed so powerful that they
alone can bring redemption? One of our rabbis comments that
this saying refers to two special shabbatoth: Shabbath Chazon
(after *chazon Isaiah*, the vision of Isaiah, at the beginning of this
prophetic book, which is read on the Shabbath before Tisha
be-Av—the fifteenth day of the month of Av) and Shabbath
Nachamu, the Shabbath following Tisha be-Av, when we read
the Torah portion *Ve-Etchanan*. In other words, if we would

283

succeed to live our lives according to the precepts of these two shabbatoth, redemption would surely come.

Tisha be-Av is a stark reminder of all our suffering during the centuries, the humiliation that countless generations of Jews have had to undergo at the hands of other people, the pogroms, the unimaginable bloodshed, and all the other terrors and disasters to which the Jewish people were subjected because they were defenseless and had no country of their own.

The second Shabbath, Shabbath Nachamu, on the other hand, reminds us that all this misery has not been the end of our existence. It shows that God is prepared to sustain and comfort us. Taking the ideas contained in these two shabbatoth together, we are able to overcome every conceivable misfortune and ensure our future survival.

We should remember that at the very beginning of Jewish history our father Abraham was forced to leave his family, bereft of property and protection. Yet, in the end, he became prosperous because he believed in the future and in what God had promised him. The same happened when the Children of Israel were in Egypt. They started as an assembly of tribes, and they even became slaves. But they believed; they followed Moses through the wilderness, and in the end became a prosperous nation.

The same story has repeated itself over and over again, even in our own lifetime. A people persecuted and decimated in a world war, a people who were destined for annihilation and disintegration, succeeded in rebuilding their ancient homeland. There obviously is a plan and a purpose behind it all—and yet it prompts a bitter question: Is it really necessary that we should always suffer destruction before we can build? Why does there have to be a Shabbath Chazon before Shabbath Nachamu? Why should there be destruction, in order for God to come and console us?

While we do not have a concrete answer to this question, the Midrash has a story that points into the direction where we have to look. An old man and his grandson were lost in the wilderness. They suffered from the burning sun by day, and from the cold desert air by night. Yet they struggled on, without passing any habitation or even a living soul who could offer them some food or water. At long last an object appeared on the horizon, which soon turned out to be a brick wall. Overjoyed, they believed it to be a city, until they came near and found it to be the wall of a cemetery. The grandson started to cry, but his grandfather consoled him by saying, "Where there is a cemetery, there also must be living people, and not far from here we will find the place where the people who are buried here came from."

The Midrash concludes that we must learn from this, that those who have felt the sorrow and bitterness of the cemetery— or of the destruction of their Temple and their independence— will in the end find the way to their home and survival.

The portion of *Ve-Etchanan* is read during the week of Tisha be-Av. Our sages tell us that in the days of the Temple, the fifteenth of Av and Yom Kippur were happy days for the Jewish people. According to them, it is not difficult to understand why Yom Kippur was a happy day, ever since the days of the Golden Calf. It was on this day that Moses received the second set of the Tablets of the Law, and that God said סלחתי כדבריך (*salachti ki-devareicha*), forgiving the Jewish people for their sins. Ever since, Yom Kippur has been a day of forgiveness.

But what happened on the fifteenth of Av to make it a day of celebration? Our sages give a variety of explanations, and I will restrict myself to just three. The first one is that on this day the early Jewish leaders permitted intermarriage between members of the various Hebrew tribes. During their stay in the desert following the Exodus, the Hebrews had lived in the traditional tribal context, and the descendants of our patriarch Jacob's children married only boys or girls from their own tribe. Only in Canaan, after each of the tribes had been allocated its share of the land, did the *shofetim*, the judges, permit intermarriage, and therefore only from this moment onward could the Jews begin to create a proper united nation. At first sight it might strike us as strange that the Jews were not permitted to marry a partner who was, like themselves, descended from their own kinsman Jacob. Yet we do not have to look far to realize that the answer to this question does not only apply to the days when the Jewish people first came to Canaan. Even in the *galuth* many Jews had serious reservations about marrying someone who did not hail from their own group or community. Even in our century we could see chassidim refusing to marry mitnagedim—or the reverse. Particularly during the early years of the modern Jewish state, Ashkenazim would often refuse to marry Sepharadim, while Sepharadi parents were none too keen to see their children marry Ashkenazim. At the same time, of course, the ban on intermarriage must have caused profound grief to youngsters who saw their mutual affections thwarted by "establishment" laws. So we can understand that the fifteenth of Av, when the legal restrictions on Jewish intermarriage were removed, was greeted with a sense of relief, and that in the Jewish tradition it was remembered as a day of joy.

We find a reminder of the above during the marriage ceremony. At the *chuppah* we let the bride and groom drink from the same cup, to symbolize the complete and unrestricted intertwining of their destinies. We erase, as it were, any distinctions between the couple, regardless whether they be of a social or a communal nature, to teach them—and ourselves—that marriage is not merely a contract, but a complete welding together, like the welding together of the Hebrew nation that started on the fifteenth of Av.

A second reason given by our sages is that on the 15th of Av the daughters of Jerusalem went out into the vineyards to dance and sing, all of them dressed in white. A white cotton dress, without any special ornamentation, is the simplest thing a girl can wear. There was one further condition, however, namely that no one should wear her own dress. Everyone had to borrow from a neighbor or friend, so that a poor girl, who did not have a proper dress of her own, would not have to feel ashamed. Even the daughters of the king or the high priest did not have the right to wear expensive dresses, or their own dresses, so that all the daughters of Israel would have the same opportunity of looking their best and participating in the festivities. We can imagine what a feeling of closeness and solidarity this must have produced. It is also characteristic of the morality of those days, which saw to it that, in true democratic fashion, people from all walks of life could mingle on an equal footing. We need not add that quite a few boys and girls met their future life's partners on this occasion, so taking it all together, we can understand what a joyful day this fifteenth of Av was.

A third reason has to do with the pilgrimages to the Temple in Jerusalem. Not long after King Solomon had completed his Temple — in fact, only ten years after his death — a revolt broke out and the best part of ten tribes split away from the Jewish kingdom to establish their own Kingdom of Israel. The first thing that their King Jeroboam did was to forbid the pilgrimages to Jerusalem, the central place of Jewish worship and the symbol of Israel's national unity. Instead he had two golden calves made, one of which was set up in Dan, and the other in Bethel. The *tanna* Ulla (a *tanna* is a sage of the period of the Mishnah) reports that the first king to passively permit the resumption of the pilgrimages to Jerusalem was King Elah, who removed the guards from the borders of Samaria on the fifteenth of Av. Opinions are divided on exactly how long the ban lasted, but it was a matter of several hundreds of years — sufficiently long, in fact, to destroy the unity of the Jewish nation. As a result, when soon after this the Assyrians invaded Eretz Israel, the nation was already deeply divided. Who knows whether, if the Twelve Tribes had remained united, the Assyrian attack might have been beaten off?

This brings us back to the question of how we Jews can survive and avoid being destroyed. What has history taught us that we can use to advantage in our time? We know that our sages, especially Rabbi Yochanan ben Zakkai, reminded us that if we go in the ways of the Torah we will survive. The question is how we can persuade our people. We can find the answer in the Midrash, specifically in a quotation of Rabbi Meir in the Talmud Yerushalmi, in *masechtah Shabbath*. In it, Rabbi Meir says, "When the Jewish people stood at Mount Sinai, and said, 'We will do, and after that we will hear,' God asked, 'After you will have received the Torah, who will be responsible that you will observe it?' The leaders of the Jewish people answered, 'Our guarantors will be our forefathers, Abraham, Isaac and Jacob.' But God said, 'I cannot accept them as guarantors. In the house of Abraham, the first patriarch, a son grew up who was a wild man. Isaac I cannot accept because his son Esau did not behave as I wanted. Even Jacob I cannot accept as a guarantor, because his children hated each other, and they even sold one of their brothers into slavery.' So the elders said, 'We will pledge You our children,' and to this God answered, 'Your children I will accept.'" And because of them we will survive.

This is the answer to the question at the beginning about observing the two shabbatoth. If we observe and learn from them, then — even if there should be a time of crisis — we shall have every reason to hope for renewal and redemption. God's message will never be lost — for wherever parents cease to observe, the children will continue. We have only to look at history to know this to be true. Of all the ancient civilizations among which the Jews lived — Babylonians, Assyrians, Persians, Egyptians, Greeks, and Romans — only the Jews and their faith have survived. And looking at our own generation we can observe, apart from assimilation, a constant searching for faith and renewal among young Jews. This is a true source of consolation, that Jewish faith *will* continue, despite changes and against all odds.

Parashath Ekev

ויענך וירעבך ויאכלך את־המן אשר לא־ידעת ולא ידעון
אבותיך למען הודיעך כי לא על־הלחם לבדו יחיה האדם כי
על־כל־מוצא פי־יהוה יחיה האדם.

ואמרת בלבבך כחי ועצם ידי עשה לי את־החיל הזה: וזכרת
את־יהוה אלהיך כי הוא הנתן לך כח לעשות חיל למען הקים
את־בריתו אשר־נשבע לאבתיך ביום הזה.

"He humbled you, causing you to hunger and then feeding
you with manna, which neither you nor your fathers had
known, to teach you that man does not live on bread alone,
but that man lives on every word that comes from the
mouth of God."

"You may say to yourselves, 'My power and the strength
of my hands have produced this wealth for me.' But
remember your God, for it is He who gives you the ability
to produce wealth, and so confirms His covenant, which he
swore to your forefathers, as it is today."

"Man does not live on bread alone." In this famous Torah
verse Moses tells us in the name of God that life does not have a
material aspect only, but that the material and the spiritual must
exist side by side; without these two, the world could not continue to exist.

The Torah, which is our guide to the spiritual and material
sides of our existence, tells us that we have to thank God for the

ability to produce wealth, rather than our own power or the strength of our hands.

The Midrash reminds us that God created all living things, and that nobody is capable of imitating the works of God. Rabbi Eliezer said in the name of Rabbi Yochanan that all the scientists in the world could not make one living thing, even a mosquito, that would be comparable to what God has created. He quotes a verse from the Book of Devarim, where in *Parashath Ha'azinu,* Moses says: הצור תמים פעלו כי כל־דרכיו משפט (*ha-tzur tamim pa'alo ki kol derachav mishpat*), "He is the rock, His works are perfect, and all His ways are just," which is interpreted as meaning that every living being has been created perfectly adapted to its needs. Man has two eyes, enabling him to see objects and distances, and few people would claim that we would have been more perfect if we possessed only one eye, or three or four eyes. The same goes for the human brain, which enables us to think, to remember, and to organize. God also created harmony between the material and the spiritual parts of our being, and human life would be impossible without one or the other.

The interesting thing is how we are inclined to accept all this as completely normal. We hardly stop to think about the perfect coordination between the movements of our hands and feet, or how the impulses of our brain are immediately translated into physical reactions. We accept as normal that it will become dark at night, and that the sun will rise again in the morning. To us this is self-evident. What would be abnormal, and result in immediate fear and panic, is if suddenly one day the sun would come up even ten minutes later than we expect it in our particular part of the world. In other words, we accept as normal the millions of miracles of creation, but we are surprised at the exceptions.

The Talmud, in the volume *Shabbath,* contains a discussion between two rabbis about an incident that happened in their lifetime. The wife of one of the inhabitants of their town had died, leaving a baby who had to be breast-fed. The father was too poor to hire a woman to feed the baby, and there certainly were no special baby foods available in those days. According to the story a miracle happened, and the father developed breasts, so that he was able to feed his baby son. Rabbi Yosef concluded that the incident proved God's greatness, because He changed the course of nature to enable the father to feed his child. Rabbi Abbaya, however, arrived at the opposite conclusion, arguing that it was a stain on society that it cared so little about a small baby that God was forced to intervene and change nature.

It is important to understand that this discussion between the two rabbis involved a point of principle. What is the biggest miracle: the fact that a mother (or, in her absence, another woman) is able to nourish her baby, or that God changes nature and causes a father to develop breasts in order to ensure the survival of his child? Most people would call everything that goes against the normal course of nature a miracle, but according to the traditional Jewish philosophical view the real miracle of our world is the normal routine, the built-in perfection as created by God. The exceptions, resulting from neglect or man's interference in nature, are merely signs of human imperfection.

At the beginning of this *parashah* we quoted the Torah's warning that man cannot live on bread alone, in other words that life may not be seen in terms of economic or material issues only. The spiritual side is equally important, and the Torah tells us that we can avoid suffering by accepting its ethics and its guidelines for everyday life. True, man is capable of many things, but too often his pride and ambition make him forget that he cannot provide answers for everything — except with the help of God.

A simple illustration of this is the developments in psychology and psychiatry during the last hundred years or so. There is no doubt that we have gained important insights into the workings of the human brain, and that as a result we are able to heal many nervous and mental disorders. Even so, although we are continually building new research laboratories and hospitals, we are still very much in the dark about the functioning of the human personality. Every answer scientists give raises new questions, and every new opinion is questioned by others as soon as it is proposed. Ever since Freud there have been so many different psychiatric "schools" and theories that even specialists in the field are confused, and the patients continue to suffer.

I will try to give just one example of how a confused medical approach can hold up the treatment of a disturbed person. A certain psychiatrist tells in one of his books how he was visited by a young lady in an acute state of depression. Soon after the start of the treatment he became aware that the lady was pathologically jealous of her more beautiful and apparently more charming older sister. This jealousy caused her to project her hatred upon everyone she considered even remotely similar to her sister. Once the psychiatrist realized the reason, he was able to relieve her condition — but only for a short time. For after a while her depression returned, and the psychiatrist decided to consult some colleagues. One of them said, "Instead of treating her jealousy of her sister, we must look at her personality to explain what causes her to be jealous in general. The underlying problem is a severe lack of self-confidence and self-esteem. The only treatment is to try to remove her obsession that she is discriminated against. This we must do by building up her self-esteem, and by teaching her that material things — beauty or talent — are not everything, for "man does not live on bread alone."

Our sages said הקנאה והתאוה מוציאים את האדם מן העולם (ha-kin'ah ve-ha-ta'avah motzeim eth ha-adam min ha-olam), "Jealousy, lust, and ambition drive a man out of the world." Even valuable and necessary properties, such as desire and ambition, that are needed for the world to exist and progress, can — when they are taken to excess — cause a person to lose himself and drive him to destruction.

People who do not know how to balance their desires and ambitions will never be able to live a normal life. It is to the *pasuk* "man shall not live on bread alone" that the misdrashic comment on an earlier Torah verse, in the Book of Devarim, refers: והסיר יהוה ממך כל-חלי וכל-מדוי מצרים הרעים אשר ידעת לא ישמם בך ונתנם בכל-שנאיך (ve-hesier ha-shem mimecha kol choli ve-chol madvei mitzra'im hara'im asher yadata lo yasimam bach u-netatam be-chol sone'eicha), "God will keep you free from every disease. He will not inflict on you the horrible diseases you knew in Egypt, but he will inflict them on all who hate you." What the Midrash wants to convey is that body and mind will remain healthy if one listens to the word of God and balances material and spiritual interests. This is why it is so important to realize that all we have received is from God, rather than the product of our own strength and intelligence. This realization also prevents us from falling victim to extreme reactions, either a feeling that we can do everything by ourselves, or a feeling of depression because nothing we do seems to be good enough.

For an even better understanding of all this, we should go back to the very first chapter of the Torah, where it is written, ויאמר אלהים נעשה אדם בצלמנו כדמותנו וירדו בדגת הים ובעוף השמים . . . (va-yomer ha-shem na'aseh adam be-tzalmenu ve-yirdu be-degat ha-yam u-be-of ha-shamayim . . .), "And God said: 'Let us make man in our image, in our likeness, and let them rule over the fish of the sea and the birds of the air. . . .'" God wanted us to rule the earth, but the question is *how* we should exercise our dominion. Man was blessed with creative intelligence, which enables him to invent, to create, and to build and—in so doing—ensure his survival and that of the generations to come. Our initiative and ambition keep the wheels turning, but initiative can turn into aggression, and ambition can become jealousy and greed. There comes a day, however, on which really thinking people ask themselves, "What am I living for? Do I live to improve my own life and that of my family and the world around me—or do I live to buy a bigger house, or an even more luxurious car to impress others, so that they can see how successful I am?" Envy has two aspects: not only are we jealous of other people's possessions, but often our own buying decisions are in turn aimed at making others jealous of us.

For a balanced view of the value of material wealth, and an intelligent appreciation of our limitations as "rulers" of this world, we must remind ourselves of Rabbi Eliezer's dictum that all the scientists in the world together could not make one living thing, even a mosquito, that would be comparable to what God has created. We know that engineers can make robots to replace human hands. Researchers are conducting experiments to imitate living organisms, but every scientist with a grain of moral sensibility is aware of the potential consequences that such a discovery would have. The specter of millions of artificially created beings, without conscience or feelings, who could be sent out to make war and to conquer other nations, would be too frightful to imagine. To demonstrate that the idea is not altogether fanciful, we can quote the "materialist" dictator Mao Tse-tung, who considered human beings "manure on the fields of the future," and who at one time declared that "for the sake of the achievement of a specific political goal, it is permissible to sacrifice half of mankind." I could imagine that many of us would not want to live in a world where such ideas were put into practice. Fortunately, however, people are not robots, for הצור תמים פעלו כי כל־דרכיו משפט (ha-tzur tamim pa'alo ki kol derachav mishpat), "He is the rock, His works are perfect, and all His ways are just." This teaches us that we cannot copy God's creation, and as long as we continue to go in the way of the Torah, we will remain aware of our responsibility to help prevent the world from sliding into the abyss of materialist ideology.

We accept as self-evident that all human beings are different. In the same way that the parts of the body differ, but work in harmony, human beings have to cooperate and support each other. If one part of the body refuses to cooperate, we go to a doctor or a hospital to get help. When help is no longer possible, the body dies. In the same way only a sense of mutual responsibility and solidarity will enable our human society to survive.

Centuries ago our sages said הקנאה והתאוה מוציאים את האדם מן העולם (ha-kin'ah ve-ha-ta'avah motzeim eth ha-adam min ha-olam), "Jealousy, lust, and ambition drive a man out of the world." Every thinking human being will recognize these drives in himself. We were born with them, and without them the world could not progress. At the same time we have to subject ourselves to the ethics of the Torah, for otherwise we will be "driven out of this world." It is up to us to see to it that our ambitions are turned into a blessing—for ourselves and for our society. Once we are convinced that what God asks us to do is for the sake of our own physical and spiritual health, we shall be able to live up to His demands, and in so doing benefit ourselves and our fellowmen.

Parashath Re'eh (1)

ראה אנכי נתן לפניכם היום ברכה וקללה: את־הברכה אשר
תשמעו אל־מצות יהוה אלהיכם אשר אנכי מצוה אתכם היום:
והקללה אם־לא תשמעו אל־מצות יהוה אלהיכם וסרתם מן־
הדרך אשר אנכי מצוה אתכם היום ללכת אחרי אלהים אחרים
אשר לא־ידעתם.

"See, I set before you today a blessing and a curse—the
blessing if you obey the commands of the Lord your God
that I am giving you today; the curse if you disobey the
commands of the Lord your God and turn from the way
that I command you today by following other gods, which
you have not known."

In 1904 Sigmund Freud published a book that for the next
half a century would profoundly influence all thinking in the
field of psychotherapy. In this book, called *Psychopathology of Everyday Life*, the father of psychoanalysis discusses the issue of free
will, and the problems facing man in making his own choices
between good and evil. Freud claimed that even seemingly accidental actions in everyday life were determined by unconscious
causes. According to him, the neurotic person had a faulty
understanding of his conflict. Without realizing it, the patient
did not want to know what the problem was, or what had caused
it. Because of this ignorance, it was impossible to blame him for
his resulting behavior.

What Freud in effect said was that man, being driven by
unconscious forces, has no free will, and is therefore unable to

choose between one action or another. For over half a century this Freudian principle went unchallenged in the world of mental health treatment. Only during the past three decades have many of the original psychoanalytical theories been reviewed, as a result of which they have been subjected to heavy criticism.

Needless to say, the people Freud talks about are in effect refusing to accept responsibility. In their innermost hearts they know very well what is right or wrong, but they tell themselves that, since they do not control their actions, they do not have to accept the consequences either. Neither do they have to abide by the laws of society or of religion, for it is their instinct that decides what happens. What a convenient—and irresponsible—sense of freedom they must have. To any intelligent observer it must be clear, however, that they are running away from their conscience, and an individual who is unable to make decisions with a sense of responsibility is anything but free.

In addition there are many people who cannot be responsible for their actions. They are the really problematic ones because, lacking an elementary sense of good and bad, they are not even aware of the wrongs they are committing. Their "freedom" is in effect nothing but license to do as they please, so that such people certainly should not be given the right to make decisions.

From the above it should be clear that we are by no means the helpless victims of circumstances that some would like to suggest. In fact, the Torah affirms one of the most fundamental and inspired principles of our Jewish faith, namely that of *bechirah*, or free will. In particular for us, who live in a free and open society, it is important to understand what this Torah concept intends to say.

The Torah says, "I have set before you life and death, the blessing and the curse; therefore choose life, that you and your seed may live." What we are told, in other words, is: you are free to do with life as you see fit. You can create with it, or use it to destroy; you can build with it, or use it to demolish; you can sanctify with it, or use it to profane. You should know, however, that you—and you alone—are responsible. What the Torah says is that you can turn your life into a *kelalah*, a curse, or into a *berachah*, a blessing. There are two ways to live your life: you can try to escape everyday problems by parties and merrymaking, or by taking refuge in pills and prescriptions, or you can live simply and realistically, by confronting problems and dealing with them as they come. You are the master of your own destiny, not merely in terms of your immediate physical or material welfare, but—far more important—your long-term psychological balance: your spiritual well-being.

Turning our life into a *berachah*, a blessing, enables it to be enjoyed without any fear of the results of our actions. On the other hand, we can turn our life into a *kelalah*, robbing it of any future hope or prospects. The word *berachah* is derived from the root ברך (*berech*), the Hebrew word for "knee." The knee is a very important part of the human anatomy. It consists of separate parts that are linked together in such a way that they can move smoothly and in perfect harmony. Without knees we would not be able to walk and move forward.

When Joseph wanted Ya'acov to bless his children, he placed them on his father's knee. A blessing is, therefore, when we and our family are able to act together and move in harmony like the knee joints. It is a blessing to have smooth and flexible contacts with our dear ones, not only in times of crisis but on ordinary days as well. When separate parts, like human individuals, feel connected and move in harmony, that is *berachah*.

The Torah says: the choice is yours—therefore choose life. Recognize the weaknesses, see the weak spots, and bend your knees to the task. Simply stated: Move! Uproot yourself! Yes, the knee is the organ that symbolizes our ability to move together.

To stand still, on the other hand, to remain immobilized in an environment that prevents spiritual growth and happiness, surely is no blessing but a *kelalah*, or curse, a word containing the root of the Hebrew word קל (*kal*), which means "easy" or "light."

A life that is "light" or "weightless," in other words entirely
lacking in physical or spiritual challenge, is indeed a curse. Of
course there are many people today who think that life can be
free and easy, without any duties and obligations. Isn't that
what modern progress and prosperity are all about—to be able
to free ourselves from cares and hard work, to live free as a bird,
to live fast, refusing to be tied down by responsibilities and
obligations? But do we really think that we can purchase happiness by freeing ourselves from all duties and restraints?

One of our foremost psychologists has pointed out that such
an attitude is entirely unrealistic. The seeming paradox is that in
order to be free, a certain amount of self-discipline is necessary.
Without it we are in effect turned into the slaves of our passions. The Torah says that we are born free—free from sin, free
from evil, free from guilt, and therefore free to steer our lives in
the direction we want. From this it follows that we are free to do
good and be a blessing, and free to do evil and become a curse,
both to ourselves and to society as a whole.

Choosing the first course means sticking to certain principles, principles that have been laid down in our unique Jewish
faith. It means moving closer to God, tying ourselves down to
the framework of His Torah, bending our knees toward His
task, and giving our life a direction and a meaning. This is how
our life can become a blessing.

Many people ask: What is so good about religion? Why
should I be religious? Isn't it sufficient to be a moral person?
After all, it is morality that counts—all the rest is not important.
As a believing person I myself am truly convinced that religion is
a direct reflection of the purposes of the Creator of our world,
and that therefore we have to obey its commandments. But
apart from this, religion also helps to ease the life of the individual who is open to the ideas of the Torah.

In the first place it gives a perspective and a direction to our
lives; it teaches us where we are going. It helps us to decide what
is the proper way to live, and therefore it is a measure of

morality. Judaism has traditionally taught that true morality means compassion. In answer to this, some people say that the observance of the *mitzvoth* has nothing to do with morality and compassion. Reality shows that this is by no means the case, for as soon as it comes to a crisis, ethics without religion breaks down and is no longer binding.

A second function of religion, which all of us at one stage or another in our lives need is to provide comfort; to give us strength, and help us to face and overcome life's problems. Our synagogues and religious institutions are not just there for prayer and study. They are community centers where people meet friends and mingle on an equal footing, because they are all children of God. However unequal people may be in society, the synagogue reminds us that human beings are all equally favored in the eyes of the Almighty. Our religious institutions reinforce Judaism's belief in man's equality and man's right to equal consideration and justice.

It is true that religious people are not perfect; that many of them even have visible faults. It is true that some people try to mask their deficiencies or compensate for their bad behavior by a show of religious dedication. But this does not mean that we should blame religion for the actions of these individuals.

Those who are really true to the Jewish religion will find it impossible to escape their moral responsibilities. The entire structure of Judaism, its fundamental teachings, its traditions, and its history combine to remind us of our obligations to our family, our community, and to the Jewish people at large.

Why, for instance, do we give charity? In order to make sure that we remain conscious of our duty to our brothers. Why are we told to provide a good education for our children? So that we can place them on the road to life, and teach them to respect the rights of others. Religion provides us with objective standards for making the correct moral choices. Of course we can avoid these choices. No one stops us from sinning again and again, for the choice is in our hands, and often there is no visible or immediate punishment. But we know that one day we shall be called to account for what we have done against God's laws. Furthermore, we will lose the respect of our fellowmen, and eventually our own self-respect as well.

The best illustration of the binding force of religion is the Shabbath. There is no greater support for the unity of the family than the Shabbath. Families who decide to give up the weekly Friday night meal hardly ever do so for economic reasons; they do it because they fail to appreciate the Jewish family ideal.

Besides stressing the Shabbath as a religious commandment, the Torah reminds us in yet another way of the importance of this elementary Jewish framework. It tells us about the so-called מעשר שני (ma'aser sheni), the "second tithe." "Tithing" means to "set aside (a tenth part, of profits)" for the support of, for instance, the priests. In biblical times, the first tithe was used for the upkeep of the cohanim and Levites, but the second tithe was in effect no tithe at all. This second tithe was given to no one. It was supposed to be taken up to Jerusalem, there to be spent on food and drink.

What a strange law, on the face of it, to tell people to set aside one tenth of their income once every seven years, in order to entertain their friends and relatives, as well as a number of the poor, with food and drink. The explanation is that religion was not intended to affect the individual's private existence only, but that it had to foster a feeling of comradeship. Its purpose was to bring people closer to their fellowmen and teach them to share their concerns, their worries, and their joys with others.

Sometimes people who feel religion is out of date remind me of the vulture, the biblical ראה (ra'ah). The vulture is considered tereifah, unkosher, and our sages explain that one of the reasons for this is its extraordinary vision, which enabled it to see across a great distance: it even was believed to see the faults of Eretz Israel all the way from Babylonia. Similarly, many people who themselves are far removed from religion are only too quick to point out the imperfections of those who make an earnest effort to live up to its morality. Like the vulture, they are observing and judging from a distance—in contrast to those on the spot, who are at least trying! Though not perfect, they do try to confront their moral choices, rather than run away or avoid them.

Summarizing, I would like to say that it pays for all of us to remain conscious of the ways of the Torah, to try to go in its ways. In particular we should avoid looking only at the faults of others, but have the strength to take a critical look at our own actions, and try to stick—of our own free will—to our known religious principles, so that we may become, every one in his own way, more loving, more compassionate, and more moral individuals.

Parashath Re'eh (2)

אלה החקים והמשפטים אשר תשמרון לעשות בארץ אשר נתן
יהוה אלהי אבתיך לרשתה כל־הימים אשר־אתם חיים על־
האדמה.

"These are the statutes and the ordinances which you shall
observe to do in the land which the Lord, the God of your
fathers, has given you, to possess it all the days that you
live upon the earth."

In the Book of Devarim—Deuteronomy—which contains
the history of the Jewish people till the moment of their entry
into the Land of Israel, we find three commandments that Jews
were told to observe:
1. To elect a king
2. To build the *Beth ha-Mikdash*, the Holy Temple
3. To destroy the Amalekites
According to the Talmud, volume *Sanhedrin*, there is no doubt
that the extermination of the Amalekites, although the third in
the list, had to be carried out first. Doesn't it seem strange that
people who were so eager to establish a national center—
especially a spiritual center—should have given a lower priority
to the construction of the *Beth ha-Mikdash* than to electing a king
and fighting their enemies? We could try to explain this oddity
by saying that only when a people are united under a ruler who
is capable of defeating all their enemies can they really concern
themselves with spiritual matters. Because of this, the appointment of a king—who is both a leader and a symbol of this
national unity—should come first. The most logical sequence of

events would therefore seem to be: the appointment of a king, after which this king rids the people of the enemy who is after their physical destruction (which is what the Amalekites intended), and only then the building of the Temple.

This explanation is a little bit too simplistic, however. Looking at the talmudic interpretation of the three above-mentioned commandments in chapters 10, 11, and 12 of Devarim, it would seem that there lies a far more profound message in the priorities than is evident on the surface. We are dealing here with a tautological necessity. We have to remember that the Children of Israel, in the period we are talking about, were a collection of tribes that still had to be welded together into a single and united nation.

A people can be united in two ways: through a common enemy or through a common cause. This is what unites people and nations. The difference between the two is that unity through a common enemy is negative, as well as temporary and most times meaningless. Unity through common values, on the other hand, can be positive, lasting and meaningful.

The *Beth ha-Mikdash* that the Jews were to build for their joint worship of God was conceived as a chosen house. This would seem to imply that this Temple had to be the product of a unanimous and collective choice by people who dwelt together, harmoniously united by a common interest, namely their acceptance of and submission to the Torah way of life.

The above-described situation is not only of historical interest but continues to be relevant till this very day. We can observe unanimity among people who are united through a common enemy, but such unanimity falls apart as soon as the enemy has disappeared, so that it cannot form the basis for building a harmonious future together.

Therefore we can say that the Jewish people could start thinking of unanimity only after the hostilities with their outside enemies had been resolved—specifically when the threat of Amalek had been removed. Only then could they establish a

unity of values and embark upon the building of their spiritual
center. Only then was there a sufficient likelihood that the
unity would be positive, and therefore stable and lasting,
because it was a unity based on common values rather than on a
common enemy.

Applying the above arguments, it becomes painfully clear
how, after forty years of Jewish sovereignty in Eretz Israel, we
do not even have the right to think about building a Temple.
Twice before the Jewish people built a sanctuary in Jerusalem,
and twice it was destroyed. This time we should really wait for
the Messiah to bring the required unity and unanimity before
we can rebuild the *Beth ha-Mikdash*. So far we have not even
succeeded in achieving peace with our fellowmen. We are
divided among ourselves, and often do not even live in peace
with our close neighbors. It is clear, therefore, that we must
first concentrate on achieving peace and understanding among
our own people.

How can we achieve real peace between ourselves? We can
find the answer in the Torah, in chapter 13 of the book of
Devarim, where it says אחרי יהוה אלהיכם תלכו ואתו תיראו ואת־מצוותיו
תשמרו ובקלו תשמעו (*acharei ha-shem eloheichem telechu ve-oto tira'u ve-eth-
mitzvotaiv tishmeru u-ve-kolo tishme'u*), "After the Lord your God you
shall walk... and Him you must revere. Keep His commandments and listen to His voice." Our narratives explain this verse
as follows: "After the Lord your God you shall walk" is a מצות עשה
(*mitzvath aseh*), a commandment that God asks you to carry out.
However, when the Torah says "Keep his commandments," this
refers to the מצות לא תעשה (*mitzvoth lo ta'aseh*), the negative commandments, the things God asks us not to do. "...and listen to
His voice," means that we shall listen to the voices of the
prophets.

From this we see that the commandments of the Torah are
divided into two kinds: the so-called positive commandments,
which God asks us to carry out, and the negative commandments, referring to the actions God wants us to avoid. In con-

nection with both kinds of commandments our sages say לפים צערי אגרי (lefim tzare agre), an Aramaic expression meaning that in almost every area of human endeavor the reward is determined by the measure of labor and sacrifice we invest in achieving the desired goal. Similarly, the measure of achievement is a function of our enthusiasm and inspiration. Enthusiasm and inspiration are not always easy to come by. For this reason, in the same book of Devarim, God says to the Jewish people in connection with the bringing of the tithe to the place of worship: "If the way is too long for you, so that you are not able to carry it... you shall go in the way that God told you to walk."

In other words, if the way appears too long, and the burden too heavy, the reason must be that we are too far from our target—that we have somehow become too far removed from God, and that we are too much estranged from His teachings and norms. Whenever a *mitzvah* becomes a burden, rather than a source of spiritual reward, it means that something is missing, and that we must adjust our attitude and behavior. By remembering this, we can avoid our spiritual fatigue.

We will not always know how to do this. Our sages of the oral tradition knew this too, for which reason they offered us a program intended to help change our attitudes and actions and to avoid spiritual fatigue. This program consists of the following points:

1.   To fulfill the *mitzvoth aseh*, the positive commands, with an emphasis upon the joys and the rewards achieved through the *mitzvoth*. For example, in conveying the traditions connected with the Shabbath laws, we should not merely emphasize everything that is forbidden on the Shabbath, in terms of the limitation on physical activities, but also the tangible gains and the happiness of *oneg Shabbath*, the joy and blessings that we derive from Shabbath observance.

2.   To be mindful of יראת אלהים (*yirath elohim*), the "fear of God." Although modern psychiatry aims to eliminate the element of fear from the human mind, we are very much aware that

many people would continue trespassing on dangerous or forbidden territory, or indulging in activities that might damage their own well-being, if it was not for the fear of being caught and punished. The fear of God will keep us alert and prevent us from doing things that could bring harm to us and society.

3. To observe the *mitzvoth lo ta'aseh*, the negative commandments. Once we have established a firm and positive attitude to the *mitzvoth*, coupled with an intelligent understanding of reward and punishment, the individual will be prepared to submit to a measure of discipline and restraint without continually lamenting that he is a martyr.

4. To live our lives and practice the commandments in the spirit of נעשה ונשמע (*na'aseh ve-nishmah*), "first we will do, and then we will hear," the cry with which the Children of Israel expressed their readiness to accept the Torah at Sinai. First to do—and after that to hear, and to understand. This attitude, more than anything else, helps us to achieve the desired positive state of mind. Our sages explain the meaning of ובקולי תשמעו (*ubekoli tishme'u*), "to the voice of God you shall listen," as meaning that we shall listen to the words of the prophets.

    The teachings of the prophets, which emphasize universal peace, social justice, love of our fellowmen and devotion to Eretz Israel, are the logical sequence in the gradual development of *yiddishkeit*, the characteristic behavior of the true Jewish personality.

5. To create a suitable environment, another requirement for positive Jewish living. People must avoid exposing themselves recklessly to a climate that might block the growth of their spiritual עץ החיים (*etz ha-chaim*), their "Tree of Life." But just avoiding an environment that clashes with our aims is not sufficient, and will not bring us the desired result. We must actively plan our lives and create the kind

of environment that enables us to live according to the goals and morality of the Torah.

6.   To prevent the sin of habit. Habit is not the same as routine. We need a measure of routine to give our lives a certain steadiness and rhythm. Without some routine, without a certain predictability, we would find our daily lives very difficult indeed. But a routine is something we follow knowingly, whereas a habit is something automatic, as a result of which it often degenerates into performing meaningless gestures. Of course there are good habits and bad habits; good habits we should cherish, and bad habits of which we should try to rid ourselves. What I want to say is that we often sin against ourselves and our fellows by practicing habits as a routine performance. It is an excellent habit to surprise someone who is dear to us occasionally with a little gift—for instance flowers. But do we really think that he or she will appreciate, or respect, such a gift when it turns out that we have given a florist a standing order to deliver flowers on certain dates? To such an extent are we creatures of habit that even intelligent people frequently catch themselves adopting courses of action and embracing patterns of thought that are habitual, even long after the circumstances have changed, and the realities warrant a new look and a new approach. We continue with our old habits and customs as if nothing has happened. We are blind to the changes in our surroundings. This is what the Torah asks us to avoid—even if the majority are continuing to practice habits that are harmful to themselves and others.

"These are the statutes and the ordinances which you shall observe to do in the land which the Lord, the God of your fathers, has given you." If we take this advice from the Torah, in the interpretation of our sages, we will not become spiritually fatigued, and we will follow the commandments and the Jewish law, which will bring us peace of mind and lead to peace among ourselves.

Parashath Re'eh (3)

ראה אנכי נתן לפניכם היום ברכה וקללה: את־הברכה אשר
תשמעו אל־מצות יהוה אלהיכם אשר אנכי מצוה אתכם היום:
והקללה אם־לא תשמעו אל־מצות יהוה אלהיכם וסרתם מן־
הדרך אשר אנכי מצוה אתכם היום ללכת אחרי אלהים אחרים
אשר לא־ידעתם.

"See, I am setting before you today a blessing and a curse—
the blessing if you obey the commands of your God that I
am giving you today; the curse if you disobey the commands of your God by following other gods, which you
have not known."

This verse from the Book of Devarim indicates that God
punishes those who do not follow His commandments. However, in the Talmud and Midrash our sages explain that God
wants to impress upon the Jewish people that they are not doing
Him a favor by observing His commandments, but that it is *in
their own* interest! The prophet Jeremiah said in the name of God,
מאתי לא תצא הרעות והטובות (*me'iti lo tetze ha-ra'oth ve-ha-tovoth*), "I [in other
words God] will cause you neither bad nor good." We must
understand this in the sense that God has shown the Jewish
people a way of life, and that it is up to them to choose. If they go
the right way, good will come to them, whereas if they go the
wrong way, they will meet bad in return.

The Midrash continues with a quote from Rabbi Haggai to
his students, according to which God said to the Jewish people: I
have shown you two ways, a good way and a bad way—but I did

you a favor by advising you to choose the good way. Our foremost Torah interpreters ask how we should understand the words of Rabbi Haggai. What exactly is the favor that God did us?

According to Jewish tradition, God separated man from the rest of His creation by giving only him a free choice between doing good or bad. Indeed, humans are capable of distinguishing between their actions, whereas animals have only their instincts to guide their survival. Even so, the Torah says: I give you a blessing if you listen to the commandments, and a curse if you do not listen. So where is our free choice, if the alternative to doing good is to be cursed? How do we understand the Torah when God says that He places a curse before us if we disobey His commandments?

From the outset we must make it clear that we are not talking here about the choice between a righteous life and a life of crime; crime has its own punishment. We are talking about normal, reasonably law-abiding citizens going about their everyday affairs. To them also applies two ways to behave: a good way and a bad way, depending upon their motivations. Jewish religious philosophers are of the opinion that everything human beings do is influenced by the behavior of Adam and Eve in the Garden of Eden, at the very beginning of human life on earth. Adam ate from the Tree of Knowledge. He ate something that did not belong to him, something God had specifically warned him not to eat. Eating from the Tree of Knowledge changed Adam's personality, and not only his, but that of all succeeding generations. Man began to covet things, to make demands—and as a result jealousy, greed, lust, and ambition came into the world.

Adam and Eve were created naked, but in their innocence they were not aware of it. They did not need clothes, they felt no inclination to be either good or bad, and they did not know dissatisfaction or desire. However, as soon as Adam had eaten from the forbidden fruit, they became conscious of their nakedness. They covered themselves, but it was not enough to hide their sense of shame and imperfection. People have been covering themselves ever since, with clothes, jewelry, and cosmetics—but they continue to feel "naked." Society ladies who own five hundred dresses and two hundred pairs of shoes have been heard to complain "that they have nothing to put on". Some people feel ashamed because they are afraid that their car is old-fashioned! And so we could go on giving examples.

Even among basically good people, we can recognize two kinds. The first kind wants to create, but its ultimate goal is to achieve wealth or fame. These people are ambitious; they are continuously striving for more, even if the means by which this is achieved are not always above suspicion. I do not want to be misunderstood; it is my profound belief that the world cannot progress without human ambition. Ambition is the motor. Nothing can move without it, as an engine cannot move without steam or electricity. Honest efforts deserve to be rewarded! However, it is the *kind* of reward that we are talking about—and this brings us to the second kind of people we talked about. They are not motivated by material rewards; they are not eaten by jealousy or fear that others will be considered more intelligent or richer, or will be more honored. Their reward is to do good, to help create progress for the benefit of their fellowmen, to make the world an easier and more prosperous—and maybe happier—place to live in. This is the motivation that drives many scientists: the people who have given us the electric light, the motor car, the microscope; the people to whom we owe it that we no longer die of the plague, malaria, tuberculosis, or any number of other epidemics and infectious diseases.

Lust, greed, and ambition make a person restless. This applies not only to individuals, but on a large scale to societies as well. Ultimately they are the reasons why countries fight and conquer each other. The same great inventions to which we owe our progress, are often turned against us when lust, greed, pride, or ambition take the upper hand. Neither does this happen only in commerce, industry, or science. Most religious students are motivated by love of the Torah, but there are some who are driven by unhealthy ambitions, in order to know more or better than others, to show off, or to be the first.

While I am writing this, I am reminded of a famous passage in the Book of Ezekiel , where the prophet describes his vision of the heavens—a passage that is also recited in our daily prayers. "As I looked," Ezekiel says, "at the living creatures [the angels], I saw a wheel on the ground beside each creature...." These "wheels" were the אופנים (ophanim), wheel-like, angelic creatures residing around the throne of God: והאופנים וחיות הקדש ברעש גדול מתנשאים לעמת שרפים (ve-ha-ofanim ve-chayoth ha-kodesh be-ra'ash gadol mitnase'im le'umath serafim) "And the Ophanim and the holy Chayoth with a great rushing noise, upraising themselves toward the Seraphim."

It is by no means my intention here to engage in kabbalistic interpretations, but I believe that the ophanim symbolize God's desire for man to move—but to move by kedushah, in other words in a sacred way, to the greater glory of God and His creation. This is why the Torah says: "See, I am setting before you today a blessing and a curse." If you act the right way, it will prove to be a blessing for you; if not, your actions may become a curse. The above also explains why the Midrash says that God does us a favor by advising us to do good. Again, we are not talking about those who decide to be bad, but about those who act and create in a positive way, even though their motivations are selfish. God advises us, if we are already doing good, to do it the right way and with the right intentions. This way, we do not only honor God, but we also do ourselves a favor. For the more ambitious a person is when he is creating or inventing new things or methods, the greater the risk that he will forget the joy of life and his obligations to his family.

This applies particularly when someone's ambitions are selfish. When he fails to achieve his purpose, the absence of any other goal will cause him to feel completely lost. On the other hand, people who do not in the first place act for their own interests, but for those of society, will be far better protected against any disappointments if they should fail. Their egos are far less likely to be hurt, and their sense of purpose will help them to try again and again, until they succeed.

The above helps to explain another saying by our sages. Rabbi Eliezer said, "The sword and the Book [the Torah] came together from the heavens, and God said, If you do what is written in this book, you will be saved from the sharpness of the sword. But if you do not listen, the sword will kill you." Again there appears to be this contradiction with the words of Jeremiah we quoted at the beginning, according to which "God causes us neither bad nor good." The explanation, as we realize now, is that if we do not listen to what is written in the Torah, we *ourselves* will be responsible for our destruction. The Book, the morals and ethics of the Torah, and the Sword, our actions and deeds, are connected with each other. We should not make a sword without being guided by the Book; it is in our own hands to save or kill ourselves. Man will continue to invent and develop the world. However, as long as we walk in the ways of the Torah, we can use the resulting knowledge to ease our lives and promote civilization. If not, we run a serious risk of destroying our civilization, and possibly even our planet—not necessarily because we are wicked, but through carelessness and lack of responsibility for each other.

Atoms can be used for peace and for war, to build and to destroy. Next to the many benefits of the atom as used in science and medicine, we have the example of Chernobyl. The accident that happened there was caused by a combination of human pride, carelessness, and sheer lack of responsibility. If only we allow ourselves to be guided by the morality of the Torah, particularly what it tells about our responsibility for our fellowmen, we do not have to be afraid of the destruction that human creatures are capable of bringing upon themselves.

One of the first verses of the Torah describes how God

created the light. When God saw that the light was good, He separated the light from the darkness. In the Talmud, in *masecheth Nedarim*, there is a comment to the effect that God knew that the human beings He had created were capable of infinite creativity. However, since God was afraid that their lack of maturity would create chaos, He decided to hide part of His light, to prevent man from bringing all his potential knowledge into practice at one and the same time. Researchers and philosophers alike have often asked themselves why God enabled every succeeding generation to discover only a small part of nature. We could argue that mankind might have been saved its slow and painful evolution. We could have lived longer and healthier, and enjoyed all our scientific and technical discoveries right from the start, if only we had known thousands of years ago all that has slowly been revealed—and is yet to be revealed. So why did God not give us this knowledge long ago? The answer, as indicated above, is that the Creator decided that every generation must have time to digest what it has learned, since otherwise its knowledge would overwhelm it, and man would once again destroy what he has made. It is like giving a child a hand grenade to play with! Our sages comment that since the light was so strong as to be blinding, God hid his Big Light until the דור דעה, the generation of true wisdom, when people will use their knowledge to create things for the benefit of mankind, instead of for its destruction.

This is what the Torah says in this portion of *Re'eh*: "See, I am setting before you today a blessing and a curse—the blessing if you obey the commands of your God that I am giving you today; the curse if you disobey my commands." The blessing and the curse are in our own hands, as the Torah says: ובחרת בחיים (*u-becharta be-chaim*), "and you shall choose life." Every individual has a responsibility toward himself to take the right way. Then the curse will be turned away, and no harm will come to him.

The Gaon of Vilna said: The concept of the choice between good or bad lying in people's own hands is a Jewish concept. We

Jews are not fatalists. We do not say that we cannot influence events, and that whatever has to happen will happen anyway. We believe that the choice lies in our own hands, and that if we do good, we and the whole world will benefit by it.

Parashat Re'eh (4)

כי־יהיה בך אביון מאחד אחיך באחד שעריך בארצך אשר־יהוה
אלהיך נתן לך . . . נתון תתן לו ולא־ירע לבבך בתתך לו.

"If there is a poor man among your brothers in any of the towns of the land that your God is giving you ... Give generously to him and do so without a grudging heart."

In connection with this *pasuk* about our obligation to support the poor, the Midrash reminds us of an earlier verse, in which Moses says in the name of God: ועתה ישראל מה יהוה אלהיך שאל מעמך כי אם־ליראה את־יהוה אלהיך (*ve-atah yisrael mah ha-shem eloheicha sho'el me'emach ki im-lir'ah eth ha-shem eloheicha*), "And now, O Israel, what does your God ask of you but to fear your God." For he who fears God will find it much easier to help a fellow human in distress.

But what is the connection between giving to a poor person and the fear of God? In the Talmud volume of *Berachoth*, our sages comment on the fact that Moses asked "*but* to fear your God"—in other words, *just* to fear God. The question is therefore: is the fear of God such a minor matter?" The Talmud answers, "Yes, for Moses the fear of God was a minor matter. Moses' experiences had ennobled him, and raised him to a level of spiritual attainment where he could almost instinctively do the right thing in any given situation. For Moses, following in the ways of God and the Torah had become a simple affair. Of course, Moses was a highly unusual personality. Ordinary people like us will find it much more difficult to imitate his achievement. To us יראת שמים (*yir'ath shamayim*), to fear God, and to

316

distinguish between right and wrong under the most trying circumstances, is a far more complex problem.

Wouldn't it be easy if all the problems in our lives presented themselves neatly wrapped in two packages—one black and one white? All we would have to do is to choose the white parcel and leave the black untouched, and God would be happy with our choice. Unfortunately, almost all of life's decisions come in various shades of grey, to indicate that the package contains advantages and disadvantages, good things and bad things, permissible and forbidden choices. How do we decide which is the best package under the circumstances? How do we choose the correct alternative?

God tells us that we shall not steal. But what shall a poor man do when his family is hungry and only the stolen loaf of bread stands between him and starvation? Similarly we are warned that we may not tell lies. Does this mean that we must always give our honest opinion, even in small things, as when our wife asks us how we like her new hat? What if we don't like it—even if it has cost a lot of money? I believe that often we are not obliged to tell the entire truth, provided that in so doing we are not causing damage to somebody. The same situation applies to the compliments that people routinely pay each other. There is a story about a man who told a woman that she was pretty. Thinking that he was making fun of her, she replied angrily, "I couldn't say the same about you." "Why not," the man answered, "You can always tell the same lie."

Life confronts us with various paths, one more straight or direct than the other. Each path has much to commend it, and often we know in our hearts which is the right one. However, once we have taken one path, we can no longer take the other one. The question is therefore which path to choose. And such situations do not present themselves only once, but again and again! The fear of God is therefore hardly a simple matter for ordinary mortals who have not achieved Moses' heights. The Torah says נתן תתן (naton titen), which means "you shall give generously." Our sages interpret this as meaning that we are obliged to give "even a hundred times," as long as the need continues to exist. One of our great rabbis used to apply regularly to one of the wealthy people in his community for assistance to a needy family. One day the rich man said to the rabbi:

"Rabbi, I am tired of giving. Look how much money I have been paying all these years, and their condition doesn't seem to be any better than it was at the beginning. It is like pouring money down the drain."

The rabbi looked at him and asked: "How many times do you eat every day?"

"Three times," the man answered.

The rabbi replied: "And aren't you tired yet of having eaten so many times?"

"What do you mean, Rabbi," was the reply, "you know very well that if I do not eat, I will die."

"Exactly," the rabbi said, "and if you stop assisting the ones you support, *they* will die."

Our sages were not just stating the obvious when they observed that proper conduct was easy for Moses. Moses was not born the altruistic individual that he became in his later years. There is a story in our narratives about a heathen king who had learned about the high moral character of Moses. He ordered an artist to make a likeness of the Jewish lawgiver, so that he could always have Moses' face before him as an inspiration to proper behavior. When the artist presented his work, the king became extremely angry. "Either you are playing a trick on me, or you are incompetent," he screamed at the unfortunate artist. "This is no picture of a saint, but of a corrupt and sensuous individual." The story continues that when Moses heard about the king's reaction, he sent him a message, asking him not to punish the artist. Moses said, "Your artist only painted what he saw. I was indeed a sensuous man, but strict self-discipline and a regime of good conduct enabled me to change my inherent nature, until doing the right thing became automatic to me."

This is what our sages want to say: proper conduct was a simple matter for Moses, but he had achieved it through a strict regime of Torah ethics and morality. Such a regime is not easy, but it can be achieved, even by ordinary people. Let us look at the end of Moses' statement, which is in effect an explanation of the beginning. Moses says: "What does your God ask of you? He only asks us to fear Him." How do we achieve this? "By walking in all his ways, by observing His commandments and decrees." This is the purpose of the entire regime of the מצות מעשיות (mitzvoth ma'asioth), the practical commandments. Keeping the practical command- ments, combined with an understanding of Jewish rituals and customs, forms the basis of the regime that will refine our natures, so that we, when standing at the crossroads, can choose the correct way to go.

Truly religious people do not regard the commandments as a burden. They perform them easily and without special effort. These rituals have become a part of them, in the same way as a true gentleman does not have to think whether to offer an older person his seat on the bus or let a lady precede him through the door, or to decide which fork to use during a dinner. These acts come naturally, indeed like second nature. So it is with the observance of the Jewish rituals and customs, and these, in turn, will lead a person on the road toward decency, morality, and ethical behavior.

Elsewhere in the Book of Devarim the Torah says, והיה עקב תשמעון את המשפטים האלה ושמרתם ועשיתם אתם ושמר יהוה אלהיך לך את הברית ואת־החסד אשר נשבע לאבותיך (ve-hayah ekev tishme'un eth ha-mishpatim ha-eleh u-shemartem va-asitem otam ve shamar ha-shem eloheicha lecha eth ha-brith ve-eth ha-chesed asher nishba le-avoteicha), "If you pay atten- tion to these laws and are careful to follow them, then God will keep His covenant of love with you, as He swore to your fore- fathers." The word עקב (ekev) the beginning of this pasuk means "heel." Rashi comments that he who observes all the command- ments, even those that most people are accustomed to treat lightly, as it were "with their heel," really performs God's will.

The Torah teaches us that quantity is important in life, but that quality is surely no less important. There are three areas in our practical existence to which this truth should be applied.

The first is the faithful performance of the small acts of kindness that God enables us to do. Greatness is not a matter of monumental acts or initiatives. Greatness lies in small things. There is greatness in offering unselfish love to children, in bringing cheer and joy to lonely lives, and in helping to relieve human needs.

The second area is our search for happiness. We are often deluded into believing that happiness can be found only in all kinds of exciting, faraway adventures. The truth is that happiness lies far closer to hand—in the many little things that happen in our daily lives, that we usually take for granted. In our daily prayers we are reminded of the enormous gifts with which all of us, rich and poor alike, are endowed: minds that can think, hearts that can love, hands that can lift. An awareness and appreciation of all these things is what makes our lives happy.

The third area where this truth should be applied is our Jewish consciousness, In the past, loyalty to Judaism often required great feats of courage, sacrifice, and even martyrdom. We are living in a world in which, as a people, we are only under very special circumstances called upon to make physical sacrifices. Usually all that is asked from us to ensure our survival can be spelled out in humble acts and small deeds, to be performed daily: observing the ways of the Torah, providing our children with a Jewish education, and helping our fellow Jews to survive. Our brothers in the Jewish state are as embattled as ever, and there are still millions of Jews who are unable to express their Jewish identity. All of us are obliged to assist each other. If we do not help, nobody will. These small deeds surely contain the seeds of greatness, and they will bear fruit in happiness, by nourishing the future of the Jewish nation.

Some Jews are afraid that we shall not succeed because we are so few. This is why we should see what the Torah teaches us, when it says, כי תאמר בלבבך רבים האלה ממני איכה אוכל להורישם (ki tomar bi'levavecha rabim ha-goyim ha-eleh memeni eich uchal lehorisham), "You may say to yourselves, 'These nations are stronger than we are. How can we drive them out?'" And the Torah answers: לא תירא מהם (lo tir'a mehem), "Do not be afraid of them." It is a specific *mitzvah* for a Jew not to be afraid, only when we stand up proud and erect can we survive.

From where can we get the strength to do this? According to the Torah, strength can be derived from two sources: from God and from our memory. וזכרת את יהוה אלהיך (ve-zecharta eth ha-shem eloheicha), which means, "Remember your God." If we listen to God, He will give us strength to fight. Strength is also derived from the past. We Jews have a more active collective memory than any other nation in the world. It is thanks to this memory that we know who and what we are. The very words, לא תירא מהם (lo tir'a mehem), "do not be afraid of them," are followed in the Torah by זכור תזכור (zechor tizkor), "You shall remember!" Speaking with memories means speaking of hopes and ideals. Fighting with the help of memories means fighting for dreams and aspirations. Without memories, we lose our past. Without a past we become rootless and lose our way to the future.

One of our greatest worries in this century should concern the young Jews who do not know their past—who have virtually forgotten the 1900 years of Jewish wandering from country to country. Many young Jews do not know that this exile produced the Mishnah , the Talmud , our books of prayers, the *Shulchan Aruch* (Code of Law), and thousands upon thousands of other spiritual works. We should be concerned about our Jewish youth who are totally unfamiliar with the Jewish mission, with Jewish inspiration, and with the great moments of the Jewish past—and who as a result no longer have a sense of Jewish destiny. Only a knowledgeable Jew, a Jew of faith, can stand up without being afraid.

Yes, there are dangers for Jews: Jews are being killed almost daily, and even as a nation our existence is contested. When we ask, "When will there be peace for the Jewish people; when will Jewish blood stop being shed within Israel and its borders?" the words of the prophet can serve as a consolation. In the Book of Isaiah the prophet accuses God of having forsaken the Jewish people. But God answers him with a loving reproach: "A mother may sometimes forget her child, but I will not forget you."

These words surely are among the most optimistic words in our Jewish scriptures. What they promise, in effect, is that from among the Jewish people will continue to arise new children, to infuse our people with new vitality and new hope. May this day come soon, for our children and our children's children's sake.

Parashath Shofetim

אלה החוקים והמשפטים אשר תשמרו לעשות בארץ.

"These are the statutes and the ordinances which you shall observe in the Land."

According to the Midrash, these statutes and ordinances that we are obliged to observe do not concern only the relations between God and man. Equally important, in fact, is what the Torah demands from us with regard to our relations with our fellowman.

A good example of this is the following portion of the week, called *Shofetim*. The Torah says, "If a man is found slain, lying in a field in the land the Lord your God is giving you to possess, and it is not known who killed him, your elders and judges shall go out and measure the distance from the body to the neighboring towns."

The Torah continues to describe how the elders and judges of the town that proved to be nearest to the body had to take a heifer and, after going through the prescribed ritual, wash their hands and declare: "Our hands did not shed this blood, nor did our eye see it done. Accept this atonement for your people Israel, whom you have redeemed, O God, and do not hold your people guilty of the blood of an innocent man."

This was indeed a strange statement for elders to make. From the biblical account we learn that responsibility for an anonymous killing was placed upon the town that was situated nearest the scene of the crime. This in itself seems very understandable, for somebody had to take charge of the case, and see to it that it was solved or otherwise disposed of. But why should the leaders and the judges of that town have to declare their innocence and atone for such a crime? Surely nobody suspected them of having been in any way involved?

Most probably they were not ... but in the eyes of God, they were! According to Rabbi Sa'adiah Gaon, one of our famous rabbis and a foremost leader of Babylonian Jewry in the tenth century, this Torah law reveals one of Judaism's most important principles. For once we look beyond the narrow meaning of the words—the discovery of an unknown dead body in a field—a very clear message emerges: all of us share a measure of responsibility for the things that happen in our immediate surroundings, whether a child is attacked in the street or a man is killed. We cannot absolve ourselves from any blame by saying, I did not even know the victim, or I have never been in that particular street. After all, the crime did take place in our neighborhood—in the society of which we form a part, and whose welfare we, too, help to influence for good or for bad. As our sages put it in the Talmud: הצדיק נטפס בעוון הדור (ha-tzadik nitfas ba'avon hador), meaning, "Even the most saintly person is tainted with the sins of his generation."

One of our rabbis makes an interesting remark. "Why is it," he asks, "that the Torah only asks for a ritual atonement if a dead body is found and it is not known who murdered it?" Why is no such public atonement needed if the murderer is known, or subsequently discovered? In a case like that there seems to be no public responsibility; the murderer is tried and punished, and that is the end of the affair.

Two questions seem to emerge, therefore. The first is why, in the event that the murderer is unknown, the entire society is deemed guilty? The second question, which relates to the situation where the murderer is known, seems even more pertinent. For if we know the murderer, why should there be no public atonement? Can we really claim that the community in which the murderer lived and grew up is innocent, and that the people with whom he associated are not at all responsible, although proper vigilance and care might have helped to prevent the crime?

The answer to the first question, about the community's responsibility in the case of an unknown murderer, is that the Torah wants to avoid any possibility of crimes "being swept under the carpet." After all, some people may say that the death was due to an accident, or that it was an "act of God," or perhaps that the victim deserved his death, because he was about to commit a crime, and that he was killed by his intended victim.

In other words, maybe there was no "real" crime at all. As a consequence, people may say, "Since there was no crime, no feelings of guilt are called for." The Torah, however, does not let us off so easily. Maybe no crime was committed—but maybe there was. We do not know, so at the very least a public soul-searching is required. Something terrible took place, and possibly we could in some way have prevented it. Therefore we must try to find out what happened, and why—and whether any blame could possibly, whether directly or indirectly, be attached to the leaders or our society.

The second question is why, if the murderer was known, or was subsequently discovered, the community was not required to make public atonement by performing the ritual of the heifer. Here the Torah is very realistic, for the truth is that we cannot always prevent a crime. No society is perfect, and it would therefore be impossible to demand collective atonement every time someone we know commits a crime. The real point, however, is that the Torah's purpose is not in the first place to blame society. Its chief purpose is to open our eyes to everything that happens in our surroundings. For as long as we close our eyes, the same criminal acts or transgressions will keep on happening again and again.

According to the Rabbis, the key to this commandment in *Parashath Shofetim* is to be found in the words of the prophet Jeremiah, where he says, "But I will pass judgment on you because you say, 'I have not sinned.'" God says the greatest sin that one can commit is refusing to recognize that he has sinned. And without recognition of sin, there cannot be repentance.

For an example, we should look at two of our greatest leaders, namely King Saul and King David. King Saul was asked to fight the Amalekites and totally destroy everything that belonged to them. The Torah commands: "Do not spare them; put to death men and women, children and infants, cattle and sheep, camels and donkeys." After the war had ended, and the prophet Samuel came and asked Saul why he had kept the king of the Amalekites alive, and the best of the sheep and cattle—in fact everything that was valuable and useful—Saul's answer was, "The soldiers brought them from the Amalekites; they spared the best of the sheep and the cattle to sacrifice them to God." Saul simply claimed that personally he had obeyed God's command; he was not to be blamed—it was the soldiers who were guilty! Saul did not recognize or acknowledge his guilt. God did not forgive him for this, and took away his kingdom.

The opposite happened with King David, after he had committed a grave sin toward Bathsheba and her husband, Uriah the Hittite, one of his commanders in the war against the Ammonites. The story is well known: King David first seduced Bathsheba, and then had Uriah eliminated by sending him into the front line, where he would be most exposed to the enemies' arrows. When the prophet Nathan approached David, and called him to account, the king immediately admitted his guilt. David did not lose his kingdom, because he recognized and admitted his terrible sin—even though Nathan predicted that all kinds of calamities would befall him and his house.

The commandment we are discussing here teaches us that we may never close our eyes to what happens to a stranger—not as individuals and not as a community. In fact, the Torah makes it very clear that the entire community must accept responsibility, and that we cannot say "nothing happened," or "something happened, but it was not our fault." The prophet Jeremiah warns that God will judge us for claiming categorically that something is not our sin, merely because we did not commit it ourselves. It is a crime just the same, namely the moral crime of denial of responsibility. We should never allow ourselves to fall victim to our delusions with regard to the standards of what is right and what is wrong.

How can we try to achieve this? Here again the Torah gives the answer: צדק צדק תרדוף למען תחיה בארץ אשר נתן לך יהוה אלהיך (tzedek, tzedek tirdof le-ma'an techeyeh ba-aretz asher nathan lach ha-shem eloheicha) "Justice, justice, you shall pursue, in order that you may live in the land which God gives you." This repetition of the word "justice" may be interpreted as follows: in order for the individual and the people to survive, both must pursue the justice that has become the hallmark of Judaism.

The Torah's call for justice is a critical one. In this particular portion of the week the Torah wants to stress that justice is not merely a matter of pious thoughts or expedient acts, but something very practical and real, something very closely connected with the essence of our survival. We cannot pervert justice. We cannot just close our eyes and say: I, too, believe in justice.

Justice is something we must pursue, in other words demand—so how can we know what happened when we close our eyes? And, once we know, we hope we shall not remain silent. There cannot be justice in a world of silence. That is what the Torah tells us, and that is what the Jews have been trying to tell the world every day and every year, throughout their history. Let us not be silent, but openly proclaim that we feel guilty about the evil that is happening in our lives and in the society around us.

The Torah makes it so clear when it says, "If a man is found slain, lying in a field in the land the Lord your God is giving you to possess, and it is not known who killed him, your elders and judges shall go out...." The victim was lying in the field, and it was unknown who struck him. The elders and judges went out and measured the distance between the two towns or villages nearest to the victim. And then a ceremony was enacted: a heifer was slain, after which the elders washed their hands and declared, "Our hands did not shed this blood, nor did our eye see it done."

This is how the official representatives of the Jewish people, after due investigation, cleared themselves and their community formally and publicly of any suspicion of complicity or neglect that might have led to murder in their community.

Looking back at the more recent history of our world—especially the history of the Jewish people during the present century—we may conclude that if only the responsible leaders of the modern, so-called civilized nations had in a similar way accepted responsibility, the horrors of the Second World War could not have happened. I am not referring only to the actual slaughter of innocent people by murderers in or out of uniform, but to the neglect, the dereliction of duty, the closing of the eyes by the leaders of the Free World to the injustice that was being committed under their very noses—with their knowledge and often with their tacit permission. If these leaders had felt responsibility, and if they could have been called to account in the same way as the actual murderers, how many people, how many Jews would still be alive today.

They remained silent, however, for they did not consider themselves either responsible or guilty for the crimes that were committed by others, even after they had been confronted with the extermination camps and the crematoria. When in the end they came face to face with Bergen Belsen and Auschwitz, hellish places where thousands upon thousands of Jews died every day, the nations—including the great democracies—said to themselves, "Our hands did not shed this blood, nor did our eye see it done." They knew about it, but they did not consider themselves responsible—only because they, themselves, had not been physically involved in these crimes.

How can we talk about justice? Where do we stand today, four or five decades after the Holocaust? Should we not be cynical when people talk about justice, but at the same time think they have the right to close their eyes, and refuse to acknowledge everything that happened under their responsibility? Can we continue to believe, when the Torah tells the Jewish people: You shall preach justice to this cynical world?

The answer is that the Jewish people must continue to believe in justice as a reality of life, because of the injustice and the denials of responsibility that we still see around us. Judaism must continue to teach the world its concept of justice, even when faced with leaders of nations who lack moral courage and honesty, or regimes based upon political lies.

Justice may not be perverted, neither for political reasons nor for political gains. Regardless of how much we, the Jewish people, have suffered, we cannot accept this cynical way of thinking. We shall keep on believing that there will come a day in which the Torah's demand to pursue justice will be fulfilled—a day in which justice will reign, and righteousness will prevail for every person, so that mankind, and the Jewish people among them, will be able to lead a normal and peaceful life.

Parashath Ki-Tetze

כי־תצא למלחמה על־איביך ונתנו יהוה אלהיך בידך שביו:
וראית בשביה אשת יפת־תאר וחשקת בה ולקחת לך לאשה:

"When you go to war against your enemies, and God delivers them into your hands, and you take captives, and you notice among the captives a beautiful woman and are attracted to her, you may take her as your wife."

The Torah continues to tell how the woman first should be given a whole month to mourn her father and mother, and in general adjust to her new situation, and it concludes by saying, "If you are not pleased with her, let her go whenever she wishes. You must not sell her or treat her as a slave, since you have dishonored her."

This particular portion of the week contains many different commandments, but I will take only three to exemplify the message that the Torah wants to convey to us. The first commandment, therefore, concerns the treatment of female captives in a war. The second commandment that the Torah gives us in the same *parashah* deals with the man who has a בן סורר ומורה (*ben sorer ve-moreh*), a stubborn and rebellious son, who does not obey his father and mother and will not listen to them when they discipline him; in other words, a son who does not accept their teaching and education, even if he has so far done nothing wrong in practice. In this case the father and mother are to take him out of their home and bring him to the elders of the community, and tell them: "This son of ours is stubborn and

330

rebellious. He will not obey us. He is a profligate and a drunk-ard." According to the Torah, what happens is that [after a serious hearing] all the men of the town will stone him to death, to purge the bad blood from among them. And "all Israel will hear of it and be afraid."

As I commented before, this particular portion of the week contains many other commandments, but I will mention only one more, namely the final one concerning the Amalekites: זכור את אשר עשה לך עמלק בצאתכם ממצרים (zechor eth asher asah lecha amalek be-tze'etchem me-mitzra'im), "Remember what the Amalekites did to you along the way, when you came out of Egypt ... when you were weary and worn out, they met you on your journey and cut off all who were lagging behind; they had no fear of God. Therefore, when God shall have given you rest from all your enemies around you in the land ... you shall blot out the memory of Amalek from under the heaven. Do not forget!"

There are many things in the three commandments menti-oned here that need interpretation and understanding. Let us return to the first commandment, the one about the female captives. Nations have gone to war since time immemorial, and by no means always because they were warlike or because they wanted to expand their territory. Some wars are unavoidable, because they are a matter of survival. We also know that wars are likely to bring out the worst instincts in people, and that it is often the civilian population that suffers most. In olden times it was customary that conquered cities were sacked, and their inhabitants killed or carried into captivity. Even worse were the excesses committed against those who were weak and defense-less. The female sex in particular was a prey for the rapacious warriors; women were raped and maltreated mercilessly.

It certainly requires comment, therefore, that already many centuries ago, when the world was at its most primitive and savage, the Torah commanded the Jewish people *not* to behave as others did: not to rape, not to kill or to destroy needlessly. War is bad, but—says the Torah—if you have to go to war, don't

behave like a conqueror, and do not rape the women in the
conquered cities. If you see a woman that you would like to have
for a wife, you may take her into your home, but you have to
treat her as if she is going to stay with you. You must give her
thirty days to mourn and adjust to her new situation. Maybe
you will learn to understand and like each other. But if not, do
not sell the woman. Selling captives into slavery was the
accepted custom in those times, when prisoners of war were in
every respect treated as slaves. There is a shocking story, familiar to many Israelis, about an incident that happened during one
of Israel's wars with the Arabs. A captain of the Israeli Defense
Forces entered an enemy village that had just been captured. In
one of the houses there was a commotion, and when he entered
he saw that a Jewish soldier was raping one of the local women.
Without stopping even to ask a question, he took out his
revolver and killed the soldier. When called to account, he said in
his defense, "I am not a religious man, but anyone who is
familiar with the portion כי תצא (Ki-Tetze) will not have to ask why
I acted as I did. It was the natural thing to do under the circumstances, because even in war a Jewish soldier shall never behave
like some of our enemies would; he must know that he is
expected to behave like a human being, rather than an animal."

The commandment about the female captives in the war is
immediately followed by the one about the בן סורר ומורה, the
stubborn and rebellious son. This commandment, too, dates
from a time when the Jews were not a settled people and had to
fight constant wars against the surrounding nations. It was only
to be expected that under such circumstances some children
would turn out rebellious. The Torah wants to teach us that a
family with a son who was rebellious and refused to listen was
not allowed to hide his behavior, but had to consult with the
leaders of the community. Our sages explain this requirement
by saying that where such a situation developed, it was not only
the parents who were to blame. It was the whole environment,
the climate in which the younger generation had grown up, that

was at fault. For this reason the elders were to share the responsibility for the rebelliousness with the parents and take steps to prevent the disease from spreading.

The punishment for the son's behavior, as spelled out in the Torah, seems of course extreme, but we shall have more to say on this in a moment. Meanwhile, one of the oldest and strongest Jewish traditions is that we honor our father and our mother. What does his mean? The Talmud demonstrates with the help of two examples how far this obligation is supposed to extend. One example concerns a rich farmer and merchant, called Dama ben Netina, who used to live in Ashkelon. He owned vast plots of land on which he grew all kinds of grain. One year he had such an abundant harvest that there was not enough space in his warehouses to store it all. As a result he had to look for buyers, to prevent part of his precious crop from going to waste.

Then there sailed into port a large ship whose captain was prepared to buy his entire harvest, provided that Dama ben Netina could start loading straightaway. No need to say that the merchant was delighted, and he ran home to get the keys of the warehouse. Even the price the captain was prepared to pay for the grain was right. However, on arriving home, ben Netina realized that the keys were under the pillow of the bed on which his old father was lying asleep. He returned to the captain, and told him that he could not wake his father, but that he would sell the grain even at half the price, if only he would wait until his father had woken up. The captain refused, with the result that Dama ben Netina saw a profitable transaction come to naught, only because he refused to disturb his father's rest.

The second story is about Rabbi Avihu ben Avima. Rabbi Avihu's father was so old that he spent his days alternately waking and dozing on a couch adjacent to the hall where his son was teaching Torah to hundreds of students. One day the old man woke up and asked for a drink of water. Rabbi Avihu interrupted his lesson to fetch the water, but before he returned, the old man had once again fallen asleep. So he stayed next to the couch to wait for his father to wake up. When his disciples asked him whether it was really necessary to wait, since it might be a long time until his father would wake up again, Rabbi Avihu answered, "Such is the obligation of a son to his parents."

So ingrained, therefore, is the commandment about honoring our parents, that the death sentence for a son who defies his father and mother seems an almost hypothetical situation. In fact, according to the Talmud, there is no more than one recorded instance of this sentence ever having been carried out. As one of our sages concluded, situations such as are envisaged in the commandment about the stubborn son were never encountered in practical life, and the Torah includes it simply for educational and deterrent purposes.

At this point I should add that the love and devotion of children toward their parents is not just an individual duty, or a duty toward our own parents only, merely because of the fact that they gave birth to us. It is a general duty of one generation to all other generations. Jewish tradition asks children to honor their parents not only when they are alive, but also after they have died: בחייהם ובמותם (be-chaieihem u-be-motam), as the *Shulchan Aruch* puts it. Moreover, the Torah does not say only that we shall honor our parents, but that איש את אביו ואת אמו תיראו (ish eth aviv va-et imo tira'u), "You shall fear your father and mother." Nachmanides (the "Ramban") interprets this verse as meaning that, in the same way as by honoring our parents we are raising ourselves and the entire nation onto a higher level, the opposite kind of behavior not merely hurts ourselves and our parents but causes the entire nation to suffer. In other words, we must "fear" our father and mother because of the far-reaching negative consequences that a failure to heed this commandment will produce. This explains Rabbi Ammi's conclusion, as quoted in the Talmud, that a stubborn and rebellious son was not judged by what he had done to make him deserve punishment, but because of the future damage he could expect to inflict upon his

surroundings. This is why the parents were obliged to bring him
before a court, which had to discuss the conditions prevailing in
the society in which the boy had grown up. When a sickness
breaks out that might take on epidemic proportions, and we do
not know what caused it or how to deal with it, the first thing to
do is isolate the patients to prevent even more people being
contaminated. Now we also understand the connection
between the first commandment about the war, and the second
commandment about the discovery that the war, because of its
upheavals and the resulting changes brought about in people's
individual lives, caused children to disobey and rebel against
their parents.

This brings us to the concluding commandment of this particular *parashah*, namely our obligation to blot out the memory of
Amalek. Earlier the Torah told us that war is bad, because of its
corrupting and disruptive influence on both communal and
family life. So if we can prevent a war, we should. But in this
place the Torah actually commands us to go out and actively
pursue a war, with the specific purpose of eradicating even the
memory of the Amalekites. How are we to understand that the
same Torah that is so full of compassion for the weak and
defenseless, for the young and the old, suddenly tells us to
destroy an entire nation? And who are the Amalekites, and
where are they today? Since the days of Sennacherib, the Assyrian king who conquered much of the ancient world, entire
nations have been transplanted, and—with the exception of the
Jews—none of the peoples that are mentioned in the Bible exist
any more: the Ammonites, Edomites, and Moabites and, for that
matter, the Amalekites, have long disappeared. How can we
observe the *mitzvah* to destroy this Jewish archenemy when we
do not know who or where he is? And talking about enemies,
why doesn't the Torah ask us to destroy the Egyptian nation
that enslaved the Jews for hundreds of years? On this point, it is
interesting that the Torah in fact commands us to do the opposite, when it says: לא־תתעב מצרי כי־גר היית בארצו (*lo teta'ev mitzri ki ger*

ha'ita be-artzo), "Do *not* abhor an Egyptian, because you lived as an alien in his country."

We must conclude that the term "Amalek" has to be understood in a wider context: even if the Amalekite nation itself no longer exists, its ideas and methods have survived until our own generation. These start with attacking the defenseless, the simpleminded and the underpriviliged, and end with an attempt to destroy an entire nation. We have seen it as recently as the Nazi era, which began with the elimination of the weak and the sick, and ended with wholesale slaughter of Jews, Gypsies, and other "inferior" people. Countless suggestions have been put forward to explain this profound hatred, but the Jewish consciousness denies and defies any rationalization that anyone has ever offered.

The closest explanation is the one provided by the Torah itself, where it says: כי הבדלתי אתכם מכל העמים (*ki hivdalti etchem me-kol ha'amim*), "For I separated you from all the people." Throughout much of their long history the Jewish people have lived among other nations, some of them strong and powerful, and some of them backward and poor. They lived among them, but separate. And for much of these times Jewish lives were forfeit, and nothing could make the Jews accepted by the host nations, as if their very presence, and the reminder of their special relationship with God, aroused unbounded jealousy and hatred. However, the Torah also tells that the Amalekites "had no fear of God." On a rational level we cannot, therefore, say that they fought the Jews because of their faith, given the fact that they themselves were not god-fearing. We cannot even claim that they attacked the Jews because they were so nationalistic; during their forty years in the desert the Jewish people continually clamored to be taken back to Egypt! The only answer seems therefore that the mere Jewish existence is enough to expose us to hatred. And this is why we have to continue fighting Amalek—wherever and in whatever guise he appears—from generation to generation. As a Jewish poet commented at the end of the last century: שנאת עולם לעם עולם העולם, "Eternal hatred of the eternal people." If we want to continue to exist, the only answer is to blot out the memory of Amalek—and if we don't, he will destroy us.

Parashath Ki Tavo

והיה כי תבוא אל הארץ אשר יהוה אלהיך נתן לך נחלה וירשתה
וישבת בה: ולקחת מראשית כל פרי האדמה אשר תביא מארצך
אשר יהוה אלהיך נתן לך ושמת בטנא והלכת אל־המקום אשר
יבחר יהוה אלהיך לשכן שמו שם: ובאת אל־הכהן אשר יהיה
בימים ההם ואמרת אליו הגדתי היום ליהוה אלהיך כי־באתי אל
הארץ אשר נשבע יהוה לאבתינו לתת לנו: ולקח הכהן הטנא
מידך והניחו לפני מזבח יהוה אלהיך: וענית ואמרת לפני יהוה
אלהיך ארמי אבד אבי וירד מצרימה ויגר שם במתי מעט ויהי
שם לגוי עצום ורב.

"When you have entered the land that God is giving you as
an inheritance and have taken possession of it and settled
in it, take some of the first fruits of all that you produce
from the soil of the land that God is giving you and put
them in a basket. Then you go to the place that God will
choose as a dwelling for His name and say to the priest in
office at the time, 'I declare today to God that I have come
to the land that God swore to our forefathers to give us.'
The priest shall take the basket from your hands and set it
down in front of the altar of God. Then you shall declare
before God: 'My father was a wandering Aramean, and he
went down into Egypt with a few people and lived there
and became a great nation, numerous and powerful.'"

All our interpreters ask a number of questions about this

mitzvah of bringing the first fruits of "the land." I will deal here with only a few of these questions, connected with the declarations and confessions the person who offered the first fruits had to make. The first question is why the Torah required someone who brought בכורים (*bikkurim*), the first fruits, to relate in such detail everything he did in connection with his coming to Jerusalem at this time?

Why was it necessary that the person praised himself by telling how, as it were, he had come "from rags to riches"? In none of the other *mitzvoth*, with the possible exception of the one concerning צדקה (*tzedakah*), charity — because here the knowledge about the charitable deed is bound to be to someone's advantage—is a person required to tell others about it. On the contrary, it would be considered immodest to do so, and it would invalidate the *mitzvah*.

In the second place, the man who brought the *bikkurim* had to make a confession, by saying: לא עברתי את מצוותיך (*lo avarti eth mitzvoteicha*), I did not transgress Your commandments. First the offeror made what seemed a boastful claim, as if he wanted to say, "Look, how well-to-do and dutiful I am—and how far I have come in the world," but immediately thereafter he had to confess that he did not commit any sins. Why was this necessary, and if it was necessary, why not for other *mitzvoth*, for instance for the tithe? In the book of Deuteronomy, the commandment concerning the tithe (מעשר, *ma'aser*, from the Hebrew word עשר, ten) follows immediately upon that of the *bikkurim*. The tithe was a far more substantial sacrifice, amounting—as the Hebrew word indicates—to one tenth of the farmer's income. For the *bikkurim*, on the other hand, no specific measure was fixed in Jewish law: לבכורים אין שיור (*le-bikkurim ein shi'ur*). Some *olives*, some *grapes* were sufficient. Later sages have suggested that the correct measure was "one of sixty," as a guideline, so that people would know what to do, but the Torah itself does not ask or specify it; on the contrary, it specifically states *"some* of the first fruits of all that you produce." Also the fact that the Bible verse specifically talks about a "basket," shows that a small quantity of each fruit was intended.

When bringing the *bikkurim* the donor also recited the following declaration: ושמחת בכל־הטוב אשר נתן־לך יהוה אלהיך ולביתך אתה והלוי והגר אשר בקרבך (*ve-samachta ba-kol ha-tov asher natan lecha ha-shem u-le-veteicha atah ve-ha-levi ve-ha-ger asher be-kirveicha*), "And you and the Levites and the aliens among you shall rejoice in all the good things your God has given to you and your household." This requirement also did not apply to the tithe. We could indeed ask why there was a difference, and why the Torah did not require the donor of the far bigger sacrifice to be happy that he was in the fortunate position to give. After all, isn't it much better to be a giver than a taker, like a beggar?

When we enter a little bit deeper into what the Torah tells us here, and into the explanations that our sages have provided, we will get a more complete picture and begin to understand the underlying ethics of this commandment and the morality that it has brought into Jewish life.

The Midrash , in discussing the practice as it was carried out in the days of the Temple, says that when someone brought *bikkurim* he was not obliged to carry them himself all the way to Jerusalem. He could give the basket containing the fruits to one of his children or to his slave, and they would carry it in turn until they arrived at the *Har ha-Bayit*, the entrance to the Temple. At this point the owner had to take the basket and carry it personally into the Temple. This obligation applied to everyone, no matter how rich or how poor, how lowly or how influential he was; even the king himself had to take his own basket to the priests.

The Tosephta, a halachic work containing much material not included in the Mishnah, tells of a king during the days of the Second Temple who carried the *bikkurim* on his own back, which earned him the admiration of the people.

The Midrash provides an extensive account of everything connected with the bringing of the first fruits to Jerusalem.

After entering Jerusalem, the bearers were upon their approach to the Temple met by groups of singing and dancing people to welcome their arrival. Again it is interesting that they were welcomed in this manner only when bringing the *bikkurim*, and not when bringing the tithe. All this goes to show that this *mitzvah* must have carried considerable weight, and indeed חג הבכורים (*chag ha-bikkurim*) was one of the most important festivals in Jerusalem of old.

There is no doubt that מצות הבכורים (*mitzvath ha-bikkurim*) teaches us a very important lesson. What the Torah says is that it is not always important how much we give to others, but *how* we give. Let us see what happened here. Much like his present-day counterpart, the farmer worked a whole year in the hope of being able to harvest a plentiful crop. Until this moment arrived, he had to tend his fields and orchards, hoping that weather conditions would be favorable, that there would not be too much—or too little—rain, and that the plants and trees would not be damaged by pests. Then came the time when the crops began to ripen, and his greatest desire was to see the first fruits, and to taste them.

At this point the Torah said: *Do not* take the first fruits for yourself and your family. Take them to Jerusalem for others. This was why the farmer had to take them personally to the priests, so that he would feel the sacrifice that he was bringing. To forgo the taste of his ripe fruit, to give it to others, rather than eat it himself, required a measure of spirituality and belief, an acceptance that man does not live merely for himself and his family. Man has to learn that not his own intelligence, not only his own strength and capability has given him his harvest, but that everything he receives is from God, and that God has given it to him so that he in turn can take care of others.

Psalm 24 begins with the words, ליהוה הארץ ומלואה תבל יושבי בה (*la-shem ha-aretz u-melo'ah tevel ve-yoshevei bah*): "The earth is the Lord's, and everything in it, the world, and all who live in it." In another psalm it says that the heavens belong to God, and the

earth to mankind. Our sages explain this seeming contradiction
by observing that the very fact that man blesses God for everything He has given him clearly implies the recognition that all
these things in the first place belong to God. In other words,
only after we have acknowledged that everything we possess is
a result of divine supervision may we take it as our own and
enjoy it. At the same time this helps us to realize that our
possessions are not meant for our own use only, but that we
have to share with others less fortunate than ourselves.

Sharing our plenty with less fortunate members of society is
very important, but it has to be done happily and spontaneously,
and in such a way that the other person does not see himself as a
beggar. In other words, the other individual should not be made
to feel that he is the recipient of a rich person's charity. Once we
understand this, and learn to act accordingly, our contributions
will also be accepted more easily. Thus we help prevent society
from being divided into two groups, namely givers and re-
ceivers.

Our society is one family, in which each has to have his
share. The most important lesson of the sacrifice of the *bikkurim*
is that it does not matter how much we give; what is important
is that the receiver is not degraded by being made to feel dependent. This is another reason why the giver of the *bikkurim* was not
allowed to give anonymously or through others; by bringing the
sacrifice with his own hands, he showed that he felt himself a
part of the Jewish people.

The above also helps to put into a clearer perspective the
earlier mentioned declaration about how the donor's forefathers had been poor nomads, and how from a small and vulnerable
group they had turned into a powerful nation. The declaration
was intended to demonstrate that the giver, however successful
and powerful he appeared to be, remembered his humble begin-
nings and was not ashamed of his own less than impressive past.
In effect he was telling those around him, "I too have known bad
times. I am fortunate that I am better off now, and to those who

are less fortunate, I want to say that I am sure your time will also come."

For this reason every person, regardless of his or her condition, should remain conscious of the following two fundamental truths in order to lead a stable and happy existence. If he is fortunate enough to be prosperous and wealthy, he has to remember that he himself or his parents were not always rich. This will remind him to be grateful, so that he will enjoy his present prosperity all the more. If, on the other hand, a person falls upon bad times, or if he is so unfortunate never to have known prosperity, he should remember that people's fortunes are continuously shifting, so that his own bad luck may indeed be a passing phase. This will help him to look ahead and keep up his courage until better days arrive. And finally, the prosperous must know that their fortune is not theirs by right, and that it is not promised forever.

There is an old anecdotal folk tale that illustrates the above point. There once was a simple villager who had never been in the city and had never even heard of restaurants. One day he finally traveled to the nearest town, and he was astonished at all the new and unknown things he saw. When he got hungry he ate the bread he had brought with him, but when it was time for the evening meal, he had no idea where he should buy food. He looked around, but did not find anything to eat anywhere. Then he passed a large hall, from where the sounds of festive music could be heard. Looking inside, he saw a wedding party in progress. There were long tables laden with food, and a crowd of people eating, drinking, and dancing merrily. Since he was hungry, he entered, sat down at one of the tables, and ate his fill. Nobody seemed to mind, and nobody paid. Very happy with his discovery, he went home, determined to take the first available opportunity to repeat his adventure. Several days later he again went to the hospitable hall, and once more he enjoyed a tasty meal. This went on for some time, but one day he began to wonder how people could possibly give so many parties. He asked the man sitting next to him at the table how many sons and daughters the man had who was continually giving wedding feasts. Surprised, his neighbor said, "Don't you understand? What makes you think that it is always the same man? The man who danced yesterday does not dance today, and he who dances today will not dance tomorrow." The moral of this story is: If I am able to bring *bikkurim* today, I may not take it for granted that I will be able to bring them next year.

This perspective will also remind one not to look down upon his fellowmen in good times, whereas those who in bad times succeed in remembering with gratitude the more prosperous past will gain added strength and not break down through lack of hope and confidence.

In the lines from the Torah quoted at the beginning of this *parashah* it says ועניתָ ואמרת (*ve-anita ve-amarta*). When you bring the *bikkurim*, you have to tell the community, "My forefathers were wanderers; we, too, were poor people." And the Talmud says that you should declare it in a loud voice, to show that you are not ashamed of your past. Only those who remember and acknowledge their own past will accept those who are not successful today. Only then can it indeed be said ושמחת בכל הטוב (*ve-samachta ba-chol ha-tov*), "And you and the Levites and the aliens among you shall rejoice in all the good things your God has given to you and your household." A person cannot be happy all by himself. Nor, in this case, will you be forced to enjoy yourself alone, since the whole community will be happy with you.

Parashath Nitzavim

אתם נצבים היום כלכם לפני יהוה אלהיכם ראשיכם שבטיכם
זקניכם ושוטריכם כל איש ישראל . . .

. . . והיה כי יבאו עליך כל־הדברים האלה הברכה והקללה
אשר נתתי לפניך והשבת אל־לבבך בכל־הגוים . . . ושב יהוה
אלהיך את־שבותך ורחמך ושב וקבצך מכל־העמים אשר הפיצך
יהוה אלהיך שמה.

"All of you are standing today in the presence of your
God—your leaders and chief men, your elders and offi-
cials, and all the other men of Israel....

...When all these blessings and curses I have set before
you come upon you and you take them to heart wherever
your God disperses you among the nations ... then God
will restore your fortunes and have compassion on you
and gather you again from all the nations where He scattered you."

Moses summoned the Israelites, and when they were all
gathered in front of him, he told them that they were no longer
a mere collection of tribes, but that they were about to become a
nation. This meant that they would come into contact with
other nations, who could lead them into idol worship. While
warning them in the most severe terms against abandoning
God's Covenant, Moses also held out a note of hope, by promis-
ing that if they returned to God and obeyed Him, God in turn
would have compassion with them and "gather them again from

all the nations where He scattered them, putting all the curses on their enemies who hated and persecuted them."

Anyone reading the above verses from *Parashath Nitzavim* must be somewhat confused. For the Israelites at last to become a nation surely was a blessing. Why the curses? And why should God talk about "gathering you again from the nations where He scattered you" when the Jews had not even arrived in Eretz Israel? Let us try to analyze what the Torah is telling us here.

Moses, who in this last of the five books of the Torah repeats the Law for the Jewish people, says in the name of God, "After you will have experienced both the blessings and the curses, I will take you back to the land of your fathers." What he meant, therefore, was that both the blessings and the curses *together* would cause them and their children to repent and return to the Jewish way of life.

The question at issue here is whether people do indeed learn from their blessings or afflictions. Common sense, and a look around us in the real world, suggests that maybe the opposite is the case. We often see people who are blessed with fortune and material possessions becoming even less inclined to repent and return to the observance of the commandments. Even the Torah says in one of the following chapters of Devarim, וישמן ישורין ויבעט (*va-yishman yeshurin va-yiv'at*), "When they are fat, they are kicking." People who are prosperous have both the money and the opportunity to be generous to others, but most of the time they are not. Merely being wealthy is not sufficient; one has to be a good person as well. Many rich people are far too busy with their own affairs and pleasures to think of helping others in their difficulties. So it does not look as if blessings are a reason for the Jewish people to draw nearer to the *mitzvoth*, the ways of the Torah.

Neither does the opposite condition, misfortune, create much incentive for repentance. Someone who is really in a bad situation might be inclined to say, in the words of Job's wife to her unfortunate husband, "Curse God and die!" In other words:

You cannot reverse your misfortune, but at least you can register your protest by rejecting God. In this same portion of the week we also read שלום יהיה־לי כי בשררות לבי אלך (*shalom yihyeh li ki be-shriruth libi eileich*), "If I am cursed anyway, then why shouldn't I do what I want?" In other words, "If I am going down anyway, I might as well go with a splash! What do I have to lose?"

So what does the Torah mean when it says that both blessings and curses lead to a return to God? What is it that causes us to turn back to the right ways and repent? The above arguments lead us to conclude that being blessed does not necessarily make a person better, whereas the one who feels that he is cursed is hardly in the mood to care about others who are in a similar position, or even less fortunate than himself.

So far we have been talking about individual fortunes: the luck or misfortune of this or that particular person. In my opinion, what the Torah means to say is that we should not just look at individual examples, and that speculations about whether the blessings or curses of a given individual will bring him back to God are in effect irrelevant. The Torah is referring to the Jewish people as a whole. The Torah wants to say that if we look at all the good times the Jewish people have enjoyed throughout their history, and if we look at all the curses, all the bad times, they have had to suffer during these centuries, then there is only one conclusion: if we want to exist and survive as a nation, we have to go back to the ways of the Torah.

Let us examine this explanation a little more closely, by looking at a particular era in Jewish history. The Jewish people suffered greatly during the Middle Ages. This period in European history, which until today is referred to as the "Dark Ages," was a curse. However, this same period was a dark time for everyone, Jew and Gentile alike. It was a time of wars and pestilence, a time of famine, of ignorance, and of cruelty.

So the Jews waited patiently for times to change, thinking that when the general situation improved, their own fate would also take a turn for the better. We were sure that it was just a question of time. Once people became less primitive and more understanding, everything would be different and the nations of the world would let us live without looking at distinctions of religion, race, or nationality. Then, of course, the Jewish people would also enjoy full human and civic rights.

It is interesting that the Jews themselves were the most fervent believers in the advance of civilization, which may explain why during all those black years of discrimination and persecution they refused to despair. They realized that people were primitive, but they hoped that when more civilized times arrived, their lives, too, would undergo a change for the better.

They were mistaken. The Western world developed and prospered. Every year brought new inventions; philosophers, artists, and writers flourished. In some places Jews were tolerated, but in others persecution continued. Officially sanctioned and encouraged religious discrimination reached a peak. The Jewish people waited anxiously and patiently for enlightenment to come.

The era of the Enlightenment arrived, but it brought only assimilation. Emancipation and the establishment of the European nation states created waves of national chauvinism. How little did we understand! We are now living at the end of the twentieth century, the most civilized century in the history of mankind. What has it brought the Jewish people? Hasn't this been the worst century ever? Did the march of civilization prevent the Holocaust, the killing of little children? Did civilization teach people to be less brutal, or more tolerant of different customs and traditions?

The opposite has been the case: all that civilization—and the scientific and technological advances that have followed in its wake—have achieved has been to find more efficient ways of destroying people. Far larger numbers of people have been murdered in this century than the primitives of the medieval world ever succeeded in killing. If this is civilization, then what is barbarism? Now we can understand why Moses, among his dire warnings also included the phrase, בערב תאמר מי־יתן בקר ... (ba-erev to'omar mi-yiteen boker), "...in the evening you will say, 'If only it were morning!'" What he painted was a situation that continually worsened, so that in the evening people would look back longingly to the morning of the same day, which—even though it had been bad enough—seemed at least bearable in retrospect.

And the situation *did* worsen; civilization has turned into a nightmare, reminding the Jews of the first part of Moses' warning: בבקר תאמר מי יתן ערב (ba-boker to'omar mi-yiteen erev), "In the morning you will say, 'If only it were evening!'" The morning turned out to be even more calamitous than the previous night!

The message is that not civilization, not a "Golden Age" of tolerance—and certainly not assimilation—will bring salvation for the Jewish people. We cannot rely on outsiders, hoping that they will be more civilized and more tolerant, and that they will let the Jewish people live their normal lives. Our history shows that we cannot rely on anybody—in good times or in bad. For many centuries now our people have been accustomed to being persecuted for being Jews. In more recent times they have stood accused of being Zionists, and at present it is the Israelis who are considered guilty of all kinds of transgressions against "humane behavior." Although the rationalizations may differ, the underlying reasons are always the same. We can only rely on God. *Parashath Nitzavim* teaches us our only choice: to go back to God, to our own way of life: ושבת עד יהוה אלהיך (ve-shavta ad ha-shem eloheycha), "...and you shall return to your God."

And talking of blessings and curses: whether we feel good or feel bad depends a lot upon ourselves. There is a famous story by one of our great rabbis, who was asked why it says that every individual is being judged by God every day, when we know that all creatures are judged on Rosh Ha-Shanah and Yom Kippur for their deeds during the year. The saintly rabbi said that he would explain it by means of an example. Leading his questioner to the window, he pointed at the water carrier who was passing by outside. He knocked on the glass and asked the old man to come in.

The rabbi asked him, "Tell me, how do you feel today?"

"Rabbi, don't ask!" the old man answered. "I am in terrible shape. Look at me; my back is killing me; I am well over eighty, but I have to go on working, for I never earned enough to be able to save. How long shall I be able to continue earning a living by carrying this cask of water?"

After the rabbi had offered him a drink and quietened him with a few suitable words, the old man continued on his way.

Then the rabbi said to his questioner, "Pass by tomorrow, the same time."

The next day, when the water carrier appeared, the rabbi again asked him to come in.

"How do you feel today, Moishe?" he asked.

"Wonderful, Rabbi," was the unexpected answer.

"What do you mean," the rabbi asked, "have you suddenly become younger? Have you won the lottery? Has your backache disappeared?"

"No, Rabbi," answered the old man. "I am not any younger or richer, but I was thinking about your question yesterday, and suddenly I realized: 'Moishe, you are already over eighty years old. You never had an education, you are alone and your back hurts, but you still manage to make a living and you have never had to go hungry.'"

"You see," the rabbi said to his guest, "on Rosh Ha-Shanah and Yom Kippur God judges what will happen to us—but the decision how we shall feel today and every day depends upon us ourselves."

If someone should ask why the Jewish people are always having trouble, while the rest of the world has nothing but luck, we should quickly point out to him how wrong he is. Good and bad do not exist alone; life is a "package deal." There is not a person—or a nation—in the world that has never known ups and downs. According to the Torah, whether people feel good or bad depends in many cases upon the extent that they believe in themselves.

Now we can also understand what the Torah means when it says: הברכה והקללה . . . והיה כי-יבאו עליך (ve-hayah ki tavo aleicha ha-berachah ve-ha-kelalah), one moment you will feel as if you are blessed, and another as if you are cursed. Neither feeling is correct—but the question is how we can master it. The answer is, ושבת עד יהוה אלהיך (ve-shavta ad ha-shem eloheycha . . .), "And you shall return to your God." Only belief in His Divine supervision, the knowledge that everything has a purpose, will prevent us from being high one moment, like a person taking drugs, only to sink into despair as soon as something goes wrong. A steady faith will help us to keep our daily lives on an even keel, because we know that everything that happens forms a part of God's master plan.

Parashath Va-Yelech

וילך משה וידבר את־הדברים האלה אל־כל־ישראל : ויאמר
אלהם בן־מאה ועשרים שנה אנכי היום לא־אוכל עוד לצאת
ולבוא ויהוה אמר אלי לא תעבר את־הירדן הזה . . .

"Then Moses went out and spoke these words to all Israel:
'I am now a hundred and twenty years old and I am no
longer able to lead you. God has said to me, "You shall not
cross the Jordan."'"

In this portion we read how Moses addressed a gathering of
the Jewish people to inform them officially that he was resigning his leadership of the Jewish people, since God had told him
that he was not going to cross the Jordan. But, he said, "be
strong and courageous, for God goes with you; he will never
leave you nor forsake you."

Immediately after this, Moses summoned Joshua and, still in
the presence of the people, he told him that he would be the new
leader, and that he would have to take his people into Canaan
and divide the land among them, according to God's promise to
Abraham. And he repeated the words he had used earlier: "Be
strong and courageous. God Himself goes before you and will be
with you; he will never leave you nor forsake you."

After he had finished talking, Moses wrote down his law and
gave it to the priests and to all the elders of Israel. He appealed to
them to כתבו לכם את־השירה הזאת ולמדה את־בני ישראל שימה בפיהם למען תהיה־
לי השירה הזאת לעד בבני ישראל (*kitevu lachem eth ha-shirah ha-zoth ve-lamdah
eth benei yisrael semah be-fihem lema'an tihyeh-li ha-shirah ha-zoth le'ed
bi-vnei yisrael*), "Write down for yourselves this song, and teach it

352

to the Israelites and make them sing it, so that it may be a witness for me against them."

The idea was that in the future everyone should write a copy of God's Torah for himself, so that coming generations of the Jewish people would always know how to live a Jewish life.

One of the great interpreters of the Torah writes that Moses, before he said farewell to his beloved people, told them three things, all of which are in fact implied in this *parashah*, in addition to which they are related to each other. First of all, they were told never to talk to people of the risks and dangers that might face them, unless they were certain that they would come to pass. In other words, we should avoid frightening other people—or, for that matter, ourselves—with things we are not absolutely sure will happen. When, for example, a man is ill, and he is afraid that he may die, we may agree with him that he is ill. But why worry him with all kinds of frightening stories, and possibly worsen his condition, if he may have an excellent chance to recover? When, on the other hand, God told Moses that he would not cross the Jordan, and that he would die, Moses was sure, and therefore he was obliged to tell the Jewish people.

The second advice Moses gave the Jews was never to lose their self-confidence and their belief in God's assurance that they would succeed in conquering the people who were already settled in Canaan. He was quite emphatic on this point since, as he told them, God would go before them and help them to defeat the inhabitants—even if he, Moses, would not be there to lead them.

The third thing Moses asked from them, was that everybody should write his own *Sefer Torah*, for this would oblige them to study and understand God's commandments. They should not rely on finding a *Sefer Torah* with a neighbor or a friend. They had to write it themselves, so that they would be physically in touch with the Torah in their own homes.

There is a common theme running through everything that has been said so far, namely that of fear versus security—or

anxiety versus self-confidence. In almost every life there are
moments when people are afraid that there might come a time
when they will need help, without there being anyone at their
side to support them. Such feelings of loneliness and isolation
can confuse and frighten children and grown-ups alike, and
even drive one to despair. This kind of despair may hit a person
even when he knows himself surrounded by a warm atmosphere of family and friends, particularly when for some reason
or other he is confronted with other people who are passing
through a crisis, only to find that at the crucial moment they are
all alone. There is a well-known saying, according to which,
"when you laugh, the world laughs with you; when you cry, you
cry alone." There obviously is a limit to human solidarity and
ability to help.

What a difference it must make, therefore, if someone
believes that God is with him, and will inspire and support him
in his hour of need. King David had many a harrowing day in his
life, and the Psalms are eloquent witness to his suffering. Yet, in
one of the most moving psalms, he says: גם כי־אלך בגיא צלמות לא־אירע
רע כי־אתה עמדי (gam ki elech be-geah tsalmaveth lo-ira ra ki atah imadi),
"Even though I walk through the valley of the shadow of death, I
will fear no evil, for You are with me." In short, as long as we
believe that God looks after his creatures, and that at all times
we are under the divine supervision of our Creator, there is no
longer place for fear, or a reason to feel isolated. The man who
feels that he is all alone and has nobody on whom to fall back in
time of need is a sad man—even when he is not in a crisis, for the
chances are that he will be continuously looking over his
shoulder for fear something will befall him and he will find
himself isolated.

Most people in the world are trying to save something for a
rainy day. It is the accepted thing to create a financial reserve of
some kind, for "who knows what will happen to me or my
family, and how can I be sure that when I am old or sick there
will be someone to stay at my side. At least there is some money

in the bank that I can rely upon." The question is whether
money is indeed capable of solving the problem of loneliness. I,
for one, am sure that it cannot. My own experience in the field
of social work has shown that there are many old people who
lack nothing materially, and even have all the help they need, yet
they are still lonely and sad. Even when there are children or
family members in a position to look after an aged relative, the
question is to what extent they are ready and capable of solving
the problem of isolation. Often, in fact, they are not, for however devoted children are, each of them has his own life and his
own problems, and they belong to a new generation, with a
different outlook and approach, and different expectations.

In the final analysis the only thing that can support a person
is the confident belief that God is with him in his suffering, and
that he is not alone. Again I want to refer to King David, who in
one of his incomparable psalms expresses this idea with moving
clarity and simplicity: מאין יבא עזרי: עזרי מעם יהוה עשה שמים וארץ (me'ayin
yavo ezri: ezri me'im ha-shem oseh shamayim va-aretz), "Where does my
help come from? My help comes from God, the Maker of heaven
and earth."

As long as we are on our life's journey, there may be dangers
lurking around the corner; the possibility that, sooner or later,
something may happen to us is an ever-present risk. Here,
however, we see the greatness of Moses, as a person and as a
leader. Moses did not hesitate to tell the Jewish people, "I am
going to die, but I am not afraid. I was not alone all those years,
and I am not alone today." At the same time he encouraged his
people by adding, "You, too, should know that you will not be
alone when you set out to conquer the Promised Land. For God
will go with you. I know that you are asking yourself how you
will fight those nations. You should rely on God, and He will
destroy these nations before you. He inspired Joshua by saying
to him: Get up, and show that you are a leader. Be strong, and
the people will be strong. Be not afraid, and the people will not
be afraid. Whether you succeed will depend on your faith in God

and your people. Your faith and your belief in the future will strike deep into the heart of everyone, and thus you will overcome all the difficulties that will come your way."

What goes for the individual goes for the people as a whole. Until today the Jewish people live with the feeling that they are isolated from other people. Friendship, protection, or reliance on outside agents in general have too often proved to be uncertain. Even today there exists a deep, traditional hatred of the Jewish people among many nations. Moses foresaw this even when the nation was created. This is why he exhorted the Children of Israel: "Believe in yourself and have faith that God guides you, and you will be strong and courageous. And remember: to achieve this faith and this courage, you have to study the Torah, and even write your own copy, so that it may be a witness for me against them."

Torath Moshe does not teach us how to fly off into space, or live with our heads in the clouds. It teaches us how to walk on the earth, with our feet planted firmly on the ground, secure in the knowledge that there exists a שומר ישראל (*shomer yisrael*), a guardian of Israel, who enables us to live our life and exist.

Parashath Ha'azinu

האזינו השמים ואדברה ותשמע הארץ אמרי־פי:
זכר ימות עולם בינו שנות דר־ודר שאל אביך ויגדך

Listen, O heavens, and I will speak;
hear, O earth, the words of my mouth.
. . .
Remember the days of old;
consider the generations long past.
Ask your father and he will tell you.

The Midrash refers to the words of the prophet, זכרתי לך חסד
נעוריך אהבת כלולותיך לכתך אחרי במדבר בארץ לא זרוע (zacharti lecha chesed
ne'uraicha ahavath kelulotaich lechtecha acharai be-midbar), according to
which God says, "I will remember you for the wonderful things
you did when you went after Me in the desert."

The words at the beginning of this *parashah* are from the
Song of Moses, the introduction to *Parashath Ha'azinu*, which is
the next to last chapter of the book of Devarim . In order to
understand what Moses and the prophet want to say, we shall
have to examine their words in somewhat more detail.

It is quite customary for all kinds of scholars and researchers
to devote their entire lives to the study of their chosen subjects.
Historians and archeologists, for example, often literally dig up
the past, to try to understand events that have occurred as long
ago as the beginning of recorded history—including the period
described in the Bible. They try to find out not only what
happened, but why it happened, and how. Many of these

researchers have succeeded in revealing secrets that have lain buried for thousands of years. And yet, no definitive historical or archeological sources have ever been discovered to shed light on the exact circumstances of the Jewish presence in Egypt and the Exodus of the Israelites to the Promised Land—except for what is written in the Five Books of Moses and the oral Torah. The Torah tells us that the Children of Israel lived in the land of the Nile for hundreds of years—not as a people, but as a loose collection of tribes; without a tradition or a religion of their own, except for the distant memories of their fathers who had lived in a land called Canaan, as well as God's promise to their first patriarch Abraham to return them to this land at some future time.

At first they were welcome in Egypt, thanks to Joseph's intervention at a time of famine, but eventually a pharaoh arose who did not want to know what Joseph had done for the Egyptian nation, and from that moment on their lives became a misery. How is it possible that these few small Hebrew tribes did not disperse and assimilate among the local population? Why did they not adopt the heathen religions of the surrounding peoples? From where did the Hebrews derive the strength to survive oppression and slavery? Enslavement can grind down the strongest person and drive the greatest spirit to despair. Yet, here we find a group of people—without a country, without a constitution, and without an established tradition—who suddenly, in the middle of the night, arose as one and, leaving everything behind, trekked into the desert toward an unknown and hazardous future. What force was driving them?

Some will reply that it was Moses who forced their decision, but this answer raises as many questions as it answers. For who was Moses for the Hebrews at this time? They hardly knew him. Moses was forty years old when he fled to Midian, and most of the preceding years he had lived as an Egyptian prince at the court of Pharaoh. Following his return to Egypt after several decades, following his revelation at the Burning Bush, he spent only one year in Egypt. Can we say that Moses impressed the Hebrews so much during this time that suddenly the urge to leave Egypt and to be free became overwhelming?

Historians, ethnologists, sociologists, psychologists, and other scholars trained to interpret mass phenomena are even today unable to understand from where the Children of Israel received the strength to undertake a revolt that was neither organized nor planned. It was an anarchic decision; the scenes that accompanied their Exodus must have been second only to the chaos and destruction they left behind in Egypt.

How did the Hebrews know where they were going? We already mentioned that God had promised Abraham's descendants a land of their own. How could they know whether they would like this country at all? There are no indications, either in the Torah or in historical or archeological records, of the Hebrews who lived in Egypt ever having seen the land. Nothing is known about any Jews having been left behind in Canaan, or about commercial or family contacts between the two countries. What we can assume, however, is that the parents talked about Canaan to their children, and that they were anxious to take possession of it at some future time.

Accepting this answer, the next question is what kind of conditions might have compelled the Children of Israel to begin their migration to the Promised Land. Slavery, maybe? Indeed, the Hebrews were not free—but they did not go hungry. They even had fish and lamb, which was in plentiful supply because, so Jewish tradition has it, these foods were not eaten by the Egyptians for religious or other reasons. Possibly their living conditions had become unbearable? But then, what was the logic behind 600,000 people—including women and children—uprooting themselves to start a nomadic existence in some wilderness? What about the logistics of it all? Who was going to feed them, and would there be sufficient water? In short, who could guarantee that this huge, unorganized, and unruly multitude would not disperse and perish in the desert? No wonder that Pharaoh's people predicted that the Hebrews would soon return.

We can take the argument even further, and see the mystery deepening when we look at what happened after the Exodus. Only seven weeks after the Children of Israel left Egypt, Moses appeared with his unruly band at Mount Sinai. How can we explain that these nomads, erstwhile slaves, ascended within such a short span of time to a then unknown peak of morality that enabled them to accept the Torah? Unskilled in science, law, and philosophy, they committed themselves to a code of conduct that has never been paralleled, let alone surpassed, by any civilization, and—in its printed form—is still the best-selling book in the world, the repository of the deepest and noblest thoughts humanity possesses.

We should realize that the generation that left Egypt was by no means so strong, in the sense of being equipped, physically or otherwise, for the kind of life it had taken upon itself; in this respect the next, desert-born generation was far more resistant and better adapted to its future task. A people who do not live in one place, who lead a wandering life, cannot become strong fighters. Time and again the Torah says: ויסעו ויחנו ... (va-yissu va-yachnu), "they traveled and rested...." Being continually on the move, camping out in the open, not having a sedentary life, prevents people from creating an organized existence, from planning their economy and training and maintaining a strong army. What about their chances, therefore, of fighting—let alone defeating and dislodging—a settled population such as the residents of Canaan, a large part of whom resided in fortified towns? And still the Children of Israel went, and continued.

This is why the Torah says: כי שאל־נא ראשונים אשר־היו לפניך למן־ היום אשר ברא אלהים אדם על־הארץ ... (ki she'al na rishonim asher hayu lefaneicha lemin-hayom asher bara ha-shem adam al ha-aretz), "Ask now about the former days, long before your time ... has anything so great as this ever happened, or has anything like it ever been heard of? ... Has any god ever tried to take for himself one nation out of another nation, by testings, by miraculous signs and wonders, by war, by a mighty hand and an outstretched arm, or by great and awesome deeds, like all the things your God did for you in Egypt before your very eyes?" And it continues: זכר ימות עולם בינו שנות דר־ודר שאל אביך ויגדך (*zechor yemoth olam binu shenoth dor va-dor she'al avicha ve-yagedcha*), "Remember the days of old; consider the generations long past. Ask your father and he will tell you—that something like this has never before happened in all history."

What the Torah in fact says is that considering everything that happened to the Jews in Egypt and after, we can only conclude that it was not a normal experience. The Jews who lived in the desert cannot be compared with any other generation of Jews. Despite all their faults, the Talmud says that a simple girl in the desert generation had a greater understanding of God than the subsequent prophets. The generation of the desert bequeathed knowledge and wisdom, and—above all—the recognition of the Almighty to the Jewish people for all generations to come. Only their faith and knowledge can explain what happened at that time.

There is an interesting midrash about Rabbi Jochanan, who in the course of a journey met an old man. The old man said to him, "Rabbi, don't you think that our generation is greater than the generation that came out of Egypt? That generation had only the Five Books, but ours has the entire Bible and all the commentaries." Rabbi Jochanan answered, "You are mistaken. Look, the generations after the destruction of the First Temple possessed the explanations of the written Torah. Does this mean that they were on a higher level than the generation of the Exodus? Be mindful of what God told the Jewish people through the prophet: I will always remember what you did when you were young, and you followed me in the desert in a land where nothing grows."

The Talmud tells that when the Children of Israel left Egypt, nothing happened along the way that God did not reveal and explain to them. Let us not forget that so far they had only one commandment, although a very important one. The Talmud says: When the Children of Israel left Egypt, they made a covenant to make גמילת חסדים זה לזה (gemilath chasadim zeh la zeh). Simply put, this means that they promised to care for each other.

The Talmud abounds with similar midrashim that are intended to make us realize the importance of what happened in those historic days. Only if we look at it the way the Torah tells it will we be able to understand their meaning; trying to understand them in a rational way would keep their meaning closed to us. Even worse—people might begin to say that probably these events never happened. A mere fifty years from now people may not believe that Israel succeeded in defeating 90 million Arabs during a lightning Six-Day War. So, how would they believe the events of the Exodus, which took place several thousands of years ago? This is why Moses said: האזינו השמים ואדברה ותשמע הארץ אמרי-פי (ha-azinu ha-shamayim va-adaberah ve-tishma ha-aretz imri pi). Moses called heaven and earth as witnesses to the truth of his words, since they were there at the creation—and will be there as long as the world will exist—in order to tell mankind about what happened during this period in the history of the Jewish people. What Moses wanted to say is, "Remember the history of these generations, and heavens and earth are our eternal witnesses that this is how it happened."

In the same way as Passover is the symbol of the redemption from Egypt, Shavuoth—the Feast of Weeks—reminds us of the giving of the Torah; Rosh Ha-Shanah and Yom Kippur urge the Jewish people to return to their spiritual sources, whereas Sukkoth—the Feast of Tabernacles—commemorates the history of the Jewish people. About Sukkoth it is written in the Torah, למען ידעו דורתיכם (le-ma'an yedu doroteichem): "So that all your generations will know what happened." The history of the Jewish people, from the day of their departure from Egypt until today, contains countless such reminders that the Jewish people are a miracle. Their existence and survival since that day at

Mount Sinai, when they became a nation, are not understandable by rational means. Our existence can be compared with the
Sukkah: fragile, temporary, and insecure. If nevertheless, in the
face of all odds, we continue to exist, we can only believe that it
has been the will of God to keep us alive—for otherwise surely
we would not be here today.

Parashath Ve-zoth ha-Berachah

וזאת הברכה אשר ברך משה איש האלהים את־בני ישראל לפני
מותו . . . תורה צוה־לנו משה מורשה קהלת יעקב.

"This is the blessing that Moses the man of God pronounced on the Israelites before his death ... the law that
Moses gave us, the possession of the assembly of Jacob."

Our sages tell us that as soon as a Jewish child begins to talk,
we should teach it a verse from the Torah. But not just any
verse; what we should teach it are the words: תורה צוה־לנו משה
מורשה קהלת יעקב (torah zivah lanu moshe morashah kehillath ya'acov),
"...the law that Moses gave us, the possession of the assembly
of Jacob."

Isn't it interesting that Moses did not ask us to teach our
children first of all the *aleph-beth*, or even the Ten Commandments, or the *Shema Israel*? However elementary and important
they are, they apparently were not considered the first priority.
Most important of all was to teach them the words *torah zivah
lanu moshe morashah kehillath ya'acov*. This certainly raises the question: "Why—and what does it mean?"

The Midrash reminds us that we should never forget that
Moses broke the first Tablets of the Law when he came down
the mountain and saw the Jewish people engaged in idolatry.
This, too, raises a question, and its answer is also connected
with the very first teaching of the Torah. On the face of it, it
would seem strange that we are obliged to remember Moses'
smashing of the Tablets. Is there really nothing more notable to

364

remember about him? What about the countless far more glor-
ious things he did for his people? What about the Exodus? Or
Moses' role in guiding the *B'nai Israel* to Mount Sinai? Wouldn't
this be a far better way to remember him?

It is important, therefore, that we understand what we are
asked by Moses, and why, when he told us to teach "...the law
that Moses gave us, the possession of the assembly of Jacob."
The word *morashah*, with the same Hebrew root as the word for
"possession," means "heritage," and this heritage is the Torah.
The Jewish people were originally taught the Torah by Moses;
this is how they acquired the knowledge of God's commandments, which has remained the unique heritage of every Jew
until today, both adults and children. However, in order to
acquire this heritage, the Jewish child has to be taught Torah—
but not as a part of his general learning. The basic awareness of
his Jewish identity and future has to be instilled in the child as
soon as he begins to react to his human surroundings, which is
when he utters his first words to those closest to him—his
parents. This is why it is also the parents' duty to teach the child
his first words of the Torah.

Our sages realized long ago how appropriate this first, elementary exercise in Torah is, particularly when taught by the
parents. This verse talks about "the law that Moses gave us, the
possession (i.e. heritage) of the congregation of Jacob." So if we
ask why this verse of the Torah was chosen, it is simply because
every time the parent would pronounce it, and every time the
child repeated it, the parents would be reminded that the Torah
was their heritage too—and that as such it is a parental obligation to share this heritage with the child.

There is no other verse in the Torah that combines in so few
words the three quintessential elements of our Jewish tradition:
the *Law*, which God gave to Moses at Mount Sinai, and which
the *Congregation of Jacob*, i.e. the Jewish people, promised to
observe as a *heritage* throughout their generations.

The sages chose as the initial teaching the very verse that

would serve as a catalyst for the parents' education of the child. But teaching is a two-way street. It involves the parents teaching and the child understanding. Teaching is not simply an exercise in regurgitating knowledge; it means making sure that the knowledge is properly understood and digested.

When Moses came down from Sinai, he was full of information and knowledge. But he found himself confronted with people who at that point did not appear to be receptive to anything he would like to transmit. This is why he destroyed the Tablets—and not merely out of anger and frustration.

I would like to explain this in a little more detail, for there is an important lesson in Moses' behavior—and it explains why we are told to remember that Moses smashed the Tablets of the Law at the foot of Mount Sinai. Moses decided that what was needed was soul-searching, and a reexamination of Israel's destiny. He refused to take the easy way out—and fail—and instead decided to wait and make a fresh start at the right time. So first he eradicated the alien influences and idolatry, by forcing them physically and mentally from the people's minds through the spectacular act of breaking the Tablets. This act created a more receptive climate, in which the Jewish people became eager to learn.

Only at this point was the heritage transmitted. As the leader of his people, Moses did not want to lose the Jews—but as their teacher, he realized that it was no use wasting his message, and that he would have to wait until they were able to listen and understand. Moses decided that it wasn't the proper moment to teach—so he broke the Tablets. This holding back of his teaching involved a tremendous sacrifice by Moses, which the sages regard as the greatest memorial to his life. It is only through this heroic act that the Torah could become so deeply embedded in our Jewish existence.

תורה צוה-לנו משה מורשה קהלת יעקב (torah zivah lanu moshe morashah kehillath ya'acov) therefore contains another message, namely that parents should never approach the transmission of Judaism with a fear of losing their children, but—on the contrary—on the basis that this will bind them closer to our faith. Only in this atmosphere of confident belief can the heritage be transmitted.

וזאת הברכה אשר ברך משה איש האלהים את־בני ישראל (ve-zoth ha-berachah asher berach mosheh ish ha-shem eth benei yisrael), "This is the blessing that Moses the man of God pronounced on the Israelites...." In other words, Moses gave his commandment as part of a blessing. This shows that Moses did not just give the Jews a heritage that told them how to live, he wanted them to be satisfied with it, and recognize the acceptance of the Torah as a blessing.

The portion *Ve-zoth ha-Berachah* also marks the conclusion of the annual cycle of Torah readings. How interesting it is that the members of the *Knesseth ha-Gedolah*, the Supreme Council of the Jews, also prepared a special thanksgiving prayer, recited when Jews celebrate the completion of their study of a tractate of the Talmud or Mishnah (a *sium*). Part of this prayer reads as follows: "I give thanks to God who has added my portion with those who sit in the *Beth Midrash* [the house of study] and who has not set my portion with those who sit on streetcorners." In other words, the Jew avows that he is happy that he may sit and study — both as a means of learning how to live, and for its own sake.

Present-day psychiatrists justly attribute all kinds of neuroses to stresses that burden the mind of contemporary man. These conflicts result from the most diverse human experiences, including conflicts relating to love, loyalty, and people's expectations, way of life, and beliefs. Human conflicts are caused not only by fear and anxiety, but also by people's detachment from religion and their hesitation to embrace divinely revealed norms of activity and behavior. Many people who have only a very limited religious and secular knowledge become confused due to what they consider an incompatibility between the Torah and modern life — between the *mitzvoth* and modern views on ethics and morality.

For the traditional Jew, however, religion does not pose

questions, but on the contrary presents answers. Every time we conclude our annual cycle of Torah readings, we realize that our Torah is the only real blessing in our life, because it resolves all our conflicts and answers all our questions.

About The Author

Rabbi Shmuel Werzberger, who was born in Konigsfeld, Czechoslovakia, and grew up in Borsa, is descended from an old chassidic family. A Yeshivah student at the age of eleven, he was ordained when only seventeen years old—one of the youngest alumni ever to be granted the rabbinical title.

In 1939 Rabbi Werzberger immigrated to Eretz Israel, where he studied philosophy at the Hebrew University of Jerusalem and married Miriam Hager of the illustrious Vishnitz rabbinical dynasty.

The hard times in what was then Palestine, and his responsibilities as a husband, forced him to break off his studies. At the urging of the *Mizrachi* movement he became involved in absorption activities for new immigrants, icluding those who were landed at night from illegal immigrant ships. Many of the details about this chapter in his life, and his other activities during this period will—with God's help—be related in his forthcoming biography.

From 1946 untill 1950 Rabbi Werzberger worked as the Jewish Agency's head of rehabilitation services for the handicapped and social cases for the northern part of the country.

From 1950 untill 1964 he applied his experience in the social welfare field as director of the Constructive Department of Malbon, the American Joint Distribution Committee's Israeli branch, charged with the social and economic rehabilitation of handicapped and infirm immigrants.

Between 1965 and 1968 he lived in the United States as a regional *aliyah shaliach*. Following his return to Israel, he was director of the Social Welfare Department of the Jafo-Tel Aviv municipality, until in 1973 he was called to Cleveland, Ohio, as the resident rabbi of the Menorah Park Home for the Aged.

Rabbi (emeritus, since 1948) Werzberger, who now lives in Tel Aviv, devotes his time to social welfare activities and writing. His first book, *Not in Heaven or Beyond the Sea*, a collection of *divrei Torah*, was published in 1987.